D0440014

Smart Boys:

Talent, Manhood, and the Search for Meaning

Barbara A. Kerr, Ph.D.
and
Sanford J. Cohn, Ph.D.

With contributions by Audie Alcorn, Tom Anderson,
Sam Claiborn, Megan Foley-Nicpon, James T. Webb,
and Kayoko Yokoyama

Great Potential Press, Inc.
(formerly Gifted Psychology Press, Inc.)
P.O. Box 5057
Scottsdale, AZ 85261
www.giftedbooks.com

Smart Boys: Talent, Manhood, and the Search for Meaning

Cover Design/Layout: ATG Productions, Inc.
Interior Design/Layout: Spring Winnette

Published by
Great Potential Press, Inc.
(formerly Gifted Psychology Press, Inc.)
P.O. Box 5057
Scottsdale, AZ 85261
www.giftedbooks.com

Printed and bound in the United States of America.
05 04 03 02 01   6 5 4 3 2 1

Library of Congress Cataloging-in-Publication Data
Kerr, Barbara A.
  Smart boys: talent, manhood, and the search for meaning / Barbara A. Kerr
  and Sanford J. Cohn
  p. cm.
  Includes bibliographical references and index
  ISBN 0-910707-43-X
  1. Gifted boys. 2. Gifted men. 3. Masculinity. 4. Gifted men-Longitudinal studies.
    5. Gifted men-Biography. 6. Gifted men-Employment. 7. Self-actualization
    (Psychology). 8. Achievement motivation-Case studies. 9. Success-Psychological
    aspects-Case studies. I. Cohn, Sanford J. II. Title

BF723.G48 K47 2001
155.3'32'0879-dc21   2001031388

ISBN: 0-910707-43-X

Table of Contents

Dedication

To Sam—this one's for you.
–Mom

To Medicine Horse and The White Swan,
who taught me so much.
–Sandy

Acknowledgments

We would like to thank, first of all, our contributors: Tom Anderson, who conducted the research for the follow-up study of gifted men and who co-authored Chapter 3; Kayoko Yokoyama, who interviewed gifted men of color and edited the interviews for inclusion in this book; Sam Claiborn, who wrote the essay that appears at the end of Chapter 5; and Megan Foley-Nicpon, who helped with revisions and constructed the index for us. We would also like to express our appreciation to our publisher and editor James T. Webb and co-editors Janet Gore, Audie L. Alcorn, Anna Galli, and Jen Rosso for their dogged persistence in bringing this manuscript to light, as well as their belief in the importance of this topic. They made our text say just what we wanted it to say and prevented us sometimes from making authorly flights into the realm of the speculative.

Barbara wishes to thank all of the gifted male students and clients she has taught and counseled over the years. She also wishes to acknowledge the men of the Accelerated Learning Program of the St. Louis Public Schools, who so generously shared their stories with us. And special thanks goes to Dan Siefert, who first inspired us to follow up with the men as well as the women of our class.

Barbara also thanks the male mentors of her youth, Joe Johnston and Bill Bondeson, and Nicholas Colangelo, who believed in her and who generated so much of the work that informs this book.

Finally, Barbara thanks her family, Chuck Claiborn, Grace Claiborn, and Sam Claiborn, for their love, support, and great ideas, and her mom and dad, who never had to deal with a gifted boy. She also expresses her appreciation to her "lodge of men"—those men who share their intellectual, emotional, and spiritual lives with her, teaching her so much about what it is to be a man: John McAlister, Delmar Boni, and of course, her dear co-author and guardian angel, Sandy Cohn.

Sandy wishes to thank the gifted boys and their families who have participated in programs conducted under the auspices of the Center for Academic Precocity and who have sought counsel from him during the past 25 years.

Sandy would also like to thank G. Wilson Schafer and Julian C. Stanley, who were his mentors and influences and who helped him understand the nature of men's talent development and their search for meaning, and Susan E. Schwartz for her collaboration on his self-discovery.

Finally, Sandy wishes to thank his family, Ben K. Cohn and Edward S. Cohn, with special thanks to Catherine M. G. Cohn for her steadfast care, as well as colleagues and friends who have taught him so much: Peter M. Finlay, Jesus Antonio Diaz, Steven V. Faulkner, Gary Lovejoy, and Larry V. Hedges.

Introduction

What is happening to our gifted boys? As psychologists who specialize in the development of talent, we hear disturbing news from our clients, our students, and the media. An overwhelming number of the bright boys who are referred to us and others for counseling are underachieving. That is, they are just not bothering to do their homework, and they are not getting involved in school activities. They are bored in the classroom and disengaged outside of the classroom. In some suburban high schools, it seems the girls are taking over the student government, the school paper, and the yearbook, while the boys have abdicated any and all leadership roles. Bright boys may see athletics as the one area in which they must achieve if they are to be valued and accepted, while they simultaneously camouflage being smart. Even though they may have a secret contempt for the attitudes they perceive as underlying school sports, they harbor no real hope of making any changes so that they, too, might receive the respect that athletes get.

In their adolescent relationships, they are often hesitant and distrustful. They may have only a few male friends. They dislike the superficial aspects of the dating game. Even though they may be contemptuous of the current dating system, they are confused about any alternative ways of relating to young women. Those who are gay are usually closeted, especially now in the wake of several recent conspicuous murders and other acts of violence toward gay males. Certainly, bullying is a frequent occurrence for them and their acquaintances, and they see the bumper stickers that say, "My child just beat up your honor student." The gifted boys who are shy are often called "nerd," "dork," or "geek" by their agemates.

When asked about their futures, they have modest dreams or none at all. Surprisingly, gifted boys' career dreams are often markedly unimaginative, and it seems the majority of bright boys choose careers in just a few areas, such as engineering, business, and pre-med. Our own studies of the future plans of gifted boys and girls show that many gifted boys envision having a high-paying job and a stay-at-home wife, despite the fact that gifted girls have moved on to a new vision of the future. Gifted girls paint pictures in their minds of a future featuring creative, dual-career lifestyles. This dissonance in expectations is confusing for many gifted young men who seem aware that women's roles have changed, but do not yet know how they are supposed to respond to these changes.

Furthermore, the transition to manhood for gifted boys goes largely unmarked in our society, except for those fortunate enough to have a bar mitzvah or other coming-of-age ceremony in their teen years. Most gifted young men continue to follow what they perceive to be society's dictates for the masculine role—just earn good enough grades to get into an MBA program, play and follow sports, date a series of attractive young women, get a high-paying job, marry an attractive woman, and purchase a home, cars, electronics, and other prominent signs of financial success. When a bright man fails to achieve one or more of these goals, or when fate later robs him of one of his accomplishments, he is likely to sink into a depression and then undertake a long-overdue reflection upon his identity and purpose.

The crisis in masculinity that has been predicted and promulgated by the media is often experienced by the gifted man only after a major loss. Corporate downsizing has forced many bright men to reassess the meaning of work in their lives. Similarly, the fragility of relationships with women who now have choices and power of their own is sometimes distressing to bright men, who may see their relationships as achievements. Because gifted men have so often been the prime beneficiaries of society's materialistic prosperity and power structure, they feel greatly victimized when some or all of their wealth or status is lost.

The real tragedy of the gifted male is that he has the cognitive complexity to understand the illusory nature of the quest for the masculine ideal, while at the same time feeling helpless to abstain from that quest. It is the thesis of this book that many gifted boys and men struggle throughout their lives to ignore the urgings of their intellect and creative selves in order to fulfill socially ordained masculine roles. It is our belief that parents and educators can and, indeed, must help our gifted boys tune in to their inner selves and, by doing so, help them realize their intellectual potential. This book examines and integrates current literature on boys and men with research on male giftedness in order to create new, practical approaches to guiding gifted boys. We present to the reader a new vision of what a gifted boy can become—a vision of courage, creativity, and commitment.

How We Came to Study Gifted Boys and Men

On October 4, 1957, the Soviets launched Sputnik, and thus became the first pioneers in space. Some political and educational leaders in the United States interpreted this event as a clear and foreboding sign that America was falling behind other countries in technology and in the education of its young people, especially in the fields of science and mathematics. To many, this represented a national crisis in education, and over the next several years, new educational programs and initiatives to address this concern were introduced in schools all across the country.

In one of these programs, initiated in September of 1961 in St. Louis, 30 ten-year-old children from all over the city—including some from the more economically depressed, blue-collar, and ethnic-minority neighborhoods—were brought together in a well-appointed, spacious school in a beautiful, tree-filled, upper middle class neighborhood in the heart of the city. In a freshly painted classroom, these boys and girls were taught speed-reading, accelerated math, high school science, French, music, advanced literature, composition, and art. They would put on plays of their own creation, engage in wildly creative science projects, endlessly debate the current events of the day, and carry out practical jokes on each other that would have impressed even the best sitcom writers of their day.

Why were these children selected for such a rarefied public education? Because they had been identified as "gifted," and they and their parents and teachers were told that they were the best candidates for the roles of "leaders of tomorrow." The hope was that, as adults, they would rapidly ascend to positions of leadership—in the space race, in government, and in the world of opinion and scholarship. It was believed that investments made then, in the nurturing and grooming of these young persons' gifts and talents, would return to the nation a resumption of dominance in the future of world affairs and technology.

I was one of those ten-year-olds, and I have returned to that classroom often—in my books and speeches, and in my imagination. In the books *Smart Girls, Gifted Women* and *Smart Girls (Revised Edition)*, I told the stories of the lives of the gifted girls of that class. I described how they tried to be very good little gifted girls, how they learned to camouflage their intelligence in adolescence, and how they compromised their dreams as adults. When I began to study gifted girls 20 years ago, I never thought my quest to understand feminine talent development would lead me to study gifted boys and men as well. It was inevitable, however, that in investigating the mystery of why so many gifted girls fail to achieve their goals, I would learn that gifted boys, too, often fail to realize their dreams.

For the gifted boys in that classroom, the future was a glittering promise. They were middle-class American boys in the most prosperous country on earth. They were mostly white in a nation dominated by whites; they were males in a time when nearly every leader, scientist, scholar, and professional was male. And now they had been given the label "gifted," which was to be their ticket to the best education the St. Louis public schools could offer. They would qualify for scholarships to the best colleges, and the world of work lay before them as a great feast for their enjoyment. These were boys who were told by everyone who inquired about their future plans: "Why, you can be anything you want to be!"

I can see them now, just as they were. Eddy, funny and brash, in his crewcut and thick black glasses, who loved science and found math a breeze. Theo, whose sardonic grin made him seem so much older, and who could see through adult hypocrisy more easily than the rest of us could. Tall Carl, who came from a golden family somewhat like the Kennedys': so political, idealistic, and born to lead. Stan, the bustling businessman, who seemed to know everyone on his first day at school. Tom, with his strange, lazy brilliance, who couldn't be bothered with homework, but who aced all of his tests anyway. And, finally, little Donny, the very image of Woody Allen, who wrote continually in his finely illustrated journals page after page of poems, stories, and epics full of dwarves and wizards. Recently, one of these men marveled to me, "There was so much *personality* in that group."

In high school and college, it seemed they were destined to fulfill not only their talents, but also their vivid personalities. Most did go on to excellent colleges, and when I saw them again 10 years after high school at our reunion, they were all vibrant young professionals, well on their way to success, who talked casually and modestly of their accomplishments. Eddy had wanted to be a doctor, and he became a pathologist for the Air Force. Theo had wanted to be an attorney, and was already sailing through his first years as a lawyer. Carl and Stan had completed business degrees and were working their way up the corporate ladder. While the women from our group, for the most part, had fitful careers, stopping and starting again and downsizing their dreams to fit their families' needs, the men had been quite linear in their approach to their careers. These men aimed, fired, and hit their targets. Although I did not see them at the 20th reunion because I was unable to attend, it appeared from the directory and information booklet I received that they had continued on this trajectory.

It was at my 30th reunion in 1999 that I first saw clearly that everything had changed. The gifted women, who 20 years before had seemed so quietly accepting of traditional roles, had thoroughly transformed their lives. Those who had subverted their own goals to support their husbands' goals were now deeply involved in their own careers. Many women had returned to their original interests and dreams with striking new plans for accomplishment. Several were the primary breadwinners in their families. Of those who had quietly endured unhappy marriages, many had broken free and now sang the praises of the single life or dazzled us with stories of their adventures in exotic places. As they neared the age of 50, they had thrown off the mask of middle-aged and middle-class complacence and begun to realize their potential as gifted women.

The men, however, had somehow, against all odds, become—well—ordinary. They were as funny and articulate and alert as they had ever been. But they seemed almost overly gentle and subdued. They were mostly a little chubby, a little balding. They had pictures of pretty wives (who weren't there, for the most part) and great-looking, lively kids. They didn't have much to say about their careers. Most of them had become middle managers, mid-level accountants, executives of small prosperous firms, and busy lawyers. They were contented, caring, ethical guys. However, the arching career trajectory of their youth and early adulthood seemed to have leveled out, as they pursued the pleasures of family life and a myriad avocations. And the really creative ones, such as Donny, had "disappeared" off the face of the earth. Everyone whispered about those few—"gone crazy," "got into drugs," "went to jail," or just got lost.

So what I wanted to know was: Who stole those bright-eyed boys with so much *personality* and replaced them with these nice old guys? Why weren't they glowing like the women who had hidden their lights for so long? And where the heck was Donny, with his bursting journals, his dwarves, and his elves? I decided to find the answers.

I had found clues along the way in my career. At the University of Nebraska in 1982, I had founded a Guidance Laboratory for Gifted and Talented. We brought hundreds of gifted students to the Guidance Lab, first from the state of Nebraska, and then from all over the Midwest, to provide career counseling in return for an opportunity to study gifted students up close. We also had programs for the emotional guidance of gifted students. It was there that I learned that gifted boys often struggle to meet the expectations of their families, their schools, and their communities—often at the cost of their own dreams and values. In Nebraska, I met an eleven-year-old boy who had learned everything there was to learn about the physics of skateboarding and had practiced thousands of hours to become one of the best in the region. He had won many contests, and skateboarding was his life. His parents, however, wanted him to use his extraordinary math/science skills for medicine or engineering and saw skateboarding as a silly hobby that took their son into a dangerous subculture. At the slightest act of misconduct at home, his skateboard would be taken from him and locked in a closet. How difficult it was to convince his parents that the leadership, stamina, and persistence he was exhibiting in skateboarding were the best predictors of a life of achievement and did not at all predict that he would be a failure!

At the University of Iowa from 1985 to 1991, I collaborated with Nicholas Colangelo, a mentor, and colleague who was himself a model for many gifted boys and young men. Together, we created a Counseling Laboratory for Talent Development and the Iowa Governor's Institute. Nick and I had the pleasure of working with the state's most gifted young people in language, science, arts, leadership, and invention. As the disciplinarians for the Institute, Nick and I had some fascinating discussions with creative young men who found difficulty conforming to the (*albeit* loose) structure of our Institute. I remember a delightful young man who had to be persuaded to stop disrupting classes with his "pet iron." He had taken the iron from the laundry of the dorm and now used it in "performance art." He made it sit up and beg, heel, and run along beside him while giving a running commentary on life from the perspective of an appliance. We also created a program for gifted underachievers, and we learned some very important lessons from them. One of the greatest lessons was that, often, "underachievers" were indeed high achievers in some hidden area that took all of their energies.

One year we got the opportunity to study inventors (a group of agricultural inventors approached us and asked us to study "what made them tick"). We learned that many of these extraordinarily gifted and productive men had indeed been underachievers in school, the congenial dunces of the classroom. Although they had been lonely nerds or underachievers in school, as adult inventors they were happy, humorous men with loving families and friends all over the world.

It was at Arizona State University (ASU) where I came to direct the masters of counseling program in 1991 that I met Sandy Cohn, founder of the Center for Academic Precocity (CAP) there and co-author of this book. Sandy and I had 10 years of conversation about boys, masculinity, and giftedness before beginning this book.

There were signs, both anecdotal and objective, of young Sandy's precocity. His aunt used to tell him that he was "12 going on 40," and his school principal, after reviewing Sandy's performance on an intelligence test at age 13, said that the young teen "thought like someone much older." Though his hometown was small and had no gifted programs then (in the early 1960s), the influence of the Sputnik crisis had been felt, and math and science had begun to receive heavy emphasis in school. As a result, in 1963, Sandy's high school graduating class set a school record for the highest scores ever earned on the Scholastic Aptitude Test (SAT) up to that time.

Sandy's strengths and interests as a student were extremely broad, and his high school counselor suggested that Sandy could do "anything he wanted to." He found it difficult, though, to embark on a career path, because that meant choosing from amongst his many diverse interests. His very favorite subjects, though, were literature, writing, and science, and each of these were to eventually play a role in the choices he would make as a young adult.

Prominent among his influences was a book he had read at the suggestion of his 11th-grade English teacher, Mr. Brubaker. This book was *The Immense Journey* by Loren Eiseley, the work of a philosopher-anthropologist who muses on the trajectory of man's evolution. The questions raised in Sandy's mind while reading that book have resonated in his thinking ever since. Of special interest to him was the notion that the spark of intelligence began as a highly localized event in a single individual who spawned a new species, *Homo sapiens*. Sandy discovered then that he wanted to study the emergence of intellectual talent.

After high school, Sandy enrolled as a pre-med student at Johns Hopkins University, where he was allowed to choose from a highly diversified menu of courses. He ended up with specializations in such diverse fields as chemistry, psychology, and German literature. His thesis, written under the tutelage of G. Wilson Shaffer, former dean of the university, had as its subject Sandy's own original theory of psychology. Working under Dean Shaffer also impressed upon Sandy the value and effectiveness of mentoring as an educational tool.

Later, as a biochemistry graduate student following his departure from medical school, Sandy cherished his teaching assignments, but soon became disenchanted with his own specialized area of study—nuclear chemistry. He had realized after a few months in medical school that he was less interested in what went wrong with people than in what went right with them. And the consequent painstaking focus on hard science was too narrow for him—it left out so many of the other important things he wanted to pursue and ways he wanted to interact with people and the world.

After taking some time off, during which he lived and taught for a while at an intentional community, Sandy returned to graduate school and began working with Lynn Fox in her Intellectually Gifted Child Study Group. In 1975, after attending a symposium during which early results of Professor Julian Stanley's ambitious lifetime longitudinal Studies of Intellectual Precocity were announced, Sandy decided to pursue his doctorate with Professor Stanley.

Sandy has continued the work of Julian Stanley and his Johns Hopkins colleagues as a professor at Arizona State University, where he started the Center for Academic Precocity (CAP). The Center was geared to a broader domain of abilities than simply math and verbal ability and a greater age-range of participants than the Johns Hopkins studies. For 21 years, Sandy taught, counseled, and studied gifted children at the Center, and he advised thousands of parents on ways of guiding their children. He created a model of diagnostic prescriptive education, which is a way of diagnosing the unique needs of each gifted child and prescribing precisely the challenge needed to nurture his or her talents. From the time he arrived at ASU, he met parents who told him how their children's lives had been changed by finding both him and the CAP program.

In many ways, Sandy's education and career paralleled that of most gifted boys. He loved intellectual challenge as a boy, but sometimes had difficulty finding it. He was told he could do anything, but found that having multiple potentials was as much a curse as it was a blessing; there are insufficient hours in a day to do all that one has the potential to do, and it can be quite frustrating to feel so diffused and even unfocused. He had a few mentors who showed him the way, not only toward his enthusiasms, but also toward mature masculinity. He got a little lost along the way, as many gifted men do, even after having a vision of what they might become. He found his way toward a meaningful career and meaningful life by discovering work that challenged his talents and fulfilled his deepest values.

Sandy's scholarly work and his years of listening to the concerns of gifted boys make him an appropriate co-author for this book; his own life experience as a gifted boy has also helped inform these pages.

Why Do We Need a Book about Gifted Boys?

There has been a tremendous growth of interest in the ways that the changing roles of girls and women have affected boys and men. One might get the impression that this is another book that attempts to "balance the scales" or to refocus attention that has somehow been diverted from boys by the recent emphasis on girls. However, it is not our belief that the concerns of girls and women have been overemphasized in the literature. A few decades of feminist studies and popular books can hardly tip the balance of thousands of years of male dominance in family, government, religion, art, and intellectual life.

Nor do we intend to imply that the ways in which men have been constricted by society's notions of manhood are as debilitating as the effects of the social and political oppression of women. Men's emotionality, creativity, spirituality, and self-actualization have truly been limited by the traditions of masculinity. Societal expectations have traditionally trapped men into responsibility for the protection and support of women who are perfectly capable of caring for themselves. However, it is our contention that it is better to have the means of supporting another than to be dependent, that it is better to be powerful than powerless, and that it is better to be strong and intimidating than to be weak and defenseless.

Despite the fact that gifted boys still benefit from being male, they can sometimes remain confused and concerned about what it means to be male in today's world. Many books seek to describe the world of boys today and to guide parents in raising happy and healthy boys. Some of these books are very useful to parents and teachers; we review the major ones in Chapter 3. However, both of us have worked closely in therapy and in the classroom with gifted boys. We know there are many ways in which these children are unique, and we believe a book dedicated to their unique needs will be beneficial to parents, teachers, counselors, and perhaps gifted men themselves. We believe this book can make a difference.

It is true, for example, that gifted boys are confronted with the same pressures that all men in our society face—to become independent, strong, and competitive. However, being gifted puts a special burden on boys, not only to prove their masculinity, but also to develop their gifts. It is just one more expectation to meet—one more label to constantly live up to—tacked onto a list of presumptions that was already long enough from birth. And the competitiveness that is required of all men becomes an especially high-stakes issue for gifted boys and men who may not experience failure until it is almost too late for them to learn to fail gracefully. If one gets straight A's all of one's life only to fail to get into medical school, or if one succeeds at everything until an engagement to marry is suddenly broken off, then that first failure can be devastating. Finally, there is a special brand of conformity required of men in terms of their appearance, interests, and values—and gifted men frequently diverge from the expected. It can often be troubling, for example, to a gifted young artist to feel the pressure to dress or wear his hair in a certain "currently acceptable" fashion that he considers ugly, uninteresting, and unimaginative. It can be confusing to a bright young intellectual to find that many of his classmates are more interested in, say, auto racing or professional wrestling, when he himself is more interested in collecting and cataloging insects or in reading about dinosaurs or visiting Civil War battle sites. And it can be disturbing and offensive to a sensitive young male to hear profane and disrespectful "locker room" talk about women, other cultures, homosexuals, or people of other generations.

As a result, parents of gifted boys are often puzzled about how to raise a boy in such a way as to both affirm his giftedness and help him define his own way of being a man. Teachers often want to find ways of challenging gifted boys without setting them up for bullying and mockery as the teacher's pet (the kiss of death). Teachers, counselors, and parents are eager to learn better ways of guiding gifted boys toward their academic, personal, and career goals, without pushing them too hard or too little. This book is written for all of these people.

An Overview

The first section of the book, Giftedness and Masculinity, explores the relationship of special intellectual ability to the role of males in our society. In Chapter 1, we use our own modest study of gifted men (ably implemented by Thomas Anderson) on the graduates of the accelerated learning class of 1969 as a cautionary tale. Although these men were successful by ordinary standards, many did not fulfill their dreams, and most had great difficulty in relationships. In Chapter 2, our purpose is to separate fact from fiction by explaining giftedness, presenting the research on gifted boys, and drawing whatever conclusions we can. In Chapter 3, we critically examine the current literature on masculinity to determine which of the new books on boys can be helpful to an understanding of gifted boys.

In the next section, Milestones and Danger Zones, Chapters 4 through 6 journey through the growing years of the gifted boy, from childhood to manhood, describing those issues that are unique to gifted boys. In each stage, we point out the unique concerns these boys have because they are gifted and some of the special challenges they present to parents, counselors, and teachers.

The next section, Special Challenges for Gifted Boys, describes the impact of giftedness on boys' academic and social adjustment. The gifted boy in the classroom is the topic of Chapter 7, where we point out the many forms of underachievement and what that may mean. The conduct-disordered or violent gifted boy is addressed in Chapter 8; it is our thesis here that many gifted boys, although not true sociopaths, engage in antisocial behavior because of an anger that stems from boredom, lack of attention, rejection by others, or the inappropriate expectations of adults. In Chapter 9, we take up the cases of those gifted boys who are most likely to be bullied because of their failure to fulfill traditional masculine stereotypes. We discuss how these boys become "sissies," how they become obese, and how they become social misfits, and we show ways in which acceptance and guidance can help each of these types achieve his full potential without taking on a "mask" in an attempt to be the "perfect" male. In Chapter 10, we describe the extraordinary resilience of disadvantaged gifted boys and gifted boys of color to see what can be learned from their struggles.

The last section of this book, Guiding Smart Boys, describes issues in parenting, teaching, mentoring, and guiding gifted boys and men. Chapter 11 describes parenting patterns that often are distinctive in their potentially damaging effects on gifted boys, as well as the relationship needs of gifted males. Chapter 12 provides an outline for parenting, teaching, and guiding gifted boys toward manhood, with specific suggestions from pre-kindergarten through the college years. In Chapter 13, we discuss well-known studies of creative, committed, and courageous people, and the conclusions we can draw from them about mature masculinity and talent fulfillment. We conclude this section with suggestions for guiding gifted males from infancy to maturity.

Smart Boys: Talent, Manhood, and the Search for Meaning is an initial attempt at understanding the needs of our gifted boys. By bringing together all of the research on gifted boys, the literature of masculinity studies, and our own clinical experiences, we hope to provide new insights for the boys themselves, their parents, teachers, and counselors. We also hope that *Smart Boys* provides a roadmap for a new kind of "hero's journey" for the gifted boy—a journey in which the goals are creativity, commitment, and a courageous search for meaning.

Barbara Kerr
June, 2001

Section I:
Giftedness and
Masculinity

1

Our Follow-Up Study of Gifted Men

While studies of gifted boys are few and far between, studies of gifted men are even more rare. To remedy the situation and because we truly wanted to learn what had happened to those bright boys I knew so well as a child, I decided to look closely at what happened to the boys who had graduated with me from the St. Louis Accelerated Learning Program in 1969. These were boys who had been specifically selected in the 4th grade to enter a school for gifted because their intelligence scores indicated very high potential.

At graduation, there had been 17 boys who had been in my gifted class from at least the 6th grade onwards. Tom Anderson, a graduate student in counseling psychology with a strong interest in men's issues, volunteered to help me locate the boys, now men, from the Accelerated Learning Program. Through e-mail and regular mail, we sought these men's permission to be interviewed, assuring them that we would change names and specific details in order to preserve their anonymity in this chapter and in other presentations. Tom and I conducted interviews with 13 of these men and got basic information about three more over a period of time between 1999 and 2000.

All were now approaching 50 years old. We found that six of the men still lived in the St. Louis area, and the others resided in major cities across the U.S. Among the 13 we interviewed in full were four businessmen, two accountants, two engineers, one free-lance archeological consultant, two lawyers, one physician, and one social activist. Of the three others we were able to get information about from secondary sources, there was an accountant who was deceased, one man who had been involved in drugs and was rumored to have gone to prison, and one itinerant philosophy instructor who seemed to have "disappeared"—such that even the most powerful people-finding searches could not trace him.

A few cautions to the reader are necessary here. First, this is perhaps not a representative sample of gifted men. All had grown up in the same city and all, except for one, were white, Protestant or Catholic males from blue collar or middle class families. Second, many of these men were aware that the women who had been in our class were once also the subject of a similar study and a book enti-tled *Smart Girls* (Kerr, 1985; 1995; 1997), and the men's respons-es might have been influenced by this. Third, they all knew me well, having gone to school with me every day for seven years or more. These factors might have affected their responses. Thus, Tom Anderson assisted me in conducting many of the interviews to lessen possible "experimenter bias."

We conducted phone interviews lasting approximately one hour with each of the men. We used a structured interview protocol that featured questions about childhood, adolescence, marital and family life, career history, and life satisfaction. Some of the major life themes that emerged from our interviews are described below.

Social Isolation

These men felt socially isolated from their peers as very young children. Before entry into the gifted program, they felt that their intellectual differences set them apart. They acknowledged feeling bored in school, socially awkward, and somehow discon-nected from others at a young age. Most believed they were expect-ed to excel academically. And because they were expected to outperform their contemporaries, they made sure that they did. "School was not a problem. Grades came easily," said one.

After their entry into the gifted program, they felt even further isolated from the children in their neighborhoods and old schools. Entry into the gifted program seems to have provided a culture that offered sanctuary from the demands of "normal" society, but this sanctuary came with a price. According to one former student, "Once I was at the gifted school, I didn't see any of my old friends. And at the new school, they had average kids there, too, in other classes. But we didn't even play with them at recess. So the message I got was that life is all over, and now you have to hang out only with gifted people."

Many of these men felt separated out permanently and continued to struggle to reintegrate themselves into male peer groups later in their lives. Another said, "I like to think that the kids in our class avoided elitism, but it somehow could not be helped because we were set aside from the rest of the school's 4th grade class population. There was a reason why we got special classes. Here's an example: Why didn't we get any shop classes? We got French and algebra instead. I sensed I was advantaged. I felt like people were setting aside money for things that were not offered to other people."

It was this social isolation and perhaps some guilt over preferential treatment that many of the men felt contributed to their strong desire to feel, look, and act normal. When they grew up, it became especially important to have a "normal" family, a pretty wife, and a good job. However, some of their marriages failed because the men were incapable of knowing how to be "normal," no matter how hard they tried. Given their relative social isolation, where could these brilliant men learn how to argue with a lover while still being tender, or how to be right without being impatient or condescending? Pressure to conform to the pervasively popular masculine traits of silence and strength, an over-emphasis on intelligence, and an inability to cope with emotions were problems mentioned by many men as later contributing to the failure of intimate relationships, a subject we will return to later in this chapter.

Choice between Excellence and "Normality"

Because these boys were being prodded to excel, they often became anxious about being "normal." A choice was being thrust upon them—to accept the label of giftedness and act like an intellectual, or to try very hard to prove they were "one of the guys."

Within the confines of the gifted program there was a stratification among the boys. There were boys who focused on academics but who were at the bottom of the social hierarchy; those who chose a heavy investment in socializing, sports, and/or dating; and at the top of the hierarchy, those who managed to combine a quiet academic excellence with social achievement and athletic prowess. "I think the program had a stereotype of including only the geeks and brains," said one of the men. "There were people who fit that profile, but I think the program had a broad range of people. We had great students and great athletes." In fact, most of the men made an effort to impress upon the interviewer that among their class were many popular athletes—in short, "normal" guys who also happened to be smart.

Many of the men had a strong drive to fulfill expectations of parents and teachers; they had a tremendous ability to pick up on parental expectations and to use their significant abilities to meet and exceed those expectations in an attempt to gain parental approval. Once the boys were accepted into the gifted program, their decision to attend was virtually assured: "There was never any question about whether I would go or not. My parents just told me it was an excellent opportunity. They might have mentioned I had a choice or asked me, but I knew I was going." Another said, "There was an expectation from very early on that I was going to do better than my parents, so it was a given that I was going to go to the program once I got accepted." Men reported that they had felt excited, nervous, jealous, competitive, and "resigned," but each accepted the challenge and the opportunity. None could recall anyone turning down the chance to attend the gifted school. The message from their parents, teachers, and society was that this was important and exciting and that entry into this program made you special.

These men, at a time when much of their generation was in rebellion, were highly attuned to the "accepted" needs of society and authority. Only two men spoke of any participation in anti-war activities or in the social movements of the 1960s and 1970s; one of these was a conscientious objector. It was as if the era of social transformation had passed most of them by. This is not to say that they didn't smoke marijuana (some even inhaled) or enjoy the new sexual freedom brought by the changes in the culture, but they did not see these profound social movements as having much relevance to their lives. Instead, most were working hard in college to be able to improve their original economic status. By and large, throughout school and college, these men performed exactly as expected, rose to the challenges they were given, and tried to fulfill the expectations of adults. Because most could not choose between being smart and being normal, they often camouflaged aspects of their intelligence behind a cloak of conformity.

Problems with Peer Relationships

Several of these brilliant boys had skipped at least one grade, with the result that they lagged behind their classmates in terms of physical and emotional maturity. Their rapid advancement and placement in "special classes" was now visible testimony to a long internalized fact and fear—that they were indeed different. "Smart, small, shy, weak, clumsy, naïve, and angry" are some of the words that these men used to describe themselves as young students. Here is a typical response from one of these men: "In the 5th grade I was a year younger than everyone else. In high school it had a big impact on me. I was physically and emotionally behind the others going through changes. As a result, I grew up with a different political outlook; I was shy, a bit of an oddball, even more than the other kids in the program. My image of myself is fixed in some ways to that period as a teenager. The ages of 14 to 16 played a large part in forming my identity of myself. I was a social klutz and immature. I think this had a big impact on me, staying too long in my first marriage. I was not self-confident enough to strike out on my own. It had an effect on how gregarious and social I am today." This response is typical of others we heard.

Another said, "I was one of the youngest people in my class most of the time, so when I got to high school, most of the girls were older. In my coursework, I only took classes with kids who were older. So I did not date much in high school and was limited in some of my social development." So on one hand, the young men's intellectual differences from their agemates often led to social difficulties with them, while on the other hand, the age differences with their older, gifted peers sometimes also led to embarrassment and shyness. It seemed that the boys had little support for their efforts to create the friendships they wanted and needed. Instead, they were left to fend for themselves in a world of relationships they didn't understand. Because they were bright, many of them chose to study and observe others in order to figure out how to behave. Their intense awareness of social hierarchies and the price of admission to the highest rungs of these hierarchies remained alive well into adulthood.

Ambivalence about Being Gifted

These men had learned that they shouldn't express intellectual superiority over others unless there was an actual competition. To them, being openly smart implied being an egghead—physically weak, different from the rest of the men. And they believed that academic success only creates envy and distance from the other guys. Said one of the men, "Generally, I hid my intellect; it's not too good to show off how bright you are. I've held myself back."

To these men, truly masculine heroes convert their strivings into the enhancement of something larger than themselves, but never trumpet their own abilities. Said another, "I don't tell many people that I was considered gifted. I meet a lot of smart people now who I would consider gifted who didn't go through accelerated programs. They are all bright…but I do take a little hidden pride in seeing my children are growing up bright."

The men interviewed did acknowledge that some tasks were easy for them; however, they harbored significant self-doubt about the value of their intellectual abilities, and they continually engaged in self-comparisons with others. Said one, "I don't like to think of the term 'gifted.' I am perhaps gifted in some areas, but in other areas I am below average. My artistic skills, communication skills, and personal relations are not great. When I got into the gifted program, I went into advanced math and science courses, but I struggled with French and humanities." One of the attorneys in the group said, "I don't even consider myself gifted now. It doesn't mean anything to me because when I got into law school, I saw *really* bright people there. If I was self-important before, I later learned that there were others who were *really* bright. I stayed out of areas that I didn't do well in because I didn't want to embarrass myself."

This was typical. In fact, we found that whatever the subject or ability, these men could always think of someone who was smarter or better and therefore "actually" gifted. Indeed, "gifted" seemed to be defined as "smarter than I." "Given a challenge that requires thought or analysis, I am normally not deterred," said one. "I have a lot of confidence in my mental capacity to solve problems and figure things out. I think the gifted program really enforced my confidence that I can take on any challenge. But there were others who were brighter than me, people whom I would consider truly gifted."

Typically, these men believed that their own inadequacies made it unlikely that they were truly gifted. Some were almost zealous in their descriptions of their failures.

"If I were gifted, I would know how to be a good husband; I would know how to program a VCR; I would know how to communicate with my wife; I would know how to do math as well as John does."

"Maybe it boils down to whether people read well or not if they are going to test better," said another, "but I never felt gifted. Maybe it's about aptitude, because if someone asked me to put a cable into a TV, I couldn't do it, but my stepdaughter who has dropped out of high school could."

Again, this was typical and was an attitude that spilled over into non-academic realms, too. For instance, each man interviewed offered the same several names when speaking of who the "really" smart boys in the class were. But almost without fail the guys who were mentioned as not *academically* focused were then rated highly in athletic events or socializing. There was a great deal of consensus from person to person about *other* boys' positions on these hierarchies. But when asked about his *own* place, each man insisted that others ranked higher than he did on at least one of these hierarchies. It became obvious that, even for those aware that their intellectual gifts were considerable, these men often denigrated their own abilities compared to other men in the class.

There were two main—and interestingly paradoxical—strategies used by the men to discount their giftedness. Some men claimed that they did not have to work hard for their achievements, so they saw their gift as exactly that—a gift—and therefore they could not take credit for the rewards it afforded them. Others felt that they did work hard for their achievements, and that it was this work ethic—something anyone can do—rather than anything special about themselves to which they owed their successes. The following two interview excerpts are illustrative of these strategies, respectively.

"I guess I feel pretty proud of being intelligent. I hope I don't go around acting like it. I was probably born with it because it was nothing I did. I was never prone to go overboard studying and studied less the higher I went in school. The girls studied more than the guys."

"I think in many respects I have been an overachiever as an adult. I have achieved well beyond my abilities in a lot of areas. I think the reason I have achieved is because from early on I knew there were expectations of what I should do. I can think of a few kids who had high IQs and did not work hard, but I think most of us kids achieved at a high level through hard work, because we didn't want to disappoint. Wanting to achieve and to meet others' expectations—those were the key factors."

In all of these ways—concern about hiding gifts, assuming that if one isn't good at everything one must not be gifted, concern that there is always someone smarter, "explaining away" their giftedness or accomplishments, and focusing on their shortcomings—these men showed great ambivalence about their own giftedness.

Concern about Masculinity

From a very early age, boys are groomed to become men. Thousands of sources teach boys what it means to be a man. And it seems that gifted boys learn this lesson better than most. Many of the gifted men we studied had received the same messages for "appropriate masculine" development as other men had, but because of their intelligence, they were able to more clearly understand those messages, set definitive goals regarding masculinity, and easily achieve them. For others, there was a counter-reaction. They rejected stereotyped masculinity—but then found themselves without a roadmap for alternative ways of behaving. Here's how one of the men described the quandary:

"I have spent a great deal of my life trying not to act in a stereotypically masculine fashion. And I have been about 75 percent successful, though I am not so sure I should have been. Because of my mom's high intelligence and my emotional connection with her, I always identified with her over my dad. My awareness of stereotypical male behavior and all the things wrong with it has led me to be less aggressive, more sensitive, and more aware of how my actions affect other people. Increased sensitivity is good, and less aggressiveness is mostly good, but I have always had a lot of difficulty with asking women out and being social. I am poor at picking up signals from and relating with women. Part of it comes from being socially awkward and part comes from not wanting to be a jerk. It's difficult to find a way to be me without being stereotypical."

Some of the men preserved their sense of masculinity by choosing not to compete academically. Since they did not want to be associated with the small, nerdy boys who were highly focused on academics, they sought the company of those friends who took academics less seriously. Called by girls the "locker room boys," these were gifted boys who tried for an almost exaggerated masculinity. "I was well-rounded, played sports, and enjoyed lots of camaraderie. I did not focus on academics, and my grades showed it. I didn't compete in academics at all, in fact. I got competitive on the basketball court. I did okay in academics, but I…didn't want to apply myself."

Some of the men felt that their striving for traditional masculinity had impaired their communication skills and emotional development. One said, "Some of the stereotypes about masculinity fit me pretty well. Poor communication affected my first marriage, and I am told it still affects my second marriage. I could be more communicative, more sensitive. I sometimes think I know things that others don't, because it's just so obvious to me. How I am feeling— why should I speak about it? I am perceptive about how I am feeling, but often don't really pick up on how others are feeling, and sometimes I misinterpret how my wife and others close to me are feeling. Being gifted is not a complete circle around everything."

In summary, most of the men considered themselves quite masculine and had gone to great lengths to preserve their masculine identity in their own eyes and in the eyes of others. The most frequent concern about masculinity seemed to center around difficulties with emotions and relationships with women. Here, many of the men felt that their search for masculinity—for the qualities of strength, silence, and stoicism—had distanced them from the women they most cared about.

Pursuit of Contentment

It was paramount to these gifted men that they be content. One wealthy professional man said, "I was driving down Tholozan Avenue back in South St. Louis and I saw a guy sitting on his front porch drinking a Bud and listening to the Cardinals game. And I thought to myself, you know, that's not so bad; I could be happy like that."

They did not seem to be seeking extreme wealth, but did want to have material comforts and to have their material needs well met. They wanted happy and stable families. They wanted jobs in middle-management, in which they could make good money but not necessarily have to lead or create. They sought careers in which they could use their intelligence, but without having to be overly achieving or ambitious. It's as if these men thought there was a rulebook somewhere that stated that whoever has (1) a family, (2) a job that does not require manual labor, and (3) enough money to support his family, is the winner.

One of the engineers said, "Working here is like being back in school surrounded by a stable class of people and intellects. Even before I got out of school, I could envision myself as an engineer, but I could not envision myself staying on top of the state-of-the-art of engineering. I hoped instead to get a managerial position. Ten years later, I started to drift in that direction. Now I can read schematics, but I mostly do technical and customer interfacing and a little marketing. At one time, I actually aspired to move up several levels in management, but now I am wary of stepping into a position that would require a 12-hour workday. I am still looking to step up into a position with more authority, but I'm not in a rush like I was years ago."

Another said, "I have evaluated what I may and may not be able to do in the future. I tend to be a person who, unless severely pained, doesn't feel a whole lot like moving. I worked in the same functional department for 25 years and have been supporting the same aircraft. If I shifted to a new aircraft, I would have to make new associations and it's a lot of extra work. In that regard, I am not a great risk taker."

These men pursued contentment more than they pursued excellence or achievement or recognition. Only a few took risks, and most chose conservative routes to prosperity. Given the extraordinary preparation these young people received for leadership, their outstanding education, and the high expectations of their teachers and parents, this is perhaps the most surprising finding of our small study. Perhaps their love of contentment was born of their South St. Louis cultural environment—a place of bare schoolyards, crowded houses, and large, bickering families. From the vantage point of South St. Louis, a large, airy home with room for everyone and a comfortable suburban lifestyle might have seemed the ultimate achievement. Another, more poignant conclusion might be that loneliness and unhappiness in childhood led these men to most want security and comfort in adulthood—an understandable choice for boys who wanted so much to be ordinary.

A Lack of Concern for Eminence

While all of these men wanted to do their jobs well, none of them wanted to be the best at what they did, to shine in their work, or to receive recognition for their abilities or accomplishments. There was little ambition to excel beyond their present roles. It appeared as if these men had found positions that were both comfortable and socially acceptable and then stopped. It was as if they were saying, "To do more would be offensive to others who also stopped at this position."

It seemed as if they felt a responsibility not to be too successful. These were the future leaders of our country, or so they were told, but somehow placement in a special school was all the separation they ever wanted from more average people. They spent the rest of their lives being careful not to be too achieving.

"My advisor wanted me to go to an Ivy League school, but I wasn't interested because none of them had actuarial programs. The counselor said I wasn't striving toward my highest potential. She wanted me to apply to the Ivy League schools just to show people I could get in. Both counselors beat me up about not applying to the Ivy League schools. The fact is, I applied to only two schools. Lots of people felt that if I wasn't applying to Princeton, Harvard, or Yale, I was not achieving my full potential. But to me it was a waste of time and effort. I have been very practical and career-focused and have had no desire to impress others."

"Now I manage information systems," says another of the men. "I run the computers and the database…techno junk. I learned the technology stuff on my own. When I got married, my wife and I got a computer and a lot of things went wrong with it, and I spent time fixing the problems. At the high school where I was volunteering, we had a computer lab. I would read the instruction book and start messing with the programs. When I got my job here, there was no network. I set up and now administer the network."

The brightest student in our class, our National Merit Scholar, said, "I got my degree in business in 1975; I picked it by default. I thought, 'It will work.' I had been working at a poultry factory.

After graduation I stayed there. Didn't get a job based on my degree. Later, I applied for accounting jobs and took a job as the city accountant. I've been with the city ever since."

In summary, it seems there was little concern among these men for eminence in their domain or for the development of their greatest talents toward excellence. As with their pursuit of contentment, their pursuit of moderate achievement may be related to their concern for normality and their wish not to seem to be putting other men down. However, it remains puzzling that the inspirational speeches of their early school years seem to have fallen on deaf ears. Did they burn out as children? If so, they do not remember.

Uncertainty about Vocation

These were bright, capable men who seemed to radiate good intentions and a sense of pride in their work and families, but confusion abounded when we asked about a purpose or vocation. Perhaps the gifted men in this survey had so many choices that they believed any passionate choice would inevitably limit them and exclude other paths. Also, to fully choose or be enveloped by a passion would have served to alienate these men from others, and this, they learned, is a painful situation. Whatever the reason, the gifted men we interviewed seemed to have a lack of a sense of vocation or calling.

Said one, "When I was in school, I didn't have any lofty goals. I wanted a career with no manual labor and in which I could use my brain and make a lot of money. I figured I would go into some kind of business, but I didn't know what kind."

"When I reached the end of my junior year," said another, "I went to my guidance counselor. I had advanced classes and good grades, but I didn't have any idea what I should do or what I wanted to do. My guidance counselor asked me what my strengths were. I told her my strengths were math and science. The counselor told me I could be an engineer or a math teacher. I did not want to be a math teacher, and she didn't know much about engineering, but we figured electrical engineering would be where my strengths would best lie. I knew I might design and repair TV sets."

Most of these men chose a major only when they had to. Business and law were favorite choices, but not because of a passion for enterprise or the legal system. Instead, these occupations were chosen on the basis of their fathers' occupations, a desire to "get into business and make some money," or their friends' choices. As one said, "My friend was going into the insurance business, so he got me into it."

Another said, "Since high school, I have had several jobs. I was a delivery boy for a jeweler, and then I was a laborer. I was even a bum for a number of years, living off of relatives, scraping by. I had to work as a conscientious objector during the war. I worked in hospitals for almost 20 years. I was an orderly in an operating room and a technician."

"I got information about actuarial work before starting college," reports another of the men. "My father worked in the finance department of a large chemical company, and that seemed interesting. He was the person responsible for pension plans and he knew a number of actuaries, and he got some to talk to me and explain the process and what they did. I had a tremendous amount of information about the job by the time I started college, and it sounded as interesting as anything else."

Even those who began with a passion somehow lost it along the way. "As long as I could remember, I wanted to go into medicine. My dad was a doctor and a psychiatrist. I read everything I could about the body. My play at home was being a doctor—I had a teddy bear hospital. In college, I majored in pre-med and stayed in it, took all the courses. Sometime around my sophomore year, though, I discovered anthropology. I was fascinated by Leakey, and I read about Indians and past cultures. Took a couple of courses and found the department was much smaller, professors more accessible, and I got to work with them. I got involved in research projects doing archaeology. I applied for medical school and did that for two years, but gradually got more into medical anthropology. So I changed to anthropology at Washington University. I met my wife on a dig, and after she ended a marriage we got married, and I moved with her to her faculty job. It got harder to finish the degree. I saw all the political infighting...incredible amount of feuds in archaeology. So I didn't get my Ph.D. I drifted into contract archeology, environmental consulting, and have done well."

Here's another's story: "I wanted to become a doctor and I was a physician for 20 years. But managed care, some fraudulent business situations, and the economics of it made it impossible to stay. A lot of physicians go into real estate, because that's the one investment you don't get taxed out of. I went into that because it was someplace I could invest my money."

Multipotentiality and disappointments often led to indecision and compromise for these gifted men. With their South St. Louis upbringings, they were possibly unaware of the wide variety of career options available to them. Whatever the reasons, passion and a sense of vocation seem to have played small roles in these men's lives.

Early Marriage or Multiple Marriages

Of the interviewees, two distinct relationship patterns emerged—early, long-term marriages or a series of relationship and marriage failures. The gifted men who married their first serious partner tended to have long-term, stable marriages. However, only five of the 17 men fit in this category. One of these said, "When I was with the inventory service, I met my wife. I would go out to stores with a little machine to record the information, and there were these young ladies with headsets who would transcribe. That's where I met her. She had gone to my high school and we had had a class together. She asked me out. One thing led to another. We ended up getting married in 1975. I've been very lucky. I was very fortunate to have gotten hooked up in this relationship."

Another said, "I think some of the stereotypes about men have gone away, but my family life has adhered to the stereotype pretty well. My wife worked as a nurse for a while, but she has always been more interested in the kids and what they are doing. My wife volunteers at places, but for the most part we have had a traditional family life where the husband works and the wife stays at home with the kids. It wouldn't have bothered me if my wife had wanted a full career of her own, but it would have caused more difficulties with the kids."

Of the 13 other men, six also married young, but after breaking up with their first serious girlfriend. The personal lives of these men were characterized by difficulty in relationships, multiple and unstable marriages, and a continued desire for happiness in marriage and family. For many of these men, marriage and relationships with women represented their first experience with failure. These men seemed ill-equipped to handle the emotional and communication requirements of a successful relationship. Some of them had struggled with interpersonal skills from an early age. These troubles were far from ameliorated by their entry into marriage.

"I have had down times," said one of the men, "but I guess that my biggest disappointment is that I am on my third marriage."

"I married when I was 21," said another, "and that marriage lasted for about seven years. Then I got a divorce, remarried for another five or six years, got divorced again, and remarried again— this time with no children."

Another of the men told us, "I was married just before my senior year of college. We had two daughters, and after 15 years of marriage, my wife and I got a divorce. It was not a bitter divorce; I still talk to my ex-wife."

"We moved out to Tennessee," said another, "and my wife was very unhappy. There was a lot of stress in our relationship, so we moved in 1990, and she was much happier out here. We had a child, a daughter born in 1992. Having a child changed our lives much more than we thought. I'm dad-oriented, and mom is work-oriented, and that caused a lot of strain. When my wife got tenure, another opportunity came up in Florida. She got offered the job, and I didn't want to move. She's been upset ever since. We are going through mediation."

Let's hear from one more of these men. "After I graduated, I thought, okay, now it's time to get out of this marriage. It was a mistake in the first place. It cost me a lot in alimony, but it's the best money I ever spent."

Though several of the men were on their third marriages, all of them valued success in relationships. Many men to this day consider their unsuccessful marriages their largest failures and largest sources of regret.

Said one, "If I could turn back the clock, I would probably change some issues with relationships and my two failed marriages. I would have either not gotten into the relationships or worked harder at the marriages. I felt really terrible when I discovered my marriages would not work anymore, and worse when my wives agreed it would not work."

These men, who for so long were encouraged to excel in math, science, and literature, found it difficult to turn their powerful minds off. They reported terrible discomfort and difficulty in sharing pain, sorrow, joy, grief, or anger with other people. Like most people, they would rather stick to their strengths and avoid areas of weakness. For these powerfully minded men, the emotional world is characterized by whirling and unpredictable feelings and contradictory emotions. Not only are feelings often unpredictable, they are often uncontrollable. These men reported feelings of frustration, fatigue, clumsiness, anger, and fear at operating within this rule-less and threatening frontier, and they wanted to avoid it. An overemphasis on intellect or achievement orientation had made emotional development and relationships difficult for them.

"My first wife realized she did not want to live with me," said one of the men, "and we separated without any animosity. It took me several years to recognize and believe that she had simply grown away from me. I went through counseling and began recognizing the psychological profile of engineers. Like many engineers, I feel devoid of emotional responses and have difficulty communicating my thoughts and feelings with others. And that is largely what caused our separation and divorce."

"I think if I had a higher emotional quotient and more empathy, especially with people I am close to, I would be happier," said another. "I have tried sharing feelings and communicating in more detail, but I don't seem to be able to set aside resources to keep up with sharing feelings for a long period of time. It's disappointing to my wife and ex-wife, and it's something I would like to change."

Yet another of these men put it this way: "It has been very easy to deal with intellectual issues, and then neglect and have difficulty dealing with emotions. It's been more of a struggle to come to grips with the emotionality of normal life—divorce, kids, self-doubt. It's very easy to analyze things to death, and very difficult to actually feel those things."

It seems clear that these men, who felt little disappointment in not achieving the eminence for which they were programmed, and who did not seem very concerned about their lack of a sense of vocation, were painfully aware of their failures in relationships. There was little in their masculine socialization that prepared them for heartbreak and loss in a relationship. And there was little in their academic training that educated them about the intricacies of emotions and the dance of intimacy. Therefore, they often looked back with puzzlement and sadness at the way their friendships or marriages had slipped through their fingers—and hoped that the next time would be better.

Being a Good Person and Living a Good Life

These were men who for the most part obeyed the law and abided by the standards and values of their communities. They did not aspire to higher social class or status; on the other hand, neither did they pretend interest in a bohemian or lower-class lifestyle. They wanted very much to be kind and generous, hardworking and giving. What gave them the most happiness was providing for others and doing good work. Their statements about this included the following:

"Yeah, I am pretty happy. I am getting where I want to be in life. I keep the people I love in life happy and secure. I am challenged by my job and am financially secure. In general, I am happy."

"I have been on all kinds of boards and committees to make this city a better place. I'm proud of what I've accomplished for this city."

"I'm very active in my church. I'm Catholic, and though I don't go every Sunday, I contribute a lot of service to the church."

As is often the case with people who have tried to live good lives, to fulfill their duties, and to do their jobs, there was a fleeting sensation for many of these men that they had missed something— a nagging suspicion that the path not chosen may have held something of importance. There is no doubt that these gifted men were happy with their lives. They spoke of being happy about the financial security they had acquired; they were happier still if their job provided them an environment of intellectual stimulation. Each of the men now married expressed happiness about his family life and about being able to provide for his family. Few spoke of a life rich in texture, though, and some wondered explicitly what a richer life might be like. Said one, "What if I had taken control of this situation? What if I had really pushed myself? I am smarter than most people, but...."

One of the men asked the first author about her life and marveled at her recent travels to Thailand and Brazil. "It might be too late for me, you know, to lead an exciting life like you, to have adventures, live in exotic places.... That's just not in the cards."

From the outside, these brilliant men appear to be successful, yet few have dared to go after their dreams. Many of the men, when pressed, did admit to having unfulfilled dreams of contribution, service, or creative work. Many seemed to be just now working toward this realization and were contemplating early retirement to accomplish these dreams. One wanted to do a lot of volunteer work for his community; he had served in many community leadership positions already and desired now to do it full time. One talked shyly of trying to play the piano again. One wanted to do for others what he had done for his family—create security and prosperity. Perhaps the next 10 years will be the time when many of these men retire, allowing them to fulfill the promise not only of their talent, but of their essential goodness as well.

Key Points:

1. The first author and Tom Anderson conducted the study by finding 13 of 17 graduates of an accelerated learning program in a school in South St. Louis and conducted phone interviews with them. For four of the 17 men, limited information was available.

2. At 49 years of age, half the men from the school's gifted class still lived in the St. Louis area, and the rest lived in other large urban areas.

3. All interviewees completed college; there is hearsay evidence that one who was not found did not.

4. The men were isolated as children by their gifts and were further isolated later by their selection for the special school. As a result, they behaved as if they had made a decision to be as normal as possible from then on.

5. The men were ambivalent about their own giftedness.

6. They were unconcerned about eminence and had neither a passion for their work nor a sense of vocation.

7. Many had troubled relationships with women, with well over half having had at least one divorce. Only four had sustained long-term original marriages. Most attributed their relationship problems to difficulty with expression of emotion. They saw marital failures as their greatest, and sometimes only, failure.

8. All were hard working, good providers who hoped to be able to make greater social contributions later or in retirement.

References

Kerr, B. A. (1997). *Smart Girls: A new psychology of girls, women and giftedness*. Scottsdale, AZ: Gifted Psychology Press (formerly Ohio Psychology Press).

Kerr, B. A. (1995). *Smart girls two*. Dayton, OH: Ohio Psychology Press.

Kerr, B. A. (1985). *Smart girls, gifted women*. Dayton, OH: Ohio Psychology Press.

2

Who Are These Gifted Boys?

We all have an image in our minds of gifted boys. Some of us see a little guy with thick glasses and a heavy book under his arm or with his eyes glued to a computer monitor. Some of us see a golden boy, the scholar-athlete, who is good at everything and adored by everybody. And some of us see a bohemian in black, a young rebel poet scribbling in his notebooks, or a sleepless adolescent figuring out how to hack into someone else's computer.

Gifted boys certainly do come in all of these colorful varieties. However, gifted boys often look and act just like ordinary boys, and sometimes unfortunately, they learn to act like ordinary boys, too—even if it is at the expense of their well-being and sense of self.

When we discuss gifted boys in this book, we are referring to boys who are advanced for their age in one or more talent domains. Many terms are used as synonyms for gifted, such as talented, creative, having high ability or high potential, and being an able learner. All of these words are a little fuzzy in meaning because they are used in different ways by researchers, psychologists, teachers, parents, and the media. And not only is there disagreement about defining gifted children, there is also disagreement about how to best identify them, whether or not they have special needs, and if so, how these needs are to be met.

Yet, we must all agree that children with outstanding abilities exist. So, to understand gifted boys, it is first important to understand what giftedness is and how society views it.

The term "gifted" is itself a problem for many people, since it seems to carry with it overtones of elitism. As will be seen in this chapter, early researchers in this area often *were* elitist. They were also often racist, sexist, and homophobic (as was most of the rest of society during the time gifted education was beginning). When our colleagues in education heard that we were writing a book about gifted boys, they assumed immediately that we were writing about suburban, upper middle-class, white boys, and they began to growl at us. But that was their assumption, not ours. Gifted children come in all colors, from all social classes, and from all countries and all faiths. If research on gifted children or gifted education practices have been used in the service of racist or elitist politics, then that is the fault of the policy makers, not the gifted children.

Therefore, the term "gifted" is used rather defiantly throughout this book. It is still the most commonly used term in literature and media for this phenomenon, and it is a term familiar to parents, educators, psychologists, and children. But more importantly, we, the authors, really do see high abilities of any kind as a gift from the Universe—a sort of randomly occurring, miracle-like endowment that can be used for good or evil and that bears with it a responsibility for stewardship.

For most of the 20th century, giftedness meant having a high intelligence quotient (IQ). The IQ test developed by Lewis Terman in the early 1900s for the categorization of mental abilities was considered to be the best way of identifying gifted children, and revised versions of this test, and others like it, became the standard by which intelligence and giftedness were measured. Intelligence tests continue to have extraordinary influence on identification procedures. Children identified by schools as intellectually gifted typically have mental abilities on these tests that rank them in the upper two to three percent of the population. Currently, about nine million persons in the United States are considered intellectually gifted, with less than one million of these being "highly gifted" (IQ above 145). The numbers of people with these high IQs get even smaller as we go higher.

The classic research indicates that only about 7,100 persons in the United States are estimated to have IQ scores above 160, and fewer than 120 have scores of 180 or above, which makes these individuals extremely rare. More recent findings suggest, however, that there seem to be more persons in the upper IQ ranges than the normal curve suggests, though exactly how many more is unknown. Most researchers and clinicians who have personal contact with highly gifted students have found far more subjects than they expected in their regions. It is as though there is a "bump" on the IQ curve distribution at about 160, because the number of people in that range and above may be five to ten times greater than the normal bell curve distribution would predict (Silverman, 1999; Webb & Kleine, 1993). Nobody knows why this is.

It became apparent by the late 1960s that identification of gifted students on the basis of IQ alone was fraught with problems. First of all, while intelligence tests generally do an excellent job of predicting which children will do well academically in school, they do *not* necessarily predict which children will develop to become talented adults. Second, many talents are untapped by intelligence tests—particularly leadership, interpersonal skills, and various kinds of creativity—though these talents are certainly valuable to society. Finally, intelligence tests, no matter how carefully administered, will always tend to underestimate the abilities of diverse children whose cultural world view is different from that of the makers of the test. For example, African Americans, American Indians, and members of quite a few other ethnic groups often have profoundly different ways of perceiving the world, solving problems, and relating to test administrators than do white children from middle-class homes. Children for whom English is not a first language will have little opportunity to show their true talents on a test that emphasizes one's verbal ability in English. Even more recent intelligence tests, which include less emphasis on language and add abstract or spatial reasoning components, still depend on the child having a view of the world that would impel him or her to want to perform well on the test. Some groups of children may have no such motivation.

Howard Gardner, in his theory of multiple intelligences (1983), proposed the idea that many gifts go unrecognized by educators, and his theory prepared the way for a broader conception of giftedness. Gardner proposed that people have at least six intelligences, rather than one: Linguistic, Mathematical-Logical, Spatial-Visual, Musical, Interpersonal, and Kinesthetic. His theory was greeted with relief and enthusiasm by educators who knew from their own observations that children often seem to have specific, extraordinary talents, but may be just average or only slightly above average in unrelated talent domains. Brilliant writers often can't repair the simplest mechanical device, for example, and brilliant inventors often can't write a good paragraph.

In practice, however, most school programs for gifted children still emphasize two primary areas—general intellectual ability, and specific academic aptitude (Maker & Nielson, 1995; Van Tassel-Baska, 1998; Winner, 1996). Children with specific talents, such as art or music, but who lack a measured high level of intelligence, are usually neglected and tend to "fall through the cracks." If their parents can afford it, they might receive private enrichment opportunities, but if not, these children often fail to receive the support they need to realize their potential.

Several leaders in the field, such as Linda Silverman (1998), have suggested that instead of just considering general intellectual ability when defining giftedness, we should look as well for the personality characteristics, interests, values, interpersonal skills, and other behavior qualities that so often accompany high intellectual ability. That is, instead of considering giftedness as a score on a test, we should look for particular traits and personality characteristics that seem developmentally advanced for the child's chronological age. These personality characteristics can be a vivid sense of humor, a great moral sensitivity, or an unusually creative approach to life.

Silverman has also stressed that the characteristics of giftedness typically are "asynchronous." That is, gifted individuals are seldom uniformly advanced in their development. This has significant implications. Furthermore, the more highly gifted the individual, the greater is the likelihood of asynchronous development. (See Chapter 4 for more on this topic.)

One broad set of characteristics that may signify giftedness was proposed by Webb, Meckstroth, and Tolan (1982), who noted that the following traits are the ones most generally recognized as common to all kinds of gifted children:

- Unusually large vocabulary.
- Ability to read earlier than most children, often before entering school.
- Greater comprehension of the subtleties of language.
- Longer attention span, persistence, and intense concentration.
- Ability to learn basic skills more quickly and with less practice.
- Wide range of interests.
- Highly developed curiosity and limitless supply of questions.
- Interest in experimenting and doing things differently.
- Tendency to put ideas or things together in ways that are unusual and not obvious.
- Ability to retain a great deal of information.
- Unusual sense of humor.

It is clear that many of these characteristics are not necessarily linked genetically to academic intelligence; they may be the result of children growing up "different," as well as their adapting to talents that are asynchronous with their physiological and emotional maturation. Intelligence is often like a hunger in gifted children; curiosity is its appetite, and reading, developing a wide range of interests, and experimenting are strategies for fulfilling that hunger.

An exciting model of talent development promoted by Noble, Subotnik, and Arnold (1999) suggests a relativistic approach, saying that giftedness is not just a product of intelligence or achievement, but is also affected by sociological distance from the centers of power and wealth. Thus, the more stigma, economic difficulties, and cultural barriers one must overcome, the more "gifted" one needs to be to achieve in mainstream society. In this model, for example, a traditional Navajo child who rides a bus to school for several hours a day for 12 years to receive a high school diploma with straight A's is as gifted as the white child from a wealthy suburb who completes a college degree with straight A's.

We like these new approaches to giftedness, and we think they offer great hope for a fair and just identification of gifted children. Therefore, in this book, we paint giftedness in broad strokes, and we have tried throughout to consider giftedness in the context of personality and culture.

Our definition of "gifted" for this book, then, is an inclusive one: *Any child performing significantly above his or her grade level in any academic or artistic domain, regardless of whether it is verbal, mathematical, spatial-visual, musical, interpersonal, or kinesthetic, is gifted.*

We do recognize, however, that most of the research has focused on intellectual giftedness, so when we refer to research on gifted boys, it will often be this kind of research. As a result, some of our generalizations may be limited only to our clinical observations, because the broader research simply does not exist.

Attitudes toward Gifted Children

Our society is extremely ambivalent about gifted children. On the one hand, leaders in government and business expect schools to produce bright, creative people who will be able to fulfill the roles of the managers and leaders in our community. But on the other hand, the support for gifted children, both financially and attitudinally, is greatly lacking in our current society. As a result, problems exist for gifted children, both within our schools and within our families at home.

American attitudes, unlike the attitudes of many other cultures, are fairly anti-intellectual. In the earliest years of United States history, a concern for the life of the mind was considered suspect, because intellectualism and a concern for the arts was equated with the European, elitist culture that so many immigrants left behind. A few other countries, such as Australia, also have a similar history to that of the United States. Interestingly, though, anti-intellectualism also rears its head in cultures that emphasize conformity and obedience to tradition—because creative intellectuals and artists are often the tradition-breakers. Gifted children get caught in these cultural currents of ambivalence and distrust.

There are many publicly held myths about gifted children. In the early 1900s, the prevalent myth was "early ripe, early rot." That is, a child who bloomed early in life supposedly would wither and die at a young age or at least develop a sudden post-adolescent stupidity. This simple-minded generalization has since been replaced by more recent myths, such as that gifted children who get special attention will become elitist. Unfortunately, many parents, educators, and policy makers in our society appear to be unaware that their own behavior is influenced by these false assumptions. Too often, the apathy of school boards, school administrators, and legislators has detrimental consequences for gifted students. They may make statements such as: "We don't need more programs for gifted children in our district. These kids can take care of themselves," or "Why should we provide extra services for those who already have everything going for them?" or "It's the slow kids who need the help."

Contrary to what so many people believe, a gifted mind is not necessarily able to find its own way. As Dr. Martin Seligman (1998), President of the American Psychological Association, once noted, the widespread belief that "gifted children take care of themselves...consigns a very large number of gifted children to fall by the wayside in despair and frustration...and schools too often fail to recognize or support high talents—and worse, reject them into mediocrity." Although gifted students possess exceptional capabilities, most cannot excel without opportunities, guidance, challenge, and support. They need assistance academically, and they also need assistance emotionally—through understanding, acceptance, support, and encouragement. They need adults who understand their unique abilities, and they need advocates to help them develop those abilities.

Except for programs for gifted athletes, our educational system continually de-emphasizes extraordinary talent, focusing instead, and extensively, on raising the basic minimal levels of academic achievement. The focus is now on getting average and below-average students to meet set standards, not on meeting the academic needs of those who have already mastered those standards.

This new emphasis on all students meeting "minimum standards" has been detrimental to gifted students. A sort of radical egalitarianism exists that requires not only that less-able children be raised to the average (which requires that much effort and energy be spent on these children), but that highly able children be brought down to the average. Gifted children are frequently asked to behave normally, to be more like average children. Gifted children throughout our society may often be trapped in classrooms that are, to them, intellectual wastelands in which nothing interesting is going on. Or they may find themselves in families in which they are misunderstood or in which they may be involved in intense power struggles—in short, confined to a world that can be cruel and hurtful to them.

We do recognize that many schools do have *some* sort of program for gifted children, though most schools offer such services beginning only in the third grade. And even where school programs for gifted and talented students do exist, all is not well. The program model for gifted students tends to be a minimal academic modification that is one of three types (Cox, Daniel, & Boston, 1985; Strip & Hirsch, 2000; Winner, 1996): (a) "enrichment" within the regular classroom, in which gifted children are often given additional assignments or are allowed to explore areas on their own for a brief time; (b) "cluster grouping" within the regular classroom, in which a small group of high-ability students work together for brief periods on accelerated material; or (c) "pull-out programs," in which gifted students leave their regular classes for two to four hours once each week to work on curriculum specifically designed for their group, after which they return to their regular classes.

Even though there is a general negative sentiment against special classes for gifted children, the evidence in research is heavily on the side of grouping gifted children separately from other children, at least for some part of every day, especially for children who are highly or profoundly gifted. Most research shows that special accelerated classes for gifted children pay off in terms of higher achievement and greater adjustment (Rogers, 1998; Kulik & Kulik, 1997), and that it is necessary to match the program to the child because not all programs are appropriate for all gifted children (Rogers, 2001).

Most school programs do try to emphasize "higher-order thinking skills," such as principles, concepts, and evaluative thinking, and some educators such as Dr. Susan Winebrenner (2000) have written books on how to teach gifted children in the regular classroom. Yet in the regular classroom, the emphasis still remains primarily on the acquisition of skills and facts that most gifted children already possess. Concerns tend to be more with "time on task" or covering new areas that have been added to the curriculum. Because of added pressures of standardized tests and pressure for *all* students to meet minimum standards, today's teachers are not able to place an emphasis on advanced and flexible intellectual stimulation, much less on developing an understanding of the self, the ability to relate well to others, sensitivity to feelings, or a positive self-concept.

Given the diversity of young people's gifts and talents, the tremendous difficulties in giving individualized attention, and the absence of special programs and classes, is it any wonder that so many gifted children who go to school filled with eagerness find instead frustration because their primary task is to fit in? The irony of this is that, of all of society's institutions, the one that *should* be a haven for a gifted child is the school. But too often, this is not the case.

A question worth considering, then, is this: If gifted boys cannot learn to feel good about themselves and their extraordinary talents at school, where can they? Unfortunately, outside of school settings, ambivalence about gifted children is apparent also. Parents of bright, creative, gifted children tell us how lonely they feel when they try to discuss parenting concerns with other parents (Webb, et al., 1982). People assume they are bragging or exaggerating their child's behaviors. Or worse, it is assumed that they are pushy, "yuppie" parents, desperately trying to get all the breaks for their kids. Most of these parents, in our experience, typically have mixed reactions to many of the traits of their children. These children possess extensive knowledge, intensity, unusual interests, excessive curiosity, and creative approaches to situations, all of which can be delightful and exciting, but which can also generate misunderstandings or problems for the child within his family (Strip & Hirsch, 2000).

We believe that gifted boys are often particularly misunderstood and are therefore at risk for unique, potentially serious problems. This book on smart boys has been written to help parents and teachers understand and work more effectively with the gifted boys in their homes and schools.

Studies of Giftedness in Males

Since the time when psychology was a young science, its practitioners have been fascinated by genius and giftedness. Why do some people produce great art, lead nations, and create new ideas while others seem destined for quieter, less brilliant lives? Early psychologists studied eminent men to try to find the traits that made them great. They developed tests to attempt to identify those with the greatest potential for achievement, and they observed gifted people's behaviors at school and in working situations. The emphasis on eminence as a measure of giftedness caused problems in many of these studies, because eminence is a highly subjective notion, and giftedness is an important phenomenon even without consideration of its relationship to extraordinary adult achievement. And of course, these studies of giftedness focused almost entirely on the intellectual and career lives of these men rather than upon their relationships, their innermost thoughts, or their emotional lives.

In fact, one could argue that most of psychology, until recently, was the study of boys and men. Girls and women were left out of studies of the brain (except those that were designed to prove that men had bigger, more complex, or more efficient brains!), studies of social behavior, and studies of personality development and individual differences (Tavris, 1985). In physiological studies, it was assumed that women's reproductive cycles made their systems too "unstable" to study, and women were often left out of early studies of social behavior simply because many social psychological and leadership studies were done on military personnel, who, up until recently, were almost always male. Most studies of individual differences in personality and vocational psychology also began with military testing of males for selection purposes. (It bears noting that Freud himself spent years investigating the Oedipus complex of males, and only later studied the Electra complex as an afterthought.)

Why is this important to an understanding of the research on gifted boys? Because studying men in isolation from women may not give an accurate portrait of what men are really like, because men and women all develop, grow, and change in relationship to each other. Many studies on boys continue to study boys in all-boys' schools, and men in all male groups. These boys and men may be different from those who are interacting daily with girls and women, and increasingly, our society is one of boys and girls, and men and women, working together.

Thus, the irony arises that although boys and men have been studied more, we still are quite lacking in much essential knowledge about giftedness in males. We have gleaned what has been discovered to date from the very small amount of research on gifted males, particularly from those investigations that have made some attempt to study gifted boys as "whole" people. These are studies of gifted males who live and work with and beside females, who live in families that include a mother and perhaps sisters, and who have emotional lives as well as vocational lives. That research illuminates some important aspects of giftedness in boys. In the next chapter we will add to these studies our own modest investigation into the lives of the gifted men in the first author's elementary and high school class—men who are now about 50 years old. First, though, we will summarize the key points of each of these studies, and then integrate all of these findings into descriptions of patterns that emerge in young gifted boys, gifted adolescent boys, and gifted men.

Terman's Study

The most comprehensive study of giftedness, and one of the most famous of all psychological studies, was Lewis Terman's *Genetic Studies of Genius* (1925; 1935; 1947; 1959). With thousands of measurements of 1,528 gifted individuals over their entire lifespan, the publications from these studies changed the way Americans viewed genius and giftedness.

Terman, along with his colleague Melita Oden and a group of brilliant graduate students who would go on to become great psychologists in their own right, created a series of studies in the early 1920s that followed gifted children from the time they were 11 through the rest of their lives. Over the years, this group of individuals was re-evaluated seven times by Terman and his successors in an effort to chart the growth and expression of intellectual talent.

Building upon a test that was created by French psychologist Alfred Binet (Binet & Simon, 1916) to separate mentally deficient children from average and above-average children, Terman developed an intelligence test that he believed would measure "the ability to acquire and manipulate concepts." The resulting instrument was called the Stanford-Binet Intelligence Scale, after the original author and the university where Terman was a faculty member. It soon became the most widely used intelligence test, and its updated versions continue to be the most influential tests of general intellectual ability today.

Beginning their study in 1921 and 1922, Terman and his colleagues asked hundreds of teachers in large California school districts to nominate their brightest students for testing using the Stanford-Binet. The goal was to identify the top 15 percent of the students in terms of IQ. The amount of data gathered was astonishing. In addition to an individual intelligence test, each child was administered the Stanford achievement test, a general information test, seven "character tests" (measures of personal and social adjustment), and a test of interest in and knowledge of various play activities. There were 34 anthropometric measures (height, weight, skull size, etc.), extensive medical exams, information on the student's home, information on the student's school, an interest survey, a two-month reading record, an assessment of socioeconomic indicators, and a case history. Rarely, if ever, has a group been studied so intensively.

Prior to Terman's study, the stereotype of the gifted child was that of a puny, underdeveloped, sickly child. As mentioned earlier, it was believed that those who were gifted were subject to the "early ripe, early rot" principle. Gifted boys were assumed to be hopeless at sports, nearsighted from constant reading, and so maladjusted that other boys would never want to play with them. Boys who were highly gifted experienced even stronger prejudice.

As mentioned earlier, Americans have always been, by and large, anti-intellectual. Intellectualism was associated with the decadent Old World. Americans saw themselves as rugged individuals who were both practical and strong, and they saw the British and other Europeans as effete, weak, and effeminate. In the early part of the 20th century, Oscar Wilde, the flamboyant homosexual genius, was the epitome, to Americans, of what could go wrong when a boy was too gifted. America's suspicion of the brilliant boy was more than a little tinged with homophobia.

In this cultural atmosphere of the early 20th century, a psychologist with a deep concern for young people of high ability had a difficult task: to use the young science of psychology to reshape the American concept of genius. To this task, Terman brought a veritable arsenal of techniques for observing and describing, and making statistical inferences.

If there is anything that "postmodern" philosophies have given us, it is the concept that science, no matter how objectively performed, is still the product of the personal bias of the scientist and that scientist's agenda. The questions asked, the selection of subjects, and the types of analysis all affect what knowledge emerges from the scientific work. We believe Terman had a bias—albeit a laudable one. It was a belief that gifted children should get the recognition they deserve and the education they need. Some have also accused Terman of having a racial agenda—that is, an interest in proving that the Northern European races were superior to all others in intellect. Our reading of his original work leads us to believe that he was only as racist and as ignorant of his own cultural lens, as any other scientist of the times, but no more so. In fact, his work supported the idea that there were many brilliant Jews, Irish, and people of Mediterranean descent at a time when these populations were still targets of powerful prejudices. To the degree that the tests he developed selected against, and continue to select against, non-white people, he is culpable of perpetuating America's racial stratification. How this has damaged the education and careers of gifted boys of color, and the white boys who have been deprived of diverse educations, will be dealt with later in this book.

We believe that Terman had another agenda, however, of which few have been made aware. This agenda was to masculinize the concept of genius to make giftedness acceptable to the American public. He wanted to show that gifted boys were just as much "real" boys as average boys were, and that gifted girls, although often more masculine than other girls, were still fully capable of feminine behaviors and roles. His selection criteria, measures, and inferences all supported this agenda.

The subjects Terman selected were not a nationwide sample. They were California schoolchildren born around 1910—the granddaughters and grandsons of the "Forty-niners," descendants of rugged individualists, entrepreneurs, and pioneers. They lived in cities drenched in sunshine, where it was possible to play outdoors year round, and where most everyone was full of vigor and optimism. Terman asked teachers in major California cities to select their three brightest students—by their own subjective standards—for testing. Although he cautioned them that some bright students might be shy, it is likely that teachers' choices then were the same as they might be now. That is, we believe that teachers in this study favored children with roughly the same social and behavioral characteristics generally esteemed by teachers today. And based on our work with modern-day educators, we conclude with some confidence that it is likely that Terman's study population was biased toward the inclusion of socially competent students who were pleasant, active, and enthusiastic about learning, who were not too different from the other students, who were healthy and well adjusted, and who got along well with teachers.

Some of Terman's measures and analyses also reflect a strong concern about masculinity. In addition to the standard height and weight measures, there was a strong emphasis on those physical characteristics commonly associated with manliness, such as chest width and shoulder breadth, and even an inclusion of some rather strange measurements taken of genitalia and pubic hair. The interest and activities questions also revealed a bias and concern regarding gender identity; in fact, activities were grouped together to form a "masculinity index" that supposedly reflected the degree to which a pattern of activities matched those of a masculine individual. This index was apparently devised purely for this study.

Is it any wonder, then, that the results delighted Terman by showing that the gifted boys and girls were a vigorous, healthy, well-adjusted, and gender identity-appropriate group? He said, "The gifted California children as a group arc above the best standards for American-born children in physical growth status for average standing height and weight. They also excel other California children.... A large proportion has broad shoulders and hips, strong muscles and well-developed lungs" (Terman, 1925, p. 160). He went on to say, "The gifted group is on the whole physically superior to the various groups used for comparison" (p. 211).

Terman took great pains to point out the masculinity of the gifted boys. Some of his proofs of their masculinity concerned their speedy maturation: "Pubescence, as indicated by the amount and kinkiness of the pubic hair occurs on the average somewhat earlier among the gifted than among unselected boys." He also noted that "94.2% of boys were normal in genitalia" (Terman, 1925, p. 211)!

With regard to play interests and career goals, Terman found that gifted boys were more like average boys than like average girls. Their interests in both play and careers scored high on his masculinity indices, although he noted that gifted boys liked dramatics, debating, literature, and modeling more than average boys. Average boys liked science, physiology, penmanship, manual training, drawing, geography, and painting. It would seem that gifted boys enjoyed challenging verbal activities, but Terman made little note of that, preferring to dwell on the gifted boys' similarity to other boys, rather than on their differences. The sex differences in preferences expressed by the control group were made the basis of "masculinity indices" of the activities. This made possible the calculation of a "masculinity rating" for each child, based on the total masculinity values of the activities for which his preferences were expressed. According to Terman, "The mean masculinity ratings of the gifted boys were slightly higher than those of control boys at all ages except 13" (p. 437).

At the end of his second follow-up, Terman made clear that he felt he had successfully changed the way we understand giftedness: "It is to be hoped that the superstitions so commonly accepted relative to intellectually superior children have been permanently swept away by the factual data these studies have presented. It is simply not true that such children are especially prone to be puny, overspecialized in their abilities and interests, emotionally unstable, socially unadaptable, psychotic, and morally undependable; nor is it true that they usually deteriorate to the level of mediocrity as adult life is approached" (Terman, 1930, p. 474).

Subsequent follow-ups showed this group of gifted boys to be growing into academically achieving, well-adjusted young men. They were boys with high aspirations, and they began, in a linear and logical manner, to pursue those aspirations. In high school, Terman's gifted young men had myriad interests, participating in many school activities and receiving high grades across the board in their classes. They continued to have positive and constructive views on life, and they maintained excellent health. They were leaders in their classes. The majority of Terman's gifted young men attended college, at a time—the Depression era—when only a small minority of Americans was able to go to college. They went to the best colleges, and they were highly achieving there. After college, they entered the world of work and began quickly to seek and gain success. Most married, and most of the marriages were stable and long lasting. In short, Terman's gifted men were truly "wunderkinder" in that their intelligence seemed to be associated with self-esteem, social involvement, health, and achievement in school and work. Only a small minority suffered from depression, failed to achieve vocationally, or failed in their relationships. However, we know little about those men and what prevented them from attaining their potential.

It is probably a very good thing that Terman laid to rest many of the ridiculous myths commonly held at the time about gifted people—for example, that they were prone to insanity and that early intellectual accomplishment predicted failure in adulthood. However, his studies had some unintended consequences. Because his work was so extensive, and because he and his colleagues gave their entire lives to this landmark study, it took on the quality of unimpeachable knowledge. That is, few psychologists were willing to question the methodology or dispute the findings of so grand a study by a scientist so authoritative. The psychologist and gifted pioneer Leta Hollingworth (1942) did differ with Terman's views, particularly in stating that children with an IQ of 160 or above were prone to various social and emotional problems. Her views, however, were not widely listened to, and as a result, most psychology and education textbooks even today present Terman's findings as fact, without clarifying the context in which they were developed or the methods that were used. Even now, most teachers, counselors, and psychologists will know little else about the gifted except this—that they are well-adjusted, that they are healthy and strong, that they are smart in everything, that they do well in school, and that they become leaders in the workforce.

These same educators today will expect gifted boys to be sturdy, masculine achievers. When a gifted boy is small and shy or chubby or "sissyish," or having difficulty with one subject area, or underachieving in general, it will be assumed by many that he is simply not really gifted—because he does not fit Terman's portrait.

There is another, more recent misconception based on Terman's work that is just as difficult to shake. That is the new idea, rampant among the very scholars who themselves benefited from gifted programs, that children identified as gifted are simply privileged white kids, and that intelligence tests are merely ways of enforcing the current class system and racist policies. This misconception may be just as harmful to gifted boys as the idea that they are all perfectly well adjusted and achieving.

The problem with bashing gifted education, and the kids that are identified by that system, is that although intelligence tests may be flawed, they still remain very good predictors of the child's ability to benefit from challenging, accelerated educational programs. Not only will many white boys lose out if all testing and gifted education programs based on Terman's theory are thrown out, but many boys of color will lose out as well. As the field of gifted education matures and evolves—as flaws in traditional methods and studies are uncovered and refined or replaced with more inclusive means of identification and support—the needs of a broader, more representative segment of our population of bright young males is met.

The inference that there are no gifted minority boys is simply an utterly false conclusion. And if any aspect of our gifted educational system reinforces this fiction, then the appropriate response is to improve that system, not to abolish it. Therefore, it would make sense for educators to take Terman's findings with a grain of salt, but not to throw out his work entirely. He was a product of his time. Intelligence testing and gifted education are no more flawed than any of our other institutions. Those of us who are concerned about the guidance of gifted boys need to remember that gifted boys are a diverse group. They are not all white and privileged, or well-adjusted, or masculine, or well-rounded. And even when they do fit these stereotypes, their lives are often characterized by compromise and difficult choices, as we will see throughout this book.

Key Points:

1. Terman relied upon teachers to identify boys they considered to be gifted; in general, these were boys who were well liked by teachers. Of this group, he selected for study those who scored in what he considered to be the gifted range.
2. The boys were taller, stronger, and healthier than average boys.
3. They were well-adjusted and "masculine" in their interests.
4. They had many and varied interests.

5. They did very well in school. They outperformed boys of lower IQs. Until high school, only gifted girls got better grades than they did.

6. In high school, they were very active in sports, extracurricular activities, and academic clubs.

7. They graduated with honors and went on to college in extraordinary numbers as compared to the population as a whole.

8. They chose vocations that allowed them to use their talents, and they rose to leadership positions in their professions, although few attained true eminence.

9. There were some who suffered from depression and self-destructive behaviors, but little is known about them.

James Alvino's Free Spirit Study

James Alvino and Sandford Reichert conducted a national survey of gifted children for Free Spirit Publishing in 1988 that produced some interesting insights into the lives of gifted boys. A 15-item questionnaire was used to survey 157 boys between the ages of 11 and 14. It was distributed throughout the country to teachers of the gifted, who then passed the instrument out to their students and returned them to the publisher. Alvino (1991) used these responses and interviewed key leaders in gifted education about the special problems and needs of gifted boys for his article, "An Investigation of the Needs of Gifted Boys."

One of the first and most important of Alvino's findings was the observation that, as he put it, "What is limited are boys' self- and role-identities, as well as their right and capacity to express emotions" (Alvino, 1991, pp. 174-175). Alvino pointed out that special problems were faced by sensitive and creative gifted boys who were born into families where traditional masculine roles and behaviors are valued. Gifted boys, he said, feel they must conform to a stereotype of a male who is tough, independent, aggressive, self-reliant, logical, unemotional, and lacking in sensitivity. Because gifted boys are taught, as are most boys, not to express their emotions, there are severe limitations placed upon their creativity, intuition, and spirituality. Alvino also suggested that violence among males might have its roots in the suppression of emotion. In the Free Spirit survey, gifted boys believed that expressing how they feel was one of the most difficult things for them to do. The majority believed they were less emotional than girls, and 30 percent believed it was important not to cry if they were hurt.

Second, Alvino explored how bonding and separation issues affected gifted boys. Most boys, he said, do not separate well from their mothers or bond adequately with their fathers. Gifted boys in the Free Spirit survey felt closer to their mothers than to their fathers. Alvino pointed out that when gifted boys are expected to separate from their mothers, they often have nowhere to go because their fathers are absent either physically or emotionally. Nevertheless, their most frequent complaint about their mothers was that their mothers were overprotective and didn't give them enough freedom. The second most frequent cluster of complaints had to do with "easing up on nagging."

Of the father-son relationship, Alvino said,

> Where does Dad fit in? Nowhere—and everywhere. Nowhere in the sense that in a traditional family, the father usually functions as a provider and authority figure...but from a distance, emotionally disconnected from his son.... The father fits in everywhere in the sense that the relationship, positive or negative, a gifted boy has with his father can determine whether and in what direction the former will develop his talents and sense of masculinity (1991, p. 176).

Boys in the survey said they wished their fathers would ease up on expectations, leave them alone, and give them more freedom. But they also wished they would "talk to me, do things with me, spend time with me." Many gifted boys, he concluded, feel trapped on the one hand by their own abilities and on the other hand by their fear of disappointing their fathers.

Perfectionism was a problem for a number of boys in the Free Spirit study. Because a boy's self-worth is so clearly tied to his accomplishments, perfectionism may be more of a problem for gifted boys than it is for other children. Boys in the study seemed to feel it was better not to try at all in tasks they were not sure of, than to try and possibly fail.

And at this point in their lives, these bright adolescents did not see participation in a gifted program as a way to create a successful male image—unless that participation could also be accompanied by athletic excellence. Over 50 percent of the boys in the study felt it was important to hide their intelligence, and 66 percent found that fitting in with the social group was "very hard" or "somewhat hard." As a result of both perfectionism and the lack of support for being gifted, many of these gifted boys ended up with very low self-concepts. Therefore, perfectionism and the desire to fit in both seem implicated in underachievement: many gifted boys give up trying and actually find rewards for underachievement from the peer group.

In the area of sexuality and relationships, Alvino found much ambivalence. Boys are taught to pursue the "perfect 10" and to have as many attractive females as possible. At the same time, they are taught that they must be responsible breadwinners and providers for women. They are well aware that it is acceptable in many cultures and male groups to assert that men are superior to women in intellect, leadership, and creativity. They see their male friends adopting these attitudes. Unlike many of their age peers, however, gifted boys and young men read enough and are savvy enough to know that gender roles have changed forever. Furthermore, as traditional gender role boundaries continue to be dissolved in our society, boys find that the arena of physical strength is practically the only one left in which they can distinguish themselves from girls. And because gifted boys are achievement oriented, many of them try to be stars, becoming "jocks" even when they don't feel like it, just to win the favor of, or at least to avoid rejection by, girls.

Finally, it was in the area of competitiveness that Alvino found the most distinct differences between gifted boys and gifted girls. The majority of gifted boys liked competing for grades, as opposed to the majority of gifted girls, who disliked it. A very large majority, 83 percent of the boys, said they liked athletic competition, as compared to 61 percent of girls. Competitiveness clearly seems to be one of the most commonly observed characteristics of gifted boys. This excessive competitiveness, said Alvino, "can put the ego in a straitjacket" (1991, p. 179). In this way, and in many others, gifted boys fall into what Alvino calls the Success Trap—the blind pursuit of success at the expense of their inner selves.

Key Points:

1. Alvino chose 11- to 14-year-old boys who responded to a national survey of gifted boys.

2. He found that the boys were very limited in their emotional lives; had difficulty expressing feelings, and felt that girls had more freedom than they did to express emotion.

3. Boys felt closer to their mothers; they often had a difficult time emotionally separating from their mothers.

4. Gifted boys felt distant from their fathers and wanted their fathers to be more involved with them. They also feared their fathers' high expectations for them.

5. Many had difficulties with perfectionism.

6. Half of the boys believed it was necessary to hide their intelligence, and two-thirds had problems fitting in.

7. Gifted boys tended to see relationships with girls as achievements and sought the "perfect" girl.

8. Many seemed to fall into the success trap, pursuing success at the expense of their inner selves.

The Illinois Valedictorian Study

In 1981, Terry Denny, a professor at the University of Illinois at Urbana-Champaign, attended graduation ceremonies at high schools all over the state. His goal was to enlist the valedictorians of as many high schools as possible in his study of the development of academically talented students. The 81 top achievers who agreed to participate have been tracked ever since with follow-up surveys and interviews (Arnold, 1994). Following Denny's retirement, Karen Arnold, a graduate student and former valedictorian herself, took over the project.

The Illinois valedictorian project is important in several ways. First, it is among the few studies in existence that measure giftedness by performance. These students had proven their intellectual ability by producing near-perfect performances in their high school coursework. Second, the study used an excellent combination of survey and interview material to present a truly vivid picture of these students. Third, several follow-ups were performed, in 1981, 1984, 1985, and 1988, all with high rates of return.

There were several very interesting findings about the valedictorian males. In fact, the authors found the male patterns of career and personal development to be so different from those of the women that they merited special consideration. Unlike the females, the males seemed to give little thought to marriage and family. While the females struggled with fears about balancing family and career, it never seemed to occur to the males that this might become an issue for them. Instead, these gifted males were very focused on their career goals at every follow-up. They intended to be continuously employed, and this was indeed the case for the vast majority of them.

As might be predicted, the valedictorian males did very well in college. Their college achievement was, in fact, outstanding. For the most part, they majored in technical fields and in business-related subjects. By the time the men were 26 years old, they were working full time in male-dominated professions. Their path was a linear one, with most of the men following the direct path to the career goals they had set early in college.

The researchers found these men to be a relatively homogeneous group, compared to the women. They even had difficulty assigning them to "A" or "B" groups, with the "A" group being a group of high vocational achievers/aspirers and the "B" group being somewhat lower vocational achievers/aspirers. However, with careful attention, they were able to separate out the group of men who were especially successful in high-status occupations for the "A" group. What variables predicted the occupational successes of the men in this group?

The first variable was academic ability—the boys' higher ACT scores predicted fairly well their career success in high-status occupations. The second variable was desire for career prestige, and the third was job experience while in college. Other variables such as the college they attended, intellectual self-esteem, motivation, and optimism about goals also contributed to their success—but not nearly so much as these first three variables.

Interestingly, with this group of men, socioeconomic status of the family, desire to work hard, and the desire to use one's best talents had no relationship to future success. It is noteworthy that sheer ability was able to neutralize the effects of a family's social background and even eclipse the work ethic and desire for challenge. One gets the impression of young men carried along on the current of their intellectual abilities, with little need to focus on anything else except the straightforward journey to their goals. These men simply glided along effortlessly through college and into their chosen careers with no attention to how their career goals might later interact with their relationships or even with their values.

While many were indeed successful in high status careers, these high school valedictorians were, for the most part, not outstanding or extraordinary in their career attainments. Instead, the authors said, they were beginning "solid professional careers." After their extraordinary high school academic accomplishments, the majority showed no apparent interest in further academic, intellectual, or creative activity. At the time of the 1988 study, 80 percent had not gone on to graduate school, and only three had Ph.D.'s. Furthermore, there was no exceptional intellectuality or creativity evident in the work lives of these careerist young men. In fact, the authors said, they did not appear to be the intellectual or professional leaders of the future as one might have expected at the time of their high school graduations.

The authors' interpretation of these rather disturbing findings was, first, that these young people simply reflected the careerism of their entire generation—a Reagan-era sort of vocational orientation that focused merely on material success. Their second interpretation, for which the evidence in the study is clear, had more important implications for gifted educators—high academic performance is not associated with creative lifestyles or future creative productivity. They said:

> These students were gifted as academic performers. The college entrance examination scores of the men varied far more than their high school or college grade point averages. The valedictorians were talented in school performance. Achieving a high grade point average requires organization, dutifulness, and comfort with structure and authority. This performance definition of giftedness overlaps but is not identical to conceptions of giftedness as intellectual or creative ability. Always dutiful, perhaps these men were continuing to achieve within established social structures and with defined social pathways (pp. 46-47).

Another important finding of the authors was that the men seemed "extremely disillusioned for 26-year-olds who had arrived exactly where they aspired to be" (1994, p. 48). Perhaps their narrow careerism and the awareness that they had not explored all of their options were beginning to diminish their satisfaction in their external successes.

Key Points:

1. Arnold and Denny selected for their study high-school valedictorians from the state of Illinois and followed them closely through college and young adulthood.

2. The male valedictorians as adolescents had little concern about marriage and family, especially when compared to female valedictorians.

3. The men did outstandingly well in college and chose mainly technical and business-oriented majors.

4. They entered high-level occupations and were successful in their first jobs.

5. Their career success was determined mainly by their ability. Desire for prestige and job experience during college were also important variables, but sheer talent carried the most weight.

6. No correlation was found between success in career on the one hand, and factors such as socioeconomic background, work ethic, and desire for challenge on the other.

7. Surprisingly, the men were not highly satisfied with their very linear and very successful careers, and at age 26 seemed disillusioned with the choices they had made.

The Hebert Study

In a recent study called "Defining Belief in Self: Intelligent Young Men in an Urban High School," Thomas Hebert (2000) interviewed, observed, and recorded the details of the inner and outer lives of a few young gifted men in a very poor and very troubled high school. With the help of school officials, he selected six young men who qualified as gifted in their school and who had overcome many factors that had put them at risk. He investigated how these young men both survived in their urban environment and excelled in school. He said, "They ignored drug dealers; they turned their backs on gangs; they avoided the crime in their neighborhoods; and they went on to become valedictorians, class presidents, star athletes, and scholars, and attended some of the most selective colleges in the country " (pp. 91-92).

These six adolescents reflected the multicultural composition of the student body of their school—four were Hispanic, one was white, and one was African American. Each of the young men was outstanding in one or more ways, and all had been labeled gifted as children.

During extensive interviews, the young men were first asked very general questions, such as, "Describe your middle school experience." Then, specific questions were asked to probe each topic further. The young men were also observed interacting with their peers and going about their school day. Parents, teachers, and mentors were also interviewed about each boy. Field notes, observation notes, and transcribed interviews were coded and analyzed to generate initial categories.

In the second stage of the study, consistent themes and relationships in each of the sources of information were identified. General categories were derived, and additional evidence was sought to support those categories.

The resulting themes revealed an extraordinary resiliency, an internal focus of control, and a maturing identity for each of the young men. The most important finding was that of belief in self. Hebert said of all six, "The competitive, survivor quality…appeared to be a reflection of the strong belief in self within these six young men. Several qualities merged to form this belief in self—including sensitivity, inner will, aspirations, and multicultural appreciation" (2000, p. 99). This belief in self was supported in three ways: by caring adults, by a strong family, and by experiences that gave the young men a sense of themselves as valuable individuals.

These six adolescents were characterized by a remarkable sensitivity. They were sentimental, intuitive, caring, and did not follow the dictates of the macho male stereotype. Their sensitivity extended from aesthetic awareness to intense emotional reactions to the hardships and despair they saw around them. These young men were capable of a wide range of emotional expression, and their sensitivity was praised and supported by their families.

An appreciation of diverse cultures was also vividly expressed by these young men. Unlike other students who were threatened or angered by people different from themselves, these young men were excited and happy to be in a multicultural environment. One had even passed up going to a private school because he did not want to leave the diversity of his inner-city school behind. These were young men who were fascinated by differences in languages, values, and cultural traditions. Needless to say, they all enjoyed a diverse group of friends.

The high aspirations of this group were related to their strong sense of self. Most of them had had high aspirations since they were children. They planned careers in bilingual education, public relations, law, theology, environmental studies, and engineering or architecture. Although all were "multipotential," they were concerned about focusing upon a specific career goal and were ambitious to attain that goal.

Another quality that emerged in these young men was "inner will." This phrase, used by one of the boys, describes their intense determination, their insistence on following through, and their belief that they could overcome any hardship. Most of them had endured hardships and had seen their parents make great sacrifices for them and their families. Seeing friends deal with alcoholism and difficulties at home seemed to strengthen both their appreciation of their own situations and their determination to survive.

The supportive families of the students in this study were in every way a contradiction of the stereotype of inner-city families. They provided material and emotional support to their children and assured the young men of their confidence in them. Often, the families were extended families consisting of grandparents, parents, siblings, aunts, uncles, and cousins, all of whom together formed a cohesive and caring network.

These young men also benefited from the caring support of adults beyond the family. They all described teachers who had made a difference in their lives. A certain freshman English teacher was mentioned more often than any other teacher by the group of six. She was an extraordinarily caring and enthusiastic teacher who attended to the details of nurturing—such things as bottled water for her thirsty students and a blow dryer for wet hair on rainy days. A guidance counselor was also named as very important in providing a support system. He was known for his excellent helping skills and was trusted by all. Many of the young men were also influenced by a swim coach who encouraged excellence, high ethics, and self-confidence. Finally, participation in special programs, extracurricular activities, and summer enrichment programs seemed to provide these six young men with the extra edge they needed to thrive and learn. All were involved in athletics of some sort, they participated in school clubs, and summer programs aimed at raising aspirations and enriching their education often influenced them. Visits to universities through special outreach programs gave these young men the belief that they, too, could aspire to an academic life and to the rewards that followed higher education.

Hebert interpreted his findings as a message of hope for educators, counselors, and parents. It was clear that caring adults could make a great difference in young people's lives. It was also clear that the intensity of these young men's belief in self protected them from the adversity and difficulties that surrounded them in a hostile urban environment.

Key Points:

1. Hebert's participants were boys identified as gifted who had survived and prospered in a poor and troubled high school.
2. The boys had a strong belief in self that did not waver.
3. The boys were caring and open and had great emotional sensitivity.

4. They had a strong multicultural awareness, accepting and appreciating people who were different from themselves.

5. Their high aspirations were related to belief in self and inner will; these intangible characteristics defined their ambitions better than more objective measures did.

6. Contrary to common conceptions of inner-city life, these boys' families were intact, stable, and supportive of their children. Furthermore, the boys also had the benefit of adult mentors outside the family.

R. S. Albert's Study

R. S. Albert, a social psychologist, has had a lifelong interest in the personal and environmental systems that create eminence and in the dynamics of gifted behavior. He began his study of gifted boys in 1977 with the belief, based on research, that the attainment of eminence is the result of one's possessing a variety of certain factors. His theory was that people who had attained eminence in a society were more talented than others in a particular talent domain, that they had become career-oriented earlier than their peers, and that their families were different in important ways from those of non-eminent people.

Albert wanted to find out if the patterns that had been observed in eminent people held true for two very special groups of gifted boys. The first group was a selection of 26 boys who had been identified as being in the 99th percentile on the *SAT-M* (a test of mathematical aptitude) while in seventh grade. The boys were between 11 and 14 when the study began. The second group of 28 boys, also aged 11 to 14, was a group of Southern California boys who all tested at the 150+ IQ range and who were enrolled in the program for Mentally Gifted Minors in four school districts.

Over a span of 18 years, two follow-up studies were conducted. One occurred when the boys were in high school and another four years later when they were in early adulthood. These follow-up studies consisted of further intelligence tests. And although Albert does not discuss this, it is important to note that most intelligence tests, particularly at that time, favored verbal talent. These were oral tests, administered in English, with problems requiring a mastery of language and its nuances. The SAT-M, however, being a test of purely mathematical reasoning, required little language ability. Therefore, it is to be expected that there were differences in the sort of boy that the two methods of selection produced.

For both groups, the boys' parents were much better educated than the general population—65 percent of mothers and 95 percent of fathers were college graduates. Grandparents were also extremely well educated. First-born boys were the largest group, supporting previous research on the "special" birth-order position of eminent people. There was also strong evidence that these boys identified more with their fathers than with their mothers. Many of the fathers were also first-borns, and they shared some of the same interests as their sons. In fact, of the 26 fathers in the SAT-M group, 17 worked in math-related occupations. Albert said, "It appears also that the more bases for father-son similarities, the earlier the identification of the son's particular giftedness and the more likely there will be behavioral similarities leading to subsequent reinforcements" (1994, p. 294).

Therefore, it seemed as though a father who was mathematically oriented and a first-born was likely to somehow have a great positive influence on his son's math aptitude. However, Albert also notes the negative side of this identification with the father: "Growing similarities and modeling may tightly bind the father and son, limiting the son's later explorations of self and development of interests and identity" (1994, p. 294).

Eight boys in both groups who had absent fathers due to divorce or separation at the time of the second follow-up were functioning educationally much below those of their peers who had fathers in the home. This, too, seemed to support the importance of the father-son relationship to educational achievement, although, interestingly, it did not agree with the patterns of eminent individuals, who have a very high proportion of father absence. However,

educational achievement is different from the kind of scientific creativity necessary for eminence, and creative eminence may be linked
in some way to breaking away from the father-son identification. In
fact, the math group's divergent thinking scores—one measure of
creativity—were correlated only with the mother's divergent thinking scores. This suggests that academic achievement may be related
to father-son identification, but divergent thinking among the mathematically gifted may be related to a mother's creativity.

Another interesting finding was that parents of high IQ boys
were mothers and fathers who were fairly similar to one another in
personality. When parents were dissimilar, however, there seemed
to be higher general creative potential or higher divergent thinking
in both groups of boys. For all boys, the parents' need to attain status was associated with lower creativity. Albert said, "When taken
together these results indicate that among exceptionally gifted
twelve-year-old-boys, parental differences and interfamilial stress
have a greater capacity for potentiating a gifted boy's creativeness
than parental trait similarity or high degrees of tolerance, acceptance, and conformity" (1994, p. 301). What this means is that, as
many creativity scholars have suggested, tension and differences in
a family can actually stimulate creativity, while a consistent push
toward high-status achievement may work in the opposite way.

One of the most interesting phenomena observed by Albert
was that of the "crossovers." Although personality and vocational
interests tend to be quite stable in the general population after adolescence, this was not the case with these exceptional boys. Four
years after the study began, many math/science boys had crossed
over to humanities or other non-math occupations, and many who
originally showed high verbal talent had crossed over to math/sci-
ence goals.

It was the math/science crossovers that captured Albert's attention. Albert noted that it is much harder to exit math and science than
the liberal arts because the career track is much more linear in the
former, while a certain amount of "meandering" is expected of liberal arts majors. He concluded that it was not lack of ability that
caused the math/science crossover students to change, but rather
their stronger, more dominant personalities. They were attracted to

change and felt autonomous and free. They were more creative, assertive, and self-motivated. In other words, it took a lot of independence and forcefulness to break out of a math/science major.

It may be that this breaking away was associated with a great leap forward in ego development. Perhaps because the math/science crossovers had to take a bigger risk, and perhaps because they were challenged to be more creative, they matured more quickly than those who had been required to make difficult choices. Albert said, "Just how much the math/science crossovers had changed can be seen when they are compared to the change of exceptionally high IQ crossovers and non-crossovers. At age 12, the math/science crossovers' level of ego development was lower than either of the exceptionally high-IQ subgroups. But by age 22, the math/science crossovers had moved from being primarily self-protective and wary of other persons' blame and control to an individualistic stage in which the self is the guide and decision maker.... What makes these changes thought provoking is that non-crossovers in both samples showed hardly any change in their levels of ego development between the ages of 12 and 22" (1994, p. 306).

Therefore, one of the most surprising findings of this study was that those mathematically gifted boys who are able to somehow break away from their original areas of talent applying their math/science skills to the humanities, are able to experience greater personal growth and become more psychologically mature than those boys who stay on the same track from boyhood to manhood.

Key Points:

1. Albert chose either boys who were gifted mathematically or high IQ boys who may have been more verbally oriented.
2. The families of the boys from both groups were much better educated than the average family.

3. Boys with strong father-son relationships and similarities were attracted to math/science more often than boys with strong mother-son relationships and similarities. Boys with strong mother-son relationships were more attracted to the humanities and were more creative.

4. Boys in math/science tracks found it much more difficult to cross over into the humanities than the other way around.

5. Although, in general, all of the boys were more creative than non-gifted boys, boys from very achievement-oriented families were less creative. In addition, boys from families with greater differences between the mother and father, and greater intrafamilial stress, tended to be more creative.

6. Mathematically gifted boys who did not cross over, but who stayed in the same math/science tracks, did not develop as far or as rapidly psychologically as those boys who broke from the track.

The Presidential Scholars Study

Felice Kaufmann, a well-known consultant in gifted education, chose to follow up the Presidential Scholars of 1964-1968 as her dissertation study for her Ph.D. at the University of Georgia in 1978. Part of the Baby Boom generation born after World War II, these scholars represented a rarified group of gifted high school students—the top one-tenth of one percent of the students in the nation. Each Presidential Scholar was chosen from the top-ranked National Merit Scholars in each of the 50 states. In addition to their high academic achievement, these students had extraordinary extracurricular accomplishments. They wrote brilliant essays about themselves and about their dreams for the future.

Because these students had been honored by the President and had visited the White House as a group, she assumed that at least one government office had maintained regular contact with them. To her surprise, she found that this was not the case. Kaufmann made thousands of phone calls to relatives and friends of the National Merit Scholars in order to locate 501 of them—83 percent of the original group. She then sent them a 41-item questionnaire concerning their career and personal development, and she talked to many of them in informal interviews (Kaufmann, 1981).

The lives of these young adults seemed to have been shaped by the turbulent era of the 1960s. Many had participated in the counterculture and could be considered tradition-breakers. Nevertheless, for the most part, they eventually became financially successful and rose to leadership positions in their domains. The men in particular had continued high educational and occupational attainment; their salaries were about twice those of females in similar occupations, perhaps reflecting the inequities of the workplace of the 1970s as well as the more complicated nature of women's lives. Or perhaps the society supported their drive and goal-orientation. In any case, many of those in the male group in 1978 had earned Ph.D., M.D., or J.D. degrees.

In 1986, Kaufmann followed up the Presidential Scholars using another survey with more targeted questions, focusing on mentoring relationships and critical career events in their lives. She found an interesting relationship between mentoring and career success; those Presidential Scholars who had found the most success were those who could identify a mentor who had helped them achieve their professional goals. It was clear, too, that the Presidential Scholars who found great success in achieving their goals were those who had "fallen in love with an idea," a phrase Kaufmann had learned from Paul Torrance, a well-known researcher on creativity. Mentors had spotted those men who had fallen in love with an idea and supported their drive to achieve their goals.

Throughout the next decade, Kaufmann continued to have contact with the Presidential Scholars through letters and interviews. By 1998, she was able to make some striking observations about the more subtle aspects of the lives of Presidential Scholars (Kaufmann, 2000). For example, those career paths that had appeared so linear and inevitable 20 years before had now become complex and fraught with serendipitous accident, both fortunate and unfortunate. Kaufmann was amazed at how often a chance meeting or a chance event had profoundly influenced the direction that these young people's lives had taken. Many of the men told colorful stories of fortunate acquaintances that led to opportunities. Sadly, many also told of random life events that stalled them or caused them to change direction. A second, thought-provoking observation concerned the successes of these men. Most of the men, by any measure, would be considered successful in the eyes of our society. However, they were less sure about their own power to control their destinies and often were now less sure of the value of the goals they had chosen than they were when they were younger.

Related to this new uncertainty about goals was an ambivalence about "passion." Kaufmann speaks movingly of the "dark side" of passion. Although there is clear evidence that falling in love with an idea and having a passion are necessary for great creative accomplishment, Kaufmann says that this sort of devotion can interfere with the development of relationships, can lead to depression when the desired goals are obstructed, and can fill the individual with a sense of a constant need to work and achieve. Many of these men had suffered significantly because of their passion for their work and at midlife were reconsidering the role of their intense devotion to work in their lives.

Key Points:

1. Male Presidential Scholars were some of the most extraordinary young scholars and leaders in the United States between 1964 and 1968.
2. Their lives reflected the turbulence of the 1960s, and many participated in the counterculture.
3. They went on to become successful in their fields, earning high salaries and attaining positions of leadership.

4. The most successful Presidential Scholars had mentors.
5. The most successful Presidential Scholars had "fallen in love with an idea."
6. At mid-life, they recognized the role of chance and accident in their lives.
7. They were sometimes ambivalent about the role of passion in their work, because their passion had sometimes led to social, emotional, and relationship difficulties.

Conclusion

What have we learned from this foray into the research on gifted boys and men?

First of all, the nature of the research reflects not only the changing nature of society's conception of giftedness, but also the conception of masculinity. Terman's studies were unabashedly committed to the notion that intelligence quotients defined giftedness, and to the notion that there was one acceptable model of masculinity, a masculinity defined by physical strength and heartiness, achievement and competitiveness, and an acceptance of the role of breadwinner and leader of the family and community. By the time of Arnold's, Albert's, and Kaufmann's studies, the definition of giftedness was still closely related to academic accomplishment, but there were subtle changes in the researchers' attitudes—and those of society and the men themselves—in what it means to be a successful male. Arnold found the men, and found herself, questioning the linear, conformist pursuit of career goals that Terman would have found laudable. And although Albert embarked on a quest for the origins of eminence in gifted boys' lives, he found "crossovers" the most interesting of the gifted males he studied—because they had often thrown off their fathers' influence and had turned away from the math and science careers they had been carefully guided toward and seemed destined for. Kaufmann, with her study of the Presidential Scholars, even began to question the role of vocational passion, once considered by many researchers to be the *sine qua non* of male excellence.

Alvino's and Hebert's gifted boys seem to reflect a much-changed notion of masculinity—i.e., a kinder, gentler masculinity. Alvino's boys felt closest to their mothers while longing for an emotional relationship with their fathers. Hebert's poor minority gifted boys were caring, cooperative boys who cherished diversity and showed a marked sensitivity to the needs and feelings of others. In addition, in the Alvino study, these boys were selected and labeled gifted on the basis of a dizzying variety of criteria (reflecting the diversity of identification strategies in U.S. schools) and on a new, broadly defined notion of giftedness that seems more sociological than intellectual in nature. Therefore, the research on gifted boys is fascinating, not only for the facts that we can learn about the trajectory of gifted men's lives, but also for the mirror that the research holds up to the changing conceptions of giftedness and masculinity in the 20th century.

Of course, the content itself is also fascinating. Gifted boys are hungry for better relationships with their fathers, although they often have close relationships with their mothers. They experience social isolation and problems in peer relationships. They need caring adults who will help build their belief in themselves. In fact, it appears that academic encouragement alone from parents or teachers may lead to a fast-track career, but also to less maturation. Most gifted boys do grow up to be excellent students and accomplished adults. Gifted education and special programming do seem to work, at least insofar as they provide the ideas and experiences for which gifted boys are hungry. However, it is apparent that mentoring and guidance are also critical to gifted boys' success in achieving their goals. Gifted men who do not have the "inner will" of the boys in Hebert's study and the courage of the "crossover" boys in Albert's study may find themselves, as did Arnold and Denney's men, to be unhappy to arrive at exactly where they intended to be.

References

Albert, R. S. (1994). The achievement of eminence: A longitudinal study of exceptionally gifted boys and their families. In R. F. Subotnik and K. D. Arnold (Eds.), *Beyond Terman: Contemporary longitudinal studies of giftedness and talent.* Norwood, NJ: Ablex.

Alvino, J. (1991). An investigation into the needs of gifted boys. *Roeper Review,* 13 (4), 174-180.

Arnold, K. D. (1994). The Illinois valedictorian project: Early adult careers of academically talented male high school students. In R. F. Subotnik & K. D. Arnold (Eds.), *Beyond Terman: Contemporary longitudinal studies of giftedness and talent.* Norwood, NJ: Ablex.

Binet, A. & Simon, T. (1916). *The development of intelligence in children* (E. S. Kit, trans.). Baltimore: Williams & Wilkins.

Cox, J., Daniel, N., & Boston, B. O. (1985). *Educating able learners: Programs and promising practices.* Austin: University of Texas Press.

Fox, L. H. (1981). Identification of the academically gifted. *American Psychologist,* 36, 1103-1111.

Gardner, H. (1983). *Frames of mind: The theory of multiple intelligences.* New York: Basic Books.

Hollingworth, L. S. (1942) *Children above 180 IQ Stanford-Binet: Origins and development.* Yonkers-on-Hudson, NY: World Book.

Kaufmann, F. (Summer, 2000). Gifted education and the romance of passion. *California Association for the Gifted Newsletter,* Los Angeles, CA.

Kaufmann, F. (1986). The nature, role, and influence of mentors in the lives of gifted adults. *Journal of Counseling and Development,* 64 (9), 576-578.

Kaufmann, F. (1981). The 1964 -1968 Presidential Scholars: A follow-up study. *Exceptional Children*, 48 (2), 164-169.

Kulik, J. A. & Kulik, C. C. (1997). Ability grouping. In N. Colangelo & G. A. Davis (Eds.), *Handbook of gifted education* (2nd ed., pp. 230-242). Boston: Allyn & Bacon.

Maker, C. J. & Nielson, A. B. (1995). *Teaching models in education, 2nd ed.* Austin, TX: Pro-Ed.

Noble, K., Subotnik, R., & Arnold, K. (1999). To thine own self be true: A new model of female talent development. *Gifted Child Quarterly*, 43 (3), 140-149.

Rogers, K. B. (2001). *Re-forming gifted education: Matching the program to the child.* Scottsdale, AZ: Gifted Psychology Press.

Rogers, K. B. (1998). Using current research to make good decisions about grouping. *National Association of Secondary School Principals Bulletin*, 82 (595), 38-46.

Rogers, K. B. (1991). *The relationship of grouping practices to the education of the gifted and talented learner.* Storrs, CT: The National Research Center on the Gifted and Talented, Report No. 9101.

Seligman, M. E. P. (1998). The gifted and the extraordinary. *The American Psychological Association Monitor*, 29 (11), 2.

Silverman, L. (1999). *What we have learned about gifted children.* Denver: Gifted Child Development Center.

Silverman, L. (1998). *Using test results to aid clinical judgment.* Denver: Gifted Development Center.

Silverman, L. K. (1993). *Counseling the gifted and talented.* Denver: Love Publishing Co.

Strip, C. A. & Hirsch, G. (2000). *Helping gifted children soar: A practical guide for parents and teachers.* Scottsdale, AZ: Gifted Psychology Press.

Tavris, C. (1985). *The mismeasure of woman*. New York: Touchstone.

Terman, L. M. (1959). *The gifted group at mid-life*. Palo Alto, CA: Stanford University Press.

Terman, L. M. (1925). *The mental and physical traits of a thousand gifted children*. Palo Alto, CA: Stanford University Press.

Terman, L. M. & Oden, M. H. (1947). *The gifted child grows up*. Palo Alto, CA: Stanford University Press.

Terman, L. M. & Oden, M. H. (1935). *The promise of youth*. Palo Alto, CA: Stanford University Press.

Van Tassel-Baska, J. (1998). *Excellence in education gifted and talented learners, 3rd ed.* Denver: Love.

Webb, J. T. (1993). Nurturing social-emotional development of gifted children. In K. A. Heller, F. J. Monks, & A. H. Passow (Eds.), *International handbook of research and development of giftedness and talent* (pp. 525-538). Oxford: Pergamon Press.

Webb, J. T. & Kleine, P. A. (1993). Assessing gifted and talented children. In J. Culbertson & D. Willis (Eds.), *Testing young children* (pp. 383-407). Austin, TX: Pro-Ed.

Webb, J. T., Meckstroth, E. A., & Tolan, S. S. (1982). *Guiding the gifted child*. Scottsdale, AZ: Gifted Psychology Press (formerly Ohio Psychology Press).

Winebrenner, S. (2000). *Teaching gifted kids in the regular classroom, revised edition*. Minneapolis: Free Spirit.

Winner, E. (1996). *Gifted children: Myths and realities*. New York: Basic Books.

3

All Those Books about Boys: What Can We Learn about Gifted Boys from the New Literature on Masculinity?

Only a short time ago, a parent wanting guidance about raising a boy would have had a hard time finding any help at the bookstore or library. Most of the gender-based books focused on raising healthy girls and helping them reach their goals. However, the birth of the men's movement, with its focus on the growth of both boys and men, has helped change that.

Almost since the beginning of the women's movement in the 1960s, there have been men and women who have reminded us that the liberation of women from stereotyped roles could not happen without the liberation of men from their own stereotyped roles. The men's movement crystallized around this belief and took several directions. One faction, the supportive men's movement, was enthusiastic about new roles for women. It viewed women's entry into the working world as an opportunity for men to become more involved in nurturing their children and to work as equals with women. They also saw new chances to develop men's inner lives and emotionality.

Then there were factions that were not supportive of changing women's roles. One group, the men's rights group, seized the opportunity to criticize the women's movement as an encroachment on male rights. They insisted that men, as well as women, had been oppressed, particularly in the area of child custody and unfair favoritism of women in the workplace. Another antifeminist group simply sought to reverse the women's movement, hoping to bring back the old, traditional gender roles. Still others, in the spiritual men's movement, sought to discover and nurture positive masculine identities rather than making men more like women. They looked to spirituality and connectedness, rather than to materialism and competition, as paths to meaning for men.

All of these ideas have found their way into the books about boys that suddenly began appearing in the late 1990s. This explosion of books came about for several reasons. First, the media's coverage of extreme cases of violence by boys led to widespread public concern that something was wrong with the way we were teaching and raising our boys. Second, the increasing emphasis in the schools on programs for girls prompted many educators to search for ways in which boys, too, could be helped to overcome gender stereotypes that restrict their choices. Finally, a number of psychologists, because of their interest and experience in helping men, became interested in boys' culture as a breeding ground for many of the problems experienced by adult men.

Some of the books about boys recognize that new female roles, although at times confusing to boys and men, can be a true opportunity for male growth. Some books, however, seek to "turn back the clock" and encourage the resumption of traditional gender roles. Still others focus on ways of helping boys find meaning through rites of passage, spiritual questing, and the search for a new concept of masculinity.

Those of us who have a concern for gifted boys can learn much from what the authors of these books say. Gifted boys have many of the same problems and concerns that are experienced by average boys, but their intensity, sensitivity, curiosity, and other special characteristics give their struggles with masculinity a special twist. In this chapter, we have evaluated representative books from several different points of view, and we show what these books imply for the lives of today's gifted boys.

Real Boys *by William Pollack*

William Pollack has written one of the first and best of the contemporary books about boys. As a clinical psychologist and a director of the Center for Men at the Harvard Medical School, Pollack has the experience and the credentials to debunk myths and provide practical truths to benefit gifted boys. He has years of experience counseling boys and men and has worked with the leading researchers in the area of gender studies at the Center for Men. There are many myths about boys, Pollack says, that are destructive to their lives.

First, there are the ideas that boys carry with them—the code of the boys' culture. The Boy Code, as Pollack calls it, is a type of straitjacket for boys, cruelly restricting their emotions and behaviors. Its first imperative is to be "The Sturdy Oak": stoic, stable, and independent. Boys are never to show weakness, they cannot have moods, and they must never depend on anyone for help. The second imperative is to "Give 'em Hell!"; that is, they should engage in risky, daring behavior and should act tough and macho at all times. The third is "The Big Wheel," namely that males must attain status, dominance, and power. According to this imperative, it is important to always try to be the leader of any group and to force one's way past others for success. The fourth is "No Sissy Stuff"; males must never show dependence, warmth, or sympathy. They must never show empathy or demonstrate emotional responses to another. This one, says Pollack, may be the most crippling, because it requires that boys submerge all human qualities previously, though mistakenly, attributed to females only.

The Boy Code is a valuable way of viewing the behavior of both gifted boys and average boys. Gifted boys have a tendency to want very much to fit in with societal norms. They are well adjusted and usually conforming. Their intelligence assures that they will quickly intuit the Boy Code and try to fulfill it. However, the emotional sensitivity and intellectual intensity of gifted boys may cause internal turmoil when they attempt to live by the Boy Code. Gifted boys may have a harder time shutting down their emotions. In addition, they may resent the idea that their intensity cannot be directed toward intellectual or creative activities if they are to be "real boys." As a result, gifted boys often must take their strong feelings and intense interests underground. On the outside they must be independent, tough, competitive leaders among boys, while on the inside they may long for an opportunity to exchange thoughts and feelings.

Pollack also believes that it is likely that other external societal myths keep gifted boys from expressing their true selves. These myths—these things parents and teachers and opinion makers tell each other—have a profound impact on the education and guidance of gifted boys. The first myth is: "Boys will be boys." This myth, Pollack says, makes boys the prisoners of nature. People make huge leaps of faith when they assume that where there are boys, there is testosterone; where there is testosterone, there is aggression; and where there is aggression, there is violence. In addition, the belief that nature is all-powerful leads parents and teachers to think there is little they can do to shape or redirect boys' behavior.

Pollack powerfully disputes this myth by showing how boys' behavior is shaped more by loved ones than by nature. Boys do have a natural need for action, but that action does not need to spill over into aggression. They simply prefer competitive, rigorous activities with large groups in large spaces. In addition, while testosterone may contribute to their preference for action, it is different in its effect from one boy to another, and its levels fluctuate throughout the day and over longer periods of time. At different points in a boy's lifespan, testosterone has widely differing effects, ranging from making adolescent boys more forceful to making older men more gentle. Therefore, boys are not the victims of their hormones, and their behavior *can* be shaped by those who care about them.

This myth has particularly important implications for gifted boys. Many gifted boys love to read and love to engage in quiet, creative activities. If a gifted boy does not like team sports, does that mean that he doesn't have enough testosterone and therefore is not a real boy? It is this kind of thinking that has made so many gifted boys doubt their own masculinity and fear the opinions of those who insist that aggressive boys are just being boys.

This leads to the second myth identified by Pollack, which is that "Boys *should* be boys." This is the belief that boys *must* fulfill the masculine stereotype. When boys do not act in the prescribed masculine way, then both boys and girls are quick to "tighten the gender straitjacket." Parents worry if their boy is not masculine enough and often try to search for ways of making him "more of a man." Boys who try out traditionally feminine behaviors are likely to be punished far more severely than girls who try out masculine behaviors. Boys who like to dress up or who like to be dramatic or to play-act female roles are often immediately labeled homosexuals by their peers and are quickly and strongly reprimanded by parents and teachers.

This myth is particularly destructive to creative gifted boys who may love to play roles and be as curious about female lives as they are about anything else. Learning that "boys should be boys" teaches gifted boys that there is one area about which they are not allowed to be curious—and that is the entire realm of knowledge that is called "feminine" knowledge! They learn (wrongly) that they cannot ever understand girls' or women's culture, that they can never explore the inner lives of females, and that they must never seek information about "girls'" activities, such as cooking or caring for children. Gifted boys who love to read may find themselves cut off from half of the books in the library—the ones written by female authors or featuring female characters!

Another problem arises for gifted boys regarding developmental differences. Because gifted boys like to hang out with older boys, who are, after all, their intellectual peers, they may find themselves on the receiving end of denigrating comments when they simply act their age. Boys do cry—especially young boys. A young gifted boy who is expected to hold back his tears while among the older boys may have too tall of an order to fill.

The truth, says Pollack, is that there are many ways to be a man, and there is a diversity of masculinities. He points out that different things are expected of men in different cultures, and that boys and men can create their own models of masculinity.

A third myth is that "Boys are toxic" because boys are emotionally unaware, are unsocialized, and are destructive to the social environment. This myth makes boys into unfeeling buffoons who need to be constrained at all costs. This myth also implies that girls have a civilizing influence, and thus that boys in all-male groups will quickly descend into rough or barbaric behavior. The truth, Pollack says, is that boys are empathic. Empathic fathers have empathic sons. And boys who have not been humiliated for acts of kindness, sensitivity, and cooperation are happy to collaborate and help others.

This myth denies gifted boys' civilizing influence, as well as their capacity to bring to any group a broader range of sensitivities. Gifted boys are not toxic, and although their activity levels and tendency to shout out answers can limit the behavior of quieter girls in the classroom, it is not necessary that this happen. If the need for classroom equity is explained to boys, they may be as eager as girls are to change the classroom climate so that everyone is heard.

Raising Cain: Protecting the Emotional Lives of Boys *by Dan Kindlon and Michael Thompson*

Dan Kindlon is a member of the child psychology faculty at Harvard University, and Michael Thompson is the staff psychologist for a leading boys' school in Boston. Although their book is about boys in general, one could argue that, as a teacher at Harvard and a psychologist at a prestigious school, they are both actually specialists in gifted boys and men. They are both eminently qualified to share their wisdom about the inner lives of boys, and they do so in a sensitive and practical manner.

Kindlon and Thompson are concerned about the "emotional miseducation of boys." They believe that this miseducation comes about because of the emphasis placed upon harsh punishment for boys, difficult separations from the mother, conflicted and emotionally distant relationships with the father, and boys' "culture of cruelty."

The authors show how males receive harsher punishments for misbehavior than females do throughout their lives, and how for minority boys the problem is compounded. The social perception that boys' behavior can only be controlled through harsh punishment leads to the usual problems that punishment entails: it stops the immediate behavior but teaches nothing about acceptable behavior. Parents in our society tend to administer harsher punishments for physical missteps, such as running in front of a car, than for social mistakes. However, it is boys, with their higher activity levels, that tend to commit such behaviors and thus receive physical punishment more often. Boys who are gifted, with their greater sensitivity and intensity of thought and feelings, may be deeply negatively affected by corporal punishment, for they may internalize a sense of shame and become self-punishers. Harshly treated gifted boys become harsh taskmasters of themselves—and eventually of others.

Often, mothers who don't know how to help boys make the transition from dependence to independence may push the boy away too soon or may hover over him too much. In most cases, this happens simply because social custom tells boys that they must separate from their mothers to become a man. The separation often means the end of emotional education for the son. Gifted boys may have particular difficulty with separation from their mother. As will be seen in the chapter on relationships, too often a gifted boy, because of his advanced knowledge and sensitivity, becomes his mother's surrogate spouse or constant companion during childhood—only to be forcefully taken from her later. Fathers who become worried about the mother's too close relationship with the son may feel the need to "straighten the boy out," and may begin subjecting him to a sudden introduction into the "normal" male culture.

The authors say that in therapy groups, where men often talk about almost any loss or sadness without emotion, it is always in discussions about fathers that men cry. When fathers are unsure of themselves, they may resort to control, competition, and criticism. Fathers' attempts to control their growing sons are usually doomed.

A son outgrows the father's physical control as soon as he gets his mature body; he will outgrow his father's attempts to control him socially as soon as he is able to get away from home.

Because male culture teaches men to dominate and overpower one another, fathers may respond to the discomfort of having another male in the house by competing for attention and for the satisfaction of winning. It is a father's criticism that seems to be what so many men remember from their childhoods. Many cannot, even in adulthood, forget their father's withering sarcasm or contempt, and even particular phrases will stay with them, haunting their work and their relationships. Many men feel they can never live up to their father's expectations of them.

Thus, gifted boys not only have the burden of living up to their own "potential," but also of living up to their father's expectations. Often, when boys are labeled gifted, fathers mistakenly take this as a sign that their boys will be smart at everything and that eminence is in their future. Then, when the gifted boy fails at something, the father may act out of disbelief or anger, saying things such as, "If you're so smart, why can't you figure this out?" Or, "If you're so smart, why didn't you get better grades?" It is interesting how much these authors' observations match the research we reviewed earlier by Alvino and Reichert, who said that for gifted boys, fathers were "everywhere and nowhere."

Kindlon and Thompson also state that gifted boys who do not learn how to conform perfectly may become the victims of a peer culture of cruelty. Gifted boys frequently have unusual interests—astronomy, for example, or opera, or dolphins—and often must keep these a secret if they are to survive in the "regular" boys' culture. Many gifted boys feel that they must pretend to be dumber or less sensitive than they really are to gain the approval and acceptance of their friends. It is easy for the gifted boy to get stuck in this mode—to work so hard at being ordinary that he becomes ordinary!

Finally, the culture of cruelty that their peers create forces boys into a constantly defensive posture. Any sign of weakness or deviation from group norms will lead to attacks and accusations of being a "fag" or other such epithets. Small boys are bullied, and nonconforming boys are mocked.

There was some evidence in the Alvino and Reichert study that gifted boys were well aware of this culture of cruelty. Some freely admitted that being gifted can cause social problems, and some were careful not to express their concern in any way that might imply weakness. Gifted boys need special assistance in dealing with the cruelty of their peers, and parents and teachers must be aware of this culture so they can help to change it. Open discussion between parents and sons of the various issues brought up by this book could be very valuable to all boys—but particularly to gifted boys.

Stiffed: The Betrayal of the American Man *by Susan Faludi*

Susan Faludi is a feminist known for her exhaustive research and great empathy. Few things could be more surprising in the current literature of masculinity studies than the idea of such a fervent feminist trying her hand at understanding the anger of American men. Faludi worked for six years gathering data for this book, and her work shows. She brings to this book the same compassion for her subjects that she has brought to her books about women. In this book, Faludi examines what it means to working men to be betrayed by the changes of the last 30 years.

In that time, she says, men have lost the opportunity to define themselves as men by all of the traditional measures—meaningful, productive work; bravery in war; the protection of women and children; and even the wholehearted support of the home team. To understand what has happened, she interviewed men who have been "downsized"—men who have lost traditional roles as breadwinners, militia members who have no war to fight, gang members seeking manhood, and athletes who no longer can participate with their favorite sports team.

The men in *Stiffed* are indeed sad and angry; however, the overwhelming sense readers get from the men in her book is that of puzzlement. What is wrong with their lives? How did this happen? When did everything change? They seem to be under siege from all sides, accused by women of being unfeeling and constricted, and suspecting that other men, particularly from their fathers' generation, see them as not being manly enough. Men today, Faludi suggests, have lost their old masculine roles and relationship styles and have not yet found new ones with which to replace them.

What relevance does this book have for gifted boys and men? Gifted men have more often been the victims of downsizing than average men have. This is because it is the gifted men who have often attained the highest paying jobs in American corporations, and in the cynical wave of downsizing that came in the late 1990s, the highest-paid managers were usually the first to get laid off. Their years of experience, quality of leadership, and creative contributions were often overlooked in the rush to show cost savings.

Most gifted men were once young boys who received a lot of A's in school. They got used to getting rewarded for working hard. It comes as a terrible shock to them, then, when they learn that brilliance and hard work may still lead to unemployment if they simply happen to work for the wrong corporation at the wrong time.

Gifted men may strive particularly hard to fulfill masculine roles; they have felt different since they were boys, and thus are eager to prove that they fit in. They may overcompensate for their earlier lives as nerds by attempting to create very traditional relationships with women. They may be overly adoring or overly possessive. The rejection by modern women who resist their older style of courtship and protection may seem a tremendous failure to men who see relationships as achievements.

In short, gifted men who have always been adept at following the rules may find that the rules have changed too fast even for them, and that the nimbleness required to change a lifetime of masculine role behaviors may simply be beyond their powers. The men in *Stiffed* are puzzled and exhausted, and it may be that some gifted men, confronting the same cultural dilemmas, may go beyond puzzlement to anger and hopelessness.

The men in *Stiffed* do bear some resemblance to both the young men in the study of valedictorians as well as the men in our own study. There was indeed some demoralization among the valedictorian men, and some vague sense of wanting something more among our St. Louis gifted men. The gifted men in these two studies also struggled with changing roles, a struggle that their "giftedness" had not protected them from. Perhaps the greatest evidence of this was the high rate of divorce and frequency of relationship difficulties noted in our studies.

The War Against Boys *by Christina Hoff Sommers*

This book is a horrible attempt by author Christina Hoff Sommers to slam feminists while at the same time bemoaning the fate of American boys. Much as witch-hunters used to accuse independent women of killing and eating children, Sommers accuses feminists of waging a war against boys. And much as current white supremacists insist that the Holocaust never happened, she insists that there was never any shortchanging of girls in the classroom, nor inequities in education, nor loss of the sense of self of girls during the teen years.

Most of the book is an attack upon the scholarship of the past 10 years regarding the education and guidance of girls, particularly the work of Carol Gilligan, author of *In a Different Voice* (1985), Myra and David Sadker, authors of *Failing at Fairness* (1994), and the American Association of University Women, which commissioned *Shortchanging Girls, Shortchanging America* (1991). Sommers calls the concerns about girls a "manufactured crisis." She accuses these authors of poor and shoddy research methods, although her evidence is thin. In particular, she accuses Gilligan, who has written often about the silencing of girls' voices, of using too small of a sample of women in her original qualitative study, but ignores the fact that Gilligan's conclusions were modest and appropriate to her sample size. Sommers also claims that the American Association of University Women (AAUW), by pointing out the ways in which girls receive less attention in the schools, was politically motivated to achieve feminist ends, despite the fact that the

AAUW has a long tradition of being a moderate and nonpartisan organization. Sommers also attempts to dispute findings by the Sadkers, whose observations point to gender bias in the schools— observations that have long since been carefully critiqued and then accepted by educational psychologists.

Sommers proceeds to say that it is boys who have been oppressed by the schools, because they have received lower grades and harsher treatment. She claims that attempts to bring equity to the classroom have hurt boys, because now they get even less attention than before. In addition, she claims that feminist-leaning teachers try to "feminize" boys and deny their masculinity.

She believes, above all, that we must let boys be boys—to recognize that testosterone drives their behavior, and to respect that these drives need to be expressed. It is clear that Sommers has an agenda, and that it is to encourage a return to the "good old days" when men and women had clearly differentiated roles. She romanticizes masculinity and sees it as a fixed trait rather than as a continuum of behaviors within and among men.

In brief, this book has little to offer those who want to understand gifted boys. But its very existence is a warning that there are those who are very unhappy with the changes we are seeing today in men's and women's roles. People like Sommers see feminism as the ultimate threat to the safety and happiness of boys rather than as a movement that can free men as well as women.

The Wonder of Boys *by Michael Gurian*

In much the same vein as Christina Hoff Sommers, this author, who is a therapist and educator, sets out to show how testosterone determines boys' behavior. In a simplistic way, Gurian claims that testosterone is the immutable reason for masculine behavior. As a result, he says, society needs to accommodate masculine behavior rather than subdue it.

Gurian believes that the new gender "myths" about inequities in education and in the workplace are dangerous to boys. These so-called "myths," however, have a pretty good basis in fact. For instance, there are the *facts* that males and females are more alike than they are different in personality characteristics and abilities, that males have often dominated classrooms to the detriment of females, and that females are often sexually harassed by males in schools. He, too, blames feminists for creating a world that is hostile to boys. In all of these ways, the book is another "Boohoo, the girls are getting all the attention" book.

However, this is one book that does provide some interesting suggestions for raising boys. An informal short list generated by the author and an acquaintance of his, a mother of two boys, may be more useful than the more elaborate descriptions of guidance strategies mentioned later. The list indicates 10 specific things that boys need:

- Nurturing parents/caregivers.
- A clan or tribe.
- A spiritual life.
- Important work.
- Mentors and role models.
- To know the rules.
- To learn how to lead, and how to follow.
- An adventure, and a best friend to have it with.
- Lots of games.
- An important role in life.

Some of these seem to be excellent suggestions for all boys, including boys who are gifted. However, it must be remembered that for a gifted boy, the clan or tribe might be his friends on the Internet or his Dungeons and Dragons group—not an athletic team or neighborhood group. A gifted boy's spiritual life may be very different from that of his community, or even of his "tribe." Many gifted boys are atheists or agnostics at an early age because of their love for and excitement with science and because of their dismay with the hypocrisy they so often observe in religious people and institutions. Many gifted children identify with an intellectualism that scoffs at conventional religions. Despite their atheism, though, these gifted boys may be profoundly spiritual in their intense need for understanding of the universe, their yearning for connectedness, and their capacity for transcendent experiences. And while the need for "lots of games" may be a real one for gifted boys, many of the games played by average boys may leave gifted boys bored senseless. The games of gifted boys must involve complexity, adventure, intellectual challenge, and intensity.

The need for mentors, real work, and important roles in life are undeniable needs of gifted boys, and we will say more about these topics in later chapters.

Reading Books about Boys

Current books about boys and men have much to teach us about the lives of gifted boys. It is important, however, to always pay attention to the points at which the experiences of gifted boys diverge from those of average boys, as has been discussed above. In addition to always making this distinction, it is important to keep the following issues in mind when reading books about boys.

1. *Boys are not being pushed aside by girls. Instead, boys are choosing to disengage because of status fears.* Although many of the authors, and even some of the men in Faludi's book, seem to think that boys and men have been pushed aside by girls and women in the classroom and in the world of work, the sociology of both of these settings does not support that idea. From the findings of child development specialists working with preschool groups to the findings of economists studying the labor market trends, it is clear that when girls or women enter an activity or endeavor in large numbers, boys and men flee (Kerr, 1999). It is happening in undergraduate classrooms, for instance, where boys now sometimes avoid biology because of girls' increased interests in it. ("Oh, they just all want to be marine biologists and talk to dolphins," said one gifted boy to Barb Kerr in one of our career development workshops for talented high school students at Arizona State University.)

In colleges, there is a trend among men toward choosing classes from an ever-narrowing set of majors that still confer both a high status and a potentially high salary. Even pre-law has recently lost status. In the world of work, it has long been observed that when women enter any occupation in great numbers, the status and salary of that occupation go down, and this is not due simply to an influx of additional persons in that occupation (Kerr, 1999). Therefore, "male flight" is probably very similar to "white flight" to the suburbs—one group leaves activities and occupations because they fear that the entry of too many of another group will make "property values" go down.

The solution is not to get girls to be quieter or less bossy or to give them less attention than they already receive. No, the task is much more difficult. The task is to change boys' and men's attitudes in such a way that the increasing presence of females in that activity does not lower its value in their minds. It's a tall order, but important for both boys and girls.

2. *Feminists are not in a war against boys. They are combating a system of stereotyping and gender socialization that limits both boys and girls in their life choices.* It is getting rather old to bash feminists for all the troubles between girls and boys and men and women. Most of the troubles have been there for a long time. However, the public often fears that fighting gender stereotypes and changing traditional roles will lead to the breakdown of the family and of society. So feminists get the blame for massive changes in familial roles that are actually the result of a tremendous number of economic, political, social, and individual forces. Feminists want the changes that have been incorporated into our society to stay. A society in which women can marry freely, reproduce when they wish to, and support themselves financially has never existed before our time. For this kind of society to thrive, the half that is male must support these changes. That is where our boys come in; they are our best hope for maintaining the sweeping new freedoms now being experienced by girls and women in most democratic societies.

3. *Testosterone does not "hardwire" boys for dominance, aggression, or achievement. Testosterone is complex in its effects, and its levels are profoundly affected by the rhythms and events of life experiences.* Males are not allocated a set amount of testosterone at birth that becomes a blueprint for their behavior. Instead,

males have testosterone levels that vary widely from one person to another, that ebb and flow each day and in longer cycles, and that are responsive to life events. Certain kinds of experiences can increase testosterone levels, and others can decrease the levels. Therefore, like most human attributes, masculinity is complexly determined and is not the result of a single substance. Masculinity is the result of a wide variety of both internal and external forces. As such, it is just as open to interpretation as it is to shaping.

4. *Masculinity is not a universal set of behaviors across cultures. Each culture has its own uniquely favored conception of masculinity.* An exploration of world cultures will provide a rich array of interpretations of masculinity that make the arguments of Sommers and other defenders of the "innate masculine" look hopelessly ethnocentric. Although there are no cultures in which women dominate men or own men, there are indeed many matriarchal, matrilineal, and matrilocal cultures in which women are honored as the source of life and in which males and females are regarded as equals in spiritual and temporal power. It is likely that some of these cultures, such as the Apache culture of today and the Minoan culture of ancient Crete, have much to teach us about a potential new world in which women and men are truly equals.

5. *Men who are high in masculinity and women who are high in femininity are less healthy, less happy, and less achieving than persons of either sex who are more androgynous.* People who are more balanced in masculine and feminine characteristics seem to have more flexibility in living their lives. Two decades of research on androgyny—a psychological stance that incorporates the strengths of both masculinity and femininity—has shown it to be associated with psychological health, creativity, better social functioning, and lower rates of substance abuse (Bem, 1999). The best literature on masculinity does not advise a return to a macho world in which men dominate, compete, and make all the decisions, but rather advises a society in which males are able to be strong, assertive, and constructive but are also able to be emotionally responsive, nurturing, and compassionate as well.

References

American Association for University Women (1991). *Shortchanging girls, shortchanging America*. Washington, DC: AAUW.

Faludi, S. (1999). *Stiffed: The betrayal of the American man*. New York: William Morrow.

Gilligan, C. (1985). *In a different voice*. Cambridge, MA: Harvard Press.

Gurian, M. (1996). *The wonder of boys*. New York: Tarcher.

Kerr, B. A. (1999, March). When dreams differ: Gender relations on the college campus. *Chronicle of Higher Education*, Washington, DC.

Kindlon, D. & Thompson, M. (1999). *Raising Cain: Protecting the emotional lives of boys*. New York: Ballantine.

Pollack, W. (1998). *Real boys: Rescuing our sons from the myths of boyhood*. New York: Holt.

Sadker, M. & Sadker, D. (1995). *Failing at fairness: How our schools cheat girls*. New York: Touchstone.

Sommers, C. H. (2001). *The war against boys: How misguided feminism is harming our young men*. New York: Touchstone.

Section II:
Milestones and
Danger Zones

4

The Young Gifted Boy

While his mom is cooking, five-year-old Trevor sits at the kitchen table drawing pictures of a spider from different perspectives: looking down from the top, belly up, from the side, and a very scary angle, looking up at the spider. His mom comes over and tells him that his pictures look "really neat." "Hey, Mom," he says, still drawing, "was that positive reinforcement?"

Josh is seven, the oldest kid in his kindergarten and for sure the biggest. His parents held him back because he had a summer birthday close to the cutoff day for kindergarten entry. He likes to read out loud so fast that the "littler and dumber" kids can't understand what he is saying. He knows he shouldn't be mean to the other kids, but sometimes, he explains, he "can't help it"— he just *has* to trip Jonah whenever he goes by his table, and he just *has* to break Hillary's crayons.

Eight-year-old Ricardo has not done his homework for four days, and he hasn't been caught yet. He told his parents that there was a social studies fair, and there wouldn't be any homework. They believed him. His teachers never asked him for his work either. He thinks this is interesting. Maybe they will never ask him.

It is Saturday, and Ali, who is 10, hasn't come out of his room all day. He is playing an action-packed video game, and he has almost won. It is the single most important thing in his life. He hates school, where he is so bored that he falls asleep every day. School is like a prison sentence, and homework is the torture. His homework takes hours, not because it's hard, but because it seems so stupid to him that he has to keep taking breaks from it—to re-check his e-mail or to get something to eat.

These are all gifted boys, attempting to negotiate the early trials of being bright, young, and male in America. All four are exhibiting their independence while at the same time trying to avoid boredom and the label "sissy." Yet most gifted boys, despite their trials, are joyous, funny, and delightful young people to be around.

Gifted boys enliven the classroom with their creative ideas and their vivid personalities. Because they tend to be more sensitive than other children, they are also more aware of psychological realities (such as Trevor's understanding of positive reinforcement!) and of the implications of current events. Gifted boys are quick to point out the hypocrisies of the adult world, but they often do so with good humor. Because they are fonts of knowledge, they are wonderful conversationalists who easily make friends with older kids and adults. And because their energy level is set a little higher than others,' they can accomplish a tremendous amount of work in a short time—especially for causes they believe in. Whether it is building a model car for the Pinewood Derby or writing a play about homeless people, the gifted boy is likely to invest in his work with passion and intensity. This chapter celebrates those golden boys, while also pointing out some of the conflicts that may surface when the gifted boy attempts to negotiate society's expectations about men and masculinity.

Socialization for Masculinity

The gifted boy comes into the world met by a blue blanket and all of the expectations that go along with it. As an infant, he is likely to be picked up less often than a girl baby when he cries, and people may even be amused at his cries, saying, "Look at him exercising his lungs!" No matter how androgynous his parents, they are unlikely to dress him in pink or to have any "girl" toys in his room. Instead, his toys and room decor likely will be bold and bright, featuring things such as animals and trains and cars, or the mostly male Sesame Street or Disney characters. When people see the new baby, they will comment on his size and his activity level, and not on his attractiveness or sweetness (Maccoby, 1998).

Preschool toys and games for children are rigidly segregated by gender, with pink aisles of the toy store reserved for girls, and the black and "army fatigue" green aisle for the boys. Boy toys will feature monsters, guns, swords, machines, tools, and sports gear. Parents will find no toys for nurturing, few dolls, and few items for quiet activities such as art supplies or beads.

The little boy as a toddler will wear jeans and t-shirts, and people will laugh when he gets dirty. If he is attracted by the beautiful colors and textures of his mother's clothes, it will be made clear to him that these clothes are off limits. If he has big brothers, they will tease him mercilessly if he does play dress-up—especially if he plays dress-up with girls.

For years, girls will be off limits to him as well, even though bright girls will want to play with him. In fact, smart little girls prefer his company to that of average girls. Bright girls sometimes want to be gifted boys. But boys are supposed to only want to be boys. Playing with girls interferes with that. So no matter how interesting the games might be that the girls are playing, our young boy must pretend when with the other boys that girls' games are stupid.

Even before kindergarten, the gifted boy will encounter his first trial by sports. It may be soccer or Tee-ball or midget football, but at some point in time, he will be expected to run around on the field with a bunch of other kids. When preschool kids play sports, they are as random and inattentive as loose molecules. But the dads and moms will crowd the sidelines, cheering and coaching so much that sometimes rules need to be made about parents' interventions.

Therefore, by the time they reach the primary grades, gifted boys have received very clear messages about what a boy is supposed to be like, and they may begin to be puzzled about how to be a "real boy" while at the same time pursuing those interests of theirs that diverge from those of the "real boys."

Identification

If parents have begun to suspect that their little boy is gifted, they may begin to make efforts to confirm their beliefs. Perhaps they consult a psychologist about testing. This is when the fun begins.

The psychologist takes the four-year-old boy into a testing room and begins to bring out the testing materials. Just as the materials are all laid on the table, the psychologist looks up to see that her subject has disappeared. He is under the table, looking at the gum stuck up under there and reaching for it. She reacts with horror and coaxes him out from under the table. She asks him the first question, and he responds with a funny face and a one-word answer, then jumps up and runs over to the poster on the wall to ask, "Who is that guy?" The psychologist asks him to sit down. She gets out her stopwatch for the next question. "Name as many words as you can that…" and he grabs the watch out of her hand. "Can I see that?" He begins to punch the reset button over and over, and she impatiently takes it back and explains the task again.

One of the most difficult problems in identification of preschool gifted boys is that their motor activity and curiosity combine to make the individual intelligence testing process a challenge for even the most expert test administrator. It is very difficult to get an accurate score, and it is highly likely that the resulting score will underestimate the boy's abilities. As a result, preschool-aged gifted boys may not be identified even by pediatricians or psychologists. Parents know that their son is different; preschool teachers may remark upon the boy's intelligence, but little can be done about it.

In *Guiding the Gifted Child*, Webb, Meckstroth, and Tolan (1982) noted that when parents believe their child is gifted, they are usually correct (p. 8). In fact, most parents *under*estimate their child's intelligence and often are embarrassed when talking about their child's special abilities. Nevertheless, when parents believe that their child is gifted, they should consider seeking out a psychologist who is familiar with the characteristics of gifted children to confirm this through formal testing. Most schools require some evidence of giftedness in order to provide special programming, especially in the primary and preschool grades, and test results are very helpful.

Preschool or Play at Home?

Some parents are fortunate enough to find a preschool that allows their son to learn at his own pace, even if it means that he is reading when the other children are napping. The gifted preschool boy needs an enriching, stimulating environment with plenty of challenge for his growing mind. If the preschool-aged boy is at home, it may become a tremendous task for the parent(s) to occupy him.

This leads to an important issue that often comes up in discussing preschool-aged gifted children. Should a parent stay at home to provide the needed education and guidance? It is true that a great many precocious youths and a great many boys who became eminent in their fields had mothers who provided educational opportunities at home (Bloom, 1985). But in considering whether a parent will stay home with the gifted boy, it is important to consider the following facts.

First, in the vast majority of cases, it is the mother who decides to stay home with her son. Couples who make this decision invariably tell me that it was the mother's choice and that the decision was made purely on the basis of her choice. It is nearly always the case that the father's career is considered primary and of much too great importance to be put on hold for the purpose of caring for the children.

In *Smart Girls*, Kerr (1997) showed that gifted women often compromise away their own dreams and goals to support the goals of their husbands and children and that this often leads to regret and wasted talent in later life. So we must caution: what does it teach a boy about the role of women if his mother stays home and devotes herself entirely to his care and education while the father pursues a full-time career? Too easily, boys may learn that women—no matter how talented they are—exist to serve the needs of the men in their lives, or at least, that women should put the needs of males before their own.

Second, even though many eminent adults did have mothers who stayed at home, it does not necessarily follow that mothers who teach their very young gifted boys at home are any better at stimulating them than a trained preschool teacher in a high-quality preschool. In fact, research tends to support the benefits of preschool for gifted boys, so it would seem worthwhile to seek out the best possible setting.

Kindergarten Redshirting

"Redshirting" is the sports practice of slowing down an athlete's academic progress in college so that he can play an extra year. Perhaps one of the most destructive practices for gifted boys is kindergarten redshirting, in which parents delay a child's entrance into kindergarten by a year to give him extra time to mature. Kindergarten redshirting is quite common, especially in communities where sports achievement is highly valued, and the practice has grown in recent years (Brent, May, & Kundert, 1996). More and more boys are being redshirted each year, often on the basis of parental anecdotes and suggestions in the popular press. However, there is little research evidence to support the practice, and convincing evidence demonstrates that it is in fact harmful to a gifted boy's educational, emotional, and social development.

This practice, like so many of those that harm gifted boys, is based on stereotypes of masculinity—in this case, that boys should be tall and strong and should be able to compete successfully in athletics. Often, parents will mention "social development" as their main concern, saying that they want their boy to have the opportunity to get along well with other children. Unfortunately, this is often code for, "We want him to be able to play football." Sometimes, though, kindergarten redshirting reflects parents' fears about bullying. They don't want their son to be at a disadvantage when a big kid picks on him, and they are frightened by recent media reports of the ruthless bullying that takes place in some boys' groups.

Teachers and administrators also tend to be biased in favor of holding boys back from school entrance, particularly when their birth dates fall near the cutoff, but they are thinking of the average boy, who is slower to learn to read, slower to mature socially and emotionally, and more physically active than girls. Boys who are gifted tend to read earlier than average boys (although perhaps not earlier than gifted girls). They tend to be more socially and emotionally advanced than average boys, as well. And if they are "Terman type" kids—that is, if they come from a middle or upper socioeconomic background—they even tend to be bigger, healthier, and stronger. Many educators do not recognize these great developmental differences, though, and so make the same recommendations for all boys.

So, what are the facts about kindergarten redshirting? First of all, intelligence is an important factor in determining kindergarten readiness. And bright boys may be better off entering kindergarten at a younger age than average boys are, especially if they already have preschool experience (Gullo & Burton, 1992).

Second, the belief that older children have more academic success is simply unfounded. Although older average children attain higher academic achievement than younger average children do during the first few years of school, younger gifted children generally do better than older average children do in their classes.

Third, any social disadvantage of being younger usually disappears for average children by about first grade, and they can fade for the gifted boy, too, if he is not too different in other ways. In peer nominations and ratings, in teacher nominations, and in report card grades, there were no differences between younger and older gifted students in a study by Spitzer, Cupp, and Parke (1995). When a gifted boy has difficulty relating to his peers, it is more likely because his classmates are too young for him rather than too old for him. A young gifted boy with good social skills will usually be popular with older children. It is true that giftedness may remain a social disadvantage when he is among his classmates; but it is the intellectual difference, not the age difference, that causes the asynchrony.

Fourth, delaying school entrance may have deleterious effects on both academic and social performance later on in school. In one study, boys who were delayed from entering kindergarten were more likely to be referred for learning or psycho-educational evaluation, and less likely to be referred for gifted education evaluation than boys who weren't held back (DeMeis & Stearns, 1992).

Therefore, it is likely that kindergarten redshirting is a bad strategy for gifted boys. At worst, the redshirted gifted boy is likely to become a big, bored, unhappy bully. Larger and more mature than the other boys, the redshirted gifted boy may be continually frustrated by his classmates' inability to talk about the things he wants to talk about and play at the games he wants to play. His friends can't keep up with him on the playground, and they can't keep up with him in video games either. They don't understand the movies he likes best, nor do they listen to the same kind of music or read the same kinds of books. As a result, the redshirted gifted boy may try to boss the other boys into submission, either pushing them around physically to get them moving, or raining contempt upon them for what he perceives to be their ignorance.

In school, the redshirted gifted boy may be miserably bored. If he is six or even seven in kindergarten, he may have been reading for three years—and yet reading will not come up in the curriculum for another year. He may be initially excited to enter kindergarten only to learn that they are doing "little kids stuff"—learning colors, letters, and numbers—things he mastered at age two or three. He may try to amuse himself with physical activity, jumping up, raising his hand wildly, and shouting out—but those behaviors get him reprimanded. So, even with a well-meaning teacher, he inevitably spends his day being reminded to sit down and be quiet.

It doesn't take long for him to learn to hate school and to dislike other kids. In a few years, he will be insufferable to the teachers—an obviously bright underachiever who seems to always be able to get under their skin and disrupt any teaching geared to the majority of the class. He is the kind of boy who gives a bad name to gifted kids and helps perpetuate a stereotype that is sometimes used to actually punish gifted kids for being gifted.

What are the behavioral characteristics of young gifted boys? Let's take a closer look at some of them now.

Intensity and Curiosity

Gifted boys seem to perceive the world differently from other children and have nontraditional ways of behaving (Webb, et al., 1982). Their perception of the world leads to curiosity, and this in turn creates their higher intensity. Their high general intelligence provides the gifts of efficient perception, exceptional memory, and advanced reasoning ability. What this means is that, while the gifted little boy can astound people with his insights, he can also annoy them with his constant observations of their flaws and inconsistencies. He can also use his indelible memory to make schoolwork seem easy, or he can use it to agitate for a toy he wants, recalling exactly where he saw it, its outstanding characteristic, and how much it costs. One such boy insisted on knowing how much his mother, a teacher, earned per day, and then showed his mom what a tiny fraction of her salary would go toward the purchase of the action figure toy he wanted.

The thoughts and images in the mind of the gifted boy may be more important and interesting to him than what is going on around him. With his imagination, intense curiosity, and desire for complexity, he may create entire worlds of imaginary beings and places where he can escape to when things get too boring.

Since they have always been gifted, these boys naturally expect that the world appears to others as it appears to them and that other children are just like them (Webb, et al., 1982). It usually comes as a surprise to them that others do not share their perspectives, their curiosity, or their intensity. It also surprises them that others see them differently than they see themselves.

Gifted boys not only *see* things differently, they also typically try to *do* things in non-standard ways. Therefore, they may play with toys in ways that were not intended; for example, a *Marbleworks*® game may be used to create an alarm clock that rolls marbles onto the boy's (or his brother's) forehead at wake-up time. They also like to create their own routines and master their own personal tasks in their own way. However, though these boys can see many possibilities, their limited experience often impairs their judgment, and they may have difficulty anticipating the outcome of what happens when they indulge their curiosity (Webb, et al., 1982). For example, they may ask the weight of strangers on an elevator because they want to see how close the total weight is to the maximum allowed. Or a gifted boy can get lost on a family outing simply because his curiosity took him from one sight to another until he is far afield.

In the classroom, curious questioning about possibilities and implications can quickly derail a lesson plan, and teachers often are exasperated by the gifted boy's seeming lack of ability to read subtle cues. Only in 3rd or 4th grade will he begin to notice that he is the only boy waving his hand and shouting out answers. James Webb, one of the authors of *Guiding the Gifted Child,* tells a story of a gifted boy's insistence on knowing the answers to a long string of questions—driving his parent to seek shelter in the bathroom just to get away from it all!

Just as the gifted boy's curiosity and experimentation may put a strain on family members, so, too, can his energy and enthusiasm when other family members are tired and ready to rest (Webb, et al., 1982). Gifted boys may have an unusually high level of energy, and some may need less sleep than anyone else in the family (sometimes only four or five hours per night). Parents may need to insist on regular nap times, or at least quiet times, so that they can get a little rest! Bedtime may be a battle zone, with the little gifted boy insisting that his favorite story be read over and over and becoming infuriated when the exhausted parent tries surreptitiously to skip a page here and there to shorten the ordeal.

The High Activity Level of Gifted Boys

Since their activity levels can be so high, gifted boys are sometimes misdiagnosed by parents or pediatricians as hyperactive (ADHD) or as having attention-deficit disorder (ADD). This often results in the child being placed on unnecessary medication. Some professionals (e.g., Webb, 2000) note that there is an *over*diagnosis of ADHD because physicians may not be trained to recognize the characteristics of giftedness such as intensity, curiosity, and sensitivity. Other professionals, however, suspect that attention-deficit disorder may actually be *under*diagnosed in gifted children. This is because, for the first few years of school, the gifted boy can mask his attention deficit with intelligent, on-the-spot responses, good short-term memory, and creativity (Kaufmann & Castellanos, 2000). Eventually, though, usually by the 4th or 5th grade, the boy's "disability" will manifest itself as underachievement and gross disorganization.

Because some gifted boys do indeed suffer from attention-deficit disorder, careful observation and consultation with a psychiatrist or psychologist is important when evaluating a gifted boy who has unusually high activity levels. The gifted child who truly suffers from attention-deficit disorder (with or without hyperactivity) has a very brief attention span for virtually anything except computer games and television. The healthy gifted child (without ADD) can concentrate on a single task for long periods if it is of interest to him or if ignoring it has significant consequences. The hyperactive gifted child's activity is both constant and random, and his distractibility is present in all situations (except perhaps in the most structured ones). By contrast, the healthy gifted child without ADD shows activity that is usually directed toward specific goals, and his attention problems are present only in some situations, but not in others. A gifted boy with attention-deficit disorder simply cannot get organized, no matter how terrible the potential consequences may be.

For gifted boys, the typical school setting can become boring, particularly when the child is not appropriately placed or when the system tries to force him into a preset, average mold. Most gifted children begin school full of enthusiasm, but often lose their excitement quickly. Gifted boys entering kindergarten are often stunned to find out that they are not expected to read or to know how to add and subtract.

Because gifted boys may finish their school tasks far ahead of other children, they often have a lot of time on their hands in class. Exceptionally gifted boys may experience as much as three-fourths of their class time with little to do and are often given "busywork" or are left to their own devices. In comparison with their classmates, gifted boys increasingly depart from average grade level work as they progress through school, *if their educational program permits.* What they do with their extra time varies from child to child or from day to day. In the earlier grades, they may try to help other children in the class or the teacher, or they may become "creative," often to the dismay of the teacher and their classmates! Boys who do not wish to be disruptive may become creatively inattentive and develop any number of methods for passing the time. They may develop a vivid fantasy life, for instance, making up games and stories in their mind.

Peer Relationships

Gifted boys may be hungry for the company of other gifted boys. Gifted children seem to know when another child is gifted, if they are lucky enough to find one. Miraca Gross, in Australia, has shown in her studies of young gifted children's friendships that gifted children expect to be able to discuss, create, and find like interests with their friends in the early elementary years, when other children define friendship as simply sharing toys (Gross, 2000). In some cases, however, there are not enough other children with similar abilities in the vicinity. When other gifted children are not available, the young gifted boy quickly becomes aware of the fact that he feels and acts differently from others. Even as a preschooler, he may begin to feel left out due to his differentness. Unfortunately, the child does not understand *why* he is different and may begin to feel that there is something wrong with him.

The gifted boy's interests and play activities are in many ways more sophisticated than those of the other children his same age. Some gifted boys like to lecture other children about what they have learned or involve them in their newest interests. Much of the time, these interests—astronomy, geology, history, etc.—are not interesting to the other children. Naturally, the average child frequently thinks that the gifted child is a real bore. Gifted boys don't often take the hint when other kids are bored, and their attempts to lead those children into activities that they find interesting but that the other children find odd or incomprehensible are eventually met with resistance and avoidance. Over and over, the gifted boy's enthusiasm can lead to his becoming a pariah. Finally, the gifted boy with average or below-average social skills may even be insulting or mean to other children, using his verbal skills and his wit to make fun of slower children. This will make him lasting enemies if he is not helped to see the error in his contemptuous criticism of others.

Finally, as will be seen in our many discussions about athletics in this book, the gifted boy who lags behind his male peers in motor skills may suffer a double stigma—being too clumsy as well as too smart. Other boys will quickly reject the boy who is unathletic. Because our society tends to place high stakes on the wins of the soccer team or the Little League team, the awkward boy who causes the team to lose can become the object of resentment and blame.

Sadly enough, a vicious cycle often develops—the gifted boy who cries too easily is rejected, causing him to be even more tearful, which causes him to be rejected even further. The gifted boy who has early negative experiences with team sports comes to hate those sports and avoid them, making him even less adept through lack of practice. Clearly, early successful experiences both in social relationships and in physical play are critical to peer relationships at this young age.

Sometimes by age three or four, these boys are already out of step with their friends. This could explain why they may prefer to spend time by themselves or why they so enjoy finding "peers" in books whose main characters are gifted (Halsted, 2001). Parents may think that their gifted boy is lonely when he is actually delighted by the company of the author and characters of his favorite books. Of course, sometimes the gifted boy does feel rejected and alone; however, it is important not to assume that being alone is lonely for a gifted boy.

In addition to making friends with books, gifted boys often make friends with adults and older children. These relationships may be satisfying to the child and may even be a source of pride to his parents. But mixed-age relationships can also separate the gifted child from classmates his own age, may reduce the number of his friendships, and could make him seem as though he is trying to appear "too grown up" (Webb, et al., 1982). Being accustomed to adult company can condition a child to assume a parent role with other children, often with alienating effects. On the other hand, it is important for the child to be able to share his interests with others who share his passions, regardless of their ages.

A gifted boy may need several different peer groups (Webb, et al., 1982). Thus, an *intellectual* peer group for a gifted child may not include the same persons who are his *physical* or *social* peers. Indeed, a gifted boy may need one peer group for sports, another for intellectual pursuits, and still another for emotional friendships.

Sometimes gifted boys are highly focused in their interests and seem to immerse themselves in a topic to the point of fanaticism. They may have difficulty understanding why others are not as interested as they are in dinosaurs or violins or outer space. Often, especially early in life, gifted children jump intensely from interest to interest. This may cause others to view them as "disorganized" or "scattered." But even the boy with broad and varied interests is intense about the subject that is uppermost at the moment. One peril is that this can develop into a pattern in adolescence of trying to do too many things, or even of trying to be too many things to too many people.

In adolescence and adulthood this "multipotentiality" can become a threat to focused career development as well as to healthy relationships. Multipotentiality also can be a problem because the various areas of high potential are not necessarily equally developed, and because a boy's judgment, social skills, emotional skills, and motor skills may lag behind them.

Asynchronous Development

Asynchronous development means that the gifted boy may have intellectual skills that are far ahead of his emotional and motor skills (Silverman, 1997). Emotional regulation can be a special problem for the young gifted boy. Because he is often involved in situations that frustrate him, he may have outbursts of temper or tears that surprise everyone around him. In addition, when emotional maturity does not match intellectual ability, the boy may be able to read material in books and on the Internet that he is not ready to handle emotionally. A gifted boy of eight may be able to read adult accounts of the Holocaust, for example, but may be emotionally unprepared to handle such extraordinary horror. Gifted boys may have nightmares as a result of exposure to such material.

Indeed, finding reading material for the gifted boy is often challenging, because although in elementary school he may have the reading skills of a college student, college student texts and classics of literature and philosophy may be well beyond his developmental level. That is, discussions of abstract concepts such as existentialism and postmodernism may elude him. And the subtleties of great literature, in which such things as the erotic longings or philosophical conflicts of the protagonist are central to the theme of the book, may seem weird or boring. The boy with such limited life experience simply can't relate. Therefore, gifted boys often prefer books of high vocabulary and sophisticated syntax that are nevertheless plot-driven, such as science fiction or mystery stories.

And when intellectual development outpaces motor skills, the gifted boy may be continually frustrated by his inability to make his hands and body do what his brain insists he do. He cannot write as fast as he can think. The image that is so vivid in his head or the piano melody that rings so clearly in his mind cannot be created by his young fingers. He may visualize great football plays or evocative dances, but be unable to follow through with his as yet undeveloped physical body. How wonderful the advances of technology have been for gifted boys, now that a keyboard mastery program, a computer-assisted design program, a music program, or a virtual sport software program can give him the dexterity he needs to bring his images to reality—at least on the computer screen.

For all of the reasons stated above, young gifted boys may simply decide one day to stop trying to achieve. We turn now to an example from literature to illustrate this phenomenon.

Bartleby Syndrome

For a better understanding of what happens to many congenial, bright boys when they refuse to achieve, consider this synopsis of the story of "Bartleby the Scrivener," by Herman Melville.

A Synopsis of *Bartleby the Scrivener* from Lionel Trilling's *The Experience of Literature*

The story of *Bartleby the Scrivener* is told by a businessman who does "a snug business among rich men's bonds, and mortgages, and title deeds." A pale young man comes to work for him, copying out documents. He is "a motionless young man...pallidly neat, pitiably respectable, incurably forlorn! He is a mystery to his boss: "While of other law copyists I might write a complete life, of Bartleby nothing of that sort can be done."

At first, Bartleby does an extraordinary quantity of writing, performing at an extraordinary rate. The boss becomes used to his high productivity, until one day everything changes. He says, "Being much hurried to complete a small affair I had in hand, I abruptly called to Bartleby. In my haste and natural expectancy of compliance, I sat with my head bent over the original on my desk, my right hand sideways, and somewhat nervously extended with the copy, so that Bartleby might snatch it and proceed to business without the least delay. Imagine my consternation when without moving from his privacy, Bartleby, in a singularly mild firm voice, replied, 'I would prefer not to.'

"I sat a while in perfect silence, rallying my stunned faculties. Immediately it occurred to me that my ears had deceived me, or Bartleby had entirely misunderstood my meaning. I repeated my request in the clearest tone I could assume; but in as clear a one came the previous reply, 'I would prefer not to.'

"Had there been the least uneasiness, anger, impatience or impertinence in his manner...doubtless I would have violently dismissed him from the premises.... Nothing so aggravates an earnest person as a passive resistance."

From that day on, Bartleby continues to gently refuse tasks put before him, to the complete consternation of his master. Then he begins to refuse to leave his office, even when the firm itself is moved. Finally, Bartleby is arrested for vagrancy. "As I afterwards learned, the poor scrivener, when told that he must be conducted to the Tombs, offered not the slightest obstacle, but in his pale, unmoving way, silently acquiesced." The businessman goes to visit Bartleby, who is dying of starvation, because he has preferred not to eat. "Strangely huddled at the base of the wall, his knees drawn up, and lying on his side, his head touching the cold stones, I saw the wasted Bartleby.... The round face of the grubman peered upon me now. 'His dinner is ready. Won't he dine today either? Or does he live without dining?'

"'Lives without dining,' said I, and closed the eyes.

"'Eh!—He's asleep, ain't he?'

"'With kings and counselors,' murmured I."

In this way Bartleby leaves the world—by passively refusing life.

We have given the name "Bartleby Syndrome" to a pattern of behaviors that we have found to be common in a particular type of underachieving gifted boy—a puzzling pattern of congenial refusal to do homework or to complete classroom tasks. And although few gifted boys take their apathy as far as Bartleby (there have been no recorded cases of death by boredom!), it is true that many gifted boys seem to suffer a kind of intellectual death in late elementary school, when they learn that it isn't cool to be the best student in the class (Wolfle, 1991). We begin to see Bartleby-like behaviors in gifted boys between third and fifth grade. These boys are usually friendly and mild mannered and seem to have no particular motivation for underachievement. Teachers like them and are mystified by their behavior. Parents are puzzled, frustrated, and angry.

Bartleby Syndrome usually comes to the attention of a teacher when a boy who has previously been high achieving and productive suddenly stops performing. Five or six homework assignments in a row are missing, and in-class work is turned in blank or not at all. Often, the behavior is attributed to a "bad week." But when it continues into another week and then another, the teacher becomes alarmed and contacts the parents.

Frequently, the parents are horrified to learn that their son has not been doing his homework. He has often given his parents a variety of excuses for not finishing his work, saying he did it at school or that he didn't think he had any. Later, when pressed to tell why he didn't do work that he knew he had, he may say that he doesn't know why he didn't do it—he just didn't feel like it.

What is happening here? There are several gender-related explanations.

First, gentle underachievement of this sort is an easy way for a boy to establish his independence and individuality. His newly developing masculine identity requires that he show that he can make his own decisions and can resist his teachers' wishes—particularly if the teacher is a female. He is separating himself from his mother and from mother figures, and one good way to show his friends that he is doing so is to indicate that he is not complying with his mother's or his teacher's wishes.

Second, it often takes gifted boys a few years in school to understand the costs of high achievement. By third grade, the boys who consistently get high grades begin to be teased by other boys. Often, doing all of their work and getting good grades has been a cinch—it has been easier to just get it over with and go on to do something fun. But as the teasing gets more intense, the costs for achievement rise. Eventually, it becomes easier to put up with parental frustration than to put up with bullying or teasing from the other children at school. Underachievement, particularly mild underachievement, is much more acceptable to peers than the endless perfect papers of the nerds.

Third, in classrooms where girls are beginning to be more assertive and more bold in their performance, boys may engage in Bartleby-like behaviors as a way of separating themselves from the girls. When boys have few opportunities for working together with girls and few role models for being comfortable with female leadership, they sometimes respond to girls' leadership with passivity and withdrawal. Playing with girls is often labeled by the peer culture as a low-status activity. Therefore, when forced to associate with girls in the classroom, boys may withdraw as a way of protecting their status.

The usual culprit—boredom—interacts in interesting ways with gender-identity issues. A redshirted boy may have enjoyed getting good grades and performing, as long as he was young enough to take simple pleasure in being better than everybody else at just about everything. But there comes a point at which finishing every race first begins to lose its excitement. For most gifted boys who are unchallenged, there comes a point at which they finally understand that the day when they can feel a true sense of accomplishment, when they truly will feel their limits tested, may never come. In a society that glorifies men breaking the barrier, pushing the limits, going the distance, a young boy who thinks he may never have the opportunity to prove his worth may simply give up. Just like Bartleby, he prefers just to fade away rather than keep on with the boring tasks that have filled his days. Despair has killed his desire to achieve.

In each such case, nobody is being hurt more than the boy himself. In giving away his potential to achieve, he is giving away his power. He is also missing out on opportunities to learn to achieve alongside girls and women.

It is important that Bartleby-like behaviors be identified and "nipped in the bud." Of course, the optimum is to discover topics and areas of interest that stimulate the boy's sense of excitement about learning and achieving, and to build on that motivation (Webb, et al., 1982). But some aspects of schoolwork are simply not very exciting and yet must still be done, even if they feel like drudgery. It is important to set limits and for parents and teachers to work together to monitor every day's assignments once a Bartleby pattern has been discovered. We suggest to parents who are struggling with a boy who has become passively noncompliant that they hold a family meeting in which they let their boy know that the decision to do or not do homework is not an individual decision but a family decision. Parents can suggest that if their son feels sick or feels that the homework is too much or even, very occasionally, that the homework is inappropriate, they might make a family decision that it not be completed. In that case, the parents will write a letter to the teacher. However, in all other cases, homework must be done.

Of course, it is also important for the parents to model achievement through their own behaviors—even when they, too, are faced with tasks that they might rather not do. Parents can talk about these tasks—not in a "holier than thou" manner, but simply matter-of-factly—about responsibilities that must be done and the natural and logical consequences that occur when tasks are shirked. One excellent resource for parents is the well-known book of parenting advice, *Children: The Challenge* (Dreikurs & Soltz, 1991). This book suggests ways of setting limits for children and adolescents without getting caught up in relationship-damaging power struggles.

Teachers can help prevent Bartleby Syndrome by talking honestly about boys and underachievement at the beginning of the school year. Of course, the best prevention of underachievement is to have education that is stimulating, appropriate, and flexible. Gifted boys need gifted education—learning experiences that should be directed particularly at them—even in the regular classroom. They must be encouraged to challenge themselves with more complex and difficult projects, reading material above their grade level, and more complex mathematical reasoning tasks. By finding and building upon their interests, teachers can help gifted boys maintain their motivation and excitement for learning.

For example, gifted boys, together with gifted girls, might develop videos for other children, or they could create plays, stories, and demonstrations that can delight and inform the rest of the students. Such strategies can show gifted boys that it is not only acceptable, but also exciting and fun to be both male and gifted. Several books for educators, such as *Growing Up Gifted* (Clark, 1997), *Teaching Models in Education of the Gifted* (Maker & Nielson, 1995), and *Excellence in Educating Gifted and Talented Learn*ers (Van Tassell-Baska, 1998), provide specific and detailed approaches to help teachers. Books such as *Helping Gifted Children Soar* (Strip & Hirsch, 2000) can also help parents to be more supportive of teachers' efforts to maintain motivation and prevent Bartleby Syndrome.

The Appropriately Challenged and Well-Nurtured Gifted Boy

What about the lucky ones—the boys who are properly challenged and provided with positive, healthy nurturance? Those who are allowed to enter school when their curiosity is most intense and when their readiness is at its peak? Although the path may not be completely smooth for them in a society that does not value intellect, they are at least off to a more hopeful beginning. Gifted boys who are identified in the early grades and given a rich and stimulating education are much more likely to become well-adjusted, active, achieving children excited by learning and trusting in their teachers and parents.

Studies of gifted education and special grouping are almost uniform in their findings (Rogers, 2001). Acceleration works. Grouping works. Appropriate gifted education gives bright boys a chance to be themselves, to be surrounded by boys and girls who are equally intellectually alive and capable. It gives gifted boys the hope that there will always be something new to learn and that there will be mentors and teachers who can guide them toward the ideas for which they hunger.

The gifted boy who is challenged learns to experience "flow"—that state of excitement in which the young person's abilities are just barely equal to the task, when he learns to stretch his mind and endurance to their limits and is rewarded by the joy of accomplishment (Cziksentmihalyi, 1996). He learns that there are ideas worth falling in love with, that there are values worth living for. The gifted boy who is appropriately challenged is alive to this world and full of the kind of self-esteem that results from real work done well. He achieves for the pleasure of achieving, rather than for the fulfillment of external standards, and he becomes inner-directed.

The well-nurtured gifted boy is a boy whose family supports and understands his intensity. He has been allowed to discover his own masculinity with both men and women that he trusts through the free exchange of ideas about being a man. He is a boy who has not been shamed for the expression of emotion, and who has been encouraged in his kindness and protectiveness of those who are weaker or smaller. He has a fulfilling relationship with both a strong and expressive woman, a mom, as well as with a confident and compassionate man, a dad. These adults need not be his biological parents; they may be relatives or teachers or mentors. Regardless, they play a critical role in helping him to realize both aspects of his inner self. The well-nurtured gifted boy has friendships with both boys and girls, and he enjoys smart girls rather than being threatened by them. He has a strong sense of self and an emotional resilience that will see him through the trials of adolescence.

Gifted boys are truly a joy to nurture, but there are many challenges for the parents and teachers who care about them. Active and excited about learning, they long for the stimulation of going to school only to find that sometimes school seems like being sentenced to boredom and captivity. Even when they are intellectually challenged, their uneven development can cause unexpected problems. And a theme throughout their early childhood is the difficulty of striking a balance between their growing masculine identity and their realization of the fact of being gifted, and therefore different, from the other boys. As adolescence approaches, these challenges only increase—but so does the promise.

Key Points:

1. Most gifted boys are characterized by intensity, curiosity, and high activity levels.
2. Asynchronous development can lead to difficulties with emotional expressiveness, peer relationships, and athletics.
3. Although most gifted boys are well adjusted, they do experience conflicts between expectations of masculinity and their love of learning.
4. Preschool boys may benefit more from an enriched preschool environment than from staying home with a parent.

5. Kindergarten redshirting may be very destructive to gifted boys.
6. Bartleby Syndrome may signal a need for careful monitoring of homework at home and more challenge at school.
7. Gifted boys need help in expressing emotions, support for nontraditional activities and interests, and encouragement in discovering their own true selves.

References

Bloom, B. S. (1985). *Developing talent in young people*. Chicago: University of Chicago Press.

Brent, D., May, D. C., & Kundert, D. K. (1996). The incidence of delayed school entry: A twelve year review. *Early Education and Development*, 7 (2), 1122-1135.

Clark, B. A. (1997). *Growing up gifted, 5th ed*. New York: Prentice-Hall.

Csikszentmihalyi, M. (1996). *Creativity: Flow and the psychology of discovery and invention*. New York: Harper-Collins.

DeMeis, J. L. & Stearns, E. S. (1992). Relationship of school entrance age to academic and social performance. *Journal of Educational Research,* 86 (1), 20-27.

Dreikurs, R. & Soltz, V. (1991). *Children: The challenge*. New York: Plume.

Gross, M. (May, 2000). Play pal or sure shelter: Development of friendships among gifted youth. Paper presented at the Wallace Symposium on Gifted Education, Iowa City.

Gullo, D. F. & Burton, C. B. (1992). Age of entry, preschool experience, and sex as antecedents of academic readiness in kindergarten. *Early Childhood Research Quarterly*, 7, 175-186.

Halsted, J. (2001). *Some of my best friends are books: Guiding gifted readers from preschool through high school (2nd ed).* Scottsdale, AZ: Gifted Psychology Press.

Kaufmann, F. & Castellanos, X. (2000). Gifted children and Attention Deficit Disorder. In K. A. Heller, F. J. Monks, & H. Passow (Eds.) *International handbook of research and development of gifted and talented.* London: Pergamon. (812-820).

Kerr, B. A. (1997). *Smart girls, revised edition: A new psychology of girls, women and giftedness.* Scottsdale, AZ: Gifted Psychology Press.

Maccoby, E. (1998). *The two sexes: Growing up apart and coming together.* New York: Belknap.

Maker, C. J. & Nielson, A. B. (1995). *Teaching models in education, 2nd ed.* Austin, TX: Pro-Ed.

Rogers, K. B. (2001). *Re-forming gifted education: Matching the program to the child.* Scottsdale, AZ: Gifted Psychology Press.

Silverman, L. K. (1997). The construct of asynchronous development. *Peabody Journal of Education, 72,* 36-58.

Spitzer, S., Cupp, R., & Parke, R. D. (1995). School entrance age, social acceptance, and self-perceptions in kindergarten and 1st grade. *Early Childhood Research Quarterly, 19,* 433-450.

Van Tassel-Baska, J. (1998). *Excellence in educating gifted and talented learners, 3rd ed.* Denver: Love.

Webb, J. T., Meckstroth, E. A., & Tolan, S. S. (1982). *Guiding the gifted child.* Scottsdale, AZ: Gifted Psychology Press (Formerly Ohio Psychology Press).

Wolfle, J. A. (1991). Underachieving gifted males: Are we missing the boat? *Roeper Review, 13* (4), 181-185.

5

The Adolescent Gifted Boy

Trent wears skater clothes and carries his skateboard with him wherever he goes. He used to be in the gifted program, but he got kicked out in middle school when his math scores went down. There is something about algebra he can't get, no matter how hard he tries. Even though he is talented in art, he now feels dumb and hangs out with all of the other kids who don't do well in school. He could get into a special program for students who are gifted and also learning disabled, but he doesn't want to bother.

Max is a musician and is very opinionated. Having a brother at UC Berkeley, he has a constant supply of alternative music and writings from the alternative press. When his brother was at home, they played guitar together and laughed about the stupid high-school culture. Now Max feels alone in his school. He can't stand the jocks and their girls, and he doesn't want to be a loser or a stoner. His grades are good or bad, depending on how tolerant a particular teacher is of his grunge clothes, radical opinions, and irony. If he feels that the teacher accepts him, he is likely to make an "A." If not, he will do the least amount of work required, or perhaps not even that.

Antoine considers himself to be doing time as a "meat puppet" in high school. He is really not there at all. He lives on the Internet in a number of chat rooms where he interacts with people who are as brilliant at computer hacking as he is and who are reading the same things he's reading—especially books by cyberpunk authors such as William Gibson. He wants to go straight to work after high school to create virtual-reality software with a couple of friends he met on the Internet.

Ernesto is at the top of his class and has perfect grades in an honors curriculum. He is tall and good-looking, and he plays forward on the school's championship basketball team. He isn't really associated with any clique, but because of his friendly and modest demeanor, he is well liked by everybody. Even the alternative "Goth" kids admire his independent but quietly stated opinions. Ernesto tells everyone he's going to medical school, but the truth is, he has no idea what he wants to do.

The gifted boy usually enters adolescence already knowing what his "role" is going to be in high school. By middle school, it has already been determined whether he will be a nerd, socialite, comedian, jock, nice guy, joker, criminal, stoner, skater, or social critic. By this point, he knows how he is supposed to behave, what he is supposed to wear, and with whom he is supposed to interact. Each day in high school is a matter of playing that role, competing with the other guys in his clique for whatever is valued, and avoiding criticism or even humiliation from his parents, his teachers, and the other guys.

Most gifted boys, however, inwardly aspire to something more than this superficial role, a way of belonging to the group. They want to find out who they are, they want to know what it is to be a man, and they want to know how they can make a difference in the world. Challenges for adolescent gifted boys are many. They include:

- Defining their own personal and social identities rather than being coerced into the dominant high-school culture.
- Making the passage into manhood without feeling alienated.
- Finding a meaningful career goal instead of floundering in multipotentiality.

- Discovering ways to engage in the community, not disengage from it.
- Achieving intimacy with females, as opposed to seeing relationships with girls simply as accomplishments to show off to others.

Becoming a Man

Adolescence used to be a time of initiation into manhood (Gilmore, 1990). Pollack (1999) gives passionate accounts in his book of the beauty of these ceremonies and of the sadness left behind when such initiations are lost. In these older rituals, boys were taken away from their homes by men and subjected to trials and challenges. They were taught to trust and rely upon their male peers, and they were guided in their responsibilities and in proper behavior toward women. They were taught the rituals and prayers that the adult men used in their worship, and they were encouraged to seek the vision of their lives.

Young men of the Lakota Sioux Indian tribe, for example, went out for four days on a solitary vision quest, going without food and sleep until a vision came to them that would guide them throughout their lives. Aboriginal boys in western Australia went on "walkabout" to learn the ways of the desert and to seek the wisdom of the spirits.

With the exception of bar mitzvahs and the few remaining indigenous celebrations of manhood, there are few initiation rites for today's adolescent male. He will get his driver's license and his high school diploma and take a girl to the prom, but there is virtually no other recognition by other men or by society of his passage into manhood.

Initiations have always played a critical role in integrating young men into society, preparing them to defend their community, infusing them with a sense of belonging and meaning, and preparing them to find their vocation. Without these meaningful, symbolic ceremonies, today's young men are bereft of appropriate ways of establishing their identity as men. Sports teams, hunting, and other "manly pursuits" may serve this purpose in some communities, but even here the initiation is limited. Some young men may join gangs to secure the sense of community, adventure, and heroism that once came with preparation to be a warrior. Others may make objects of girls, using them as a means of propping up their sense of masculinity. Still others may rebel against parents, teachers, and other authority figures as a way of separating themselves from childhood (Pittman, 1993).

Alienation comes about when a gifted boy does not wish to be a part of the community into which he was born, or worse, when he sees that he is not a part of any community at all. Many gifted boys have felt different and alone for much of their childhood and have felt deprived of adult male company. As mentioned before, a major complaint of the gifted boys in the Free Spirit study (Alvino, 1991) was that their dads did not do enough with them.

Adolescence often increases the sense of isolation for a gifted boy, as his peers become caught up in what may look to him like silly and self-destructive activities, such as drinking games, vandalism, pranks, and "cruising." The gifted adolescent boy may long for a "tribe" of intellectual peers and for adult gifted men who can help him feel a part of something bigger than he is, though he may not be able to articulate this longing. Ironically, the peer culture often conveys to boys that it is "not cool" to belong to a tribe of adult men. And the culture at large has given strong cautions against close relationships with male teachers, Scoutmasters, and other men who potentially could be mentors. Many of these adults now maintain a "safe distance" to protect themselves from any possibility of being accused of inappropriate close relationships.

For a gifted boy, lack of recognition for his approaching manhood may be the occasion for existential depression and a sense of alienation. He sees the shallowness of the behaviors of those around him and despairs over the hypocrisy. He is painfully aware that his idealism and his search for meaning are not concerns shared by very many other boys. When a brilliant boy has no one to guide him in his quest for his place in the world, he may come to believe that there is no place for him at all.

This depression may also engulf him when he becomes fully aware of the evils and wrongs of the world and sees no way that he can be a part of combating them. The gifted boy is often uncommonly aware of the despairing complexities of the world, such as the destruction of the earth's forests, AIDS and its devastation, and the continuing religious and ethnic wars. Perhaps because of his understanding of these complexities, he does not see how he can make a difference. Existential depression is often the consequence of feeling that one's search for meaning is fruitless (Webb, 1993). Part of a young man's initiation into manhood is learning what is to be his particular role in making the world a better place. Without a meaningful goal, the gifted boy may lapse into despair.

It is interesting that, for many gifted boys, a tribe with mentors is as close as the nearest college campus. Gifted high school boys who are fortunate enough to live in a college town often find a local group of artists, musicians, computer wizards, chess players, or conversational intellectuals that can help them become more self-aware and give them a sense of belonging. Some of the greatest art and most profound ideas have emerged from these café cultures and computer cliques.

Some gifted boys are fortunate enough to have a school group or a youth group in their local religious institution led by a caring and visionary male leader who can serve in the role of initiator and mentor. Scout leaders or Outward Bound leaders can also provide boys with a sense of challenge, purpose, structure, and belonging. But too many gifted boys do without leaders or mentors and so flounder for years in search of manhood, often jumping from cause to cause, never understanding why they remain unsatisfied.

Finding a Vocation

Gifted boys, by definition, have outstanding abilities in one or more areas. Indeed, the very breadth of their interests and abilities is an important aspect for adolescents as they struggle to ascertain what they want to do vocationally in life. Most of Terman's adolescent gifted boys in the early 1900s were the superheroes of their high schools—high-achieving students with a wide variety of extracurricular activities and athletic interests (1935). The men in our study, described in an earlier chapter, seemed to have difficulty in choosing among their many interests. The Talent Search gifted boys in Albert's study (1994), while well adjusted, were less likely to be the well-rounded scholar athletes; they were more likely to be the better-liked and higher-achieving nerds in their high schools.

A term often used in reference to people who exhibit a broad range of abilities is "multipotentiality." Multipotentiality describes a common situation in which a gifted child has the ability to select and develop any number of career options, all with an equal likelihood of success. There has been some controversy about whether all gifted students fit this mold, however (Milgram & Hong, 1999); in fact, it seems clear that some gifted children may even be overly focused and narrow in their interests and abilities. In general, though, when interest tests are given to moderately gifted students who have been selected for gifted programs by means of intelligence tests or composite achievement test scores, they tend to show a pattern of many intense interests. Not surprisingly, however, when interest tests are given to students who are selected for gifted programs because of extraordinary talents in specific areas, they are less likely to be multipotential. So it seems that, as talent in a specific domain becomes outstanding, the more narrow is the scope of the adolescent boy's interests.

To the extent that abilities reflect interests, this conclusion is borne out by achievement test studies. For example, in one study for "perfect scorers" on specific scales of the ACT (Colangelo & Kerr, 1990), the highly mathematically gifted students were likely to be just slightly above average in verbal abilities; similarly, those students who were highly verbally gifted were not likely to score in a similarly high range on math.

Furthermore, boys who were participants in the Study of Mathematically Precocious Youth program (Albert, 1994), who had been chosen on the basis of extremely high math achievement scores, were not multipotential. By contrast, boys who were chosen on the basis of high grade-point averages and composite ACT scores, such as the gifted boys selected for the Counseling Laboratory for Talent Development, were nearly all multipotential (Kerr, 1991). They tended to have high grades across the board, high achievement test scores across all domains, and high but flat interest-test profiles showing that they were interested in virtually everything, suggesting involvement in more than two career paths.

Gifted boys can experience various difficulties in setting career and college goals depending on whether the range of their interests is broad or narrow. And, of course, if their interests are narrow *and* in an unusual area, these difficulties can be even greater. Therefore, if the gifted adolescent boy is generally multipotential and academically talented, he may struggle to find a vocation because he has potential in so many areas that it is difficult for him to find the "right" one. On the other hand, if the gifted boy has a specific, extraordinary talent, he may have difficulty finding the right training and the right mentor.

At first glance, multipotentiality may not seem like much of a problem. Why would anyone complain about having too many options? Indeed, when the gifted boy goes to the guidance counselor for help in choosing a direction, he is often met with the delighted exclamation, "Why, you can be anything you want to be!" The gifted boy who may be painfully aware of the lack of clarity concerning his future may be terribly disappointed in this bland and useless advice because there simply isn't enough time to be all that one wants to be, and gifted boys often feel that there must be a "correct" career path that they somehow have not yet discovered.

Having so many options means that throughout adolescence, the gifted boy can find himself being rewarded for being "well-rounded" instead of for being focused. And despite the overwhelming evidence that most eminent, self-actualized, and content people are those who have focused on one idea or activity that they love above all others, well-roundedness continues to be a primary value that is heavily promoted among those who work with gifted students. There still exists a widespread belief that it would be dangerous to let a gifted boy get "too far out into left field."

In fact, well-meaning teachers and parents who desperately want to prevent the gifted boy from becoming "too narrow" at an early age may overwhelm him with activities and challenges. This only leads to further confusion in late adolescence. The gifted boy may be able and interested in all of the things he is involved in—academics of all kinds, sports, and perhaps a service project—but none of his accomplishments seem to help him choose a direction in life.

A related issue arises as gifted boys learn in adolescence that you can be very good at something that you don't like very much. These high ability, multi-talented boys discover a paradox—that you can be very competent in an area and yet simultaneously feel indifferent or even negative about that area. This paradox can lead to disastrous career choices. Often, the multipotential gifted boy is encouraged to pursue that activity or career that will bring the most money or status. This happened to many of the valedictorians in the Arnold study (1994), as well as to many of the men in the first author's study (Kerr & Anderson, 2001). In the absence of any other means of making a career decision, gifted young men often make the practical choice—often to their later disappointment.

If he is interested in many activities and good at many skills, the only real and lasting solution for the multipotential gifted boy is to make a career choice based on his most deeply held values. But it is difficult even for a very bright adolescent to fully understand his values, and unfortunately, he will meet few adults who challenge him to discover those values and how to act upon them. Even more unfortunately, values are not supposed to be discussed at schools, at least in the strongly held view of some parents.

The multipotential gifted boy needs competent career guidance from someone who understands the perils of too many gifts. He needs personality and values assessments to help him identify more precisely how his talents can be linked to the fulfillment of his needs and values. He needs a mentor who can challenge him to find an idea worth his commitment and loyalty—the process creativity researcher Paul Torrance calls "falling in love with an idea" (1962). Unless the gifted adolescent boy finds an idea to love, he may be doomed to wander from interest to interest, settling for an expedient career path only when forced to do so by his college or by his finite resources.

The extraordinary boy with a specific talent, on the other hand, may not have to struggle with multipotentiality. However, he is likely to have difficulty finding people who take his passion seriously. It is important here to realize that a major aspect that distinguishes men who achieve eminence in their fields from those who don't is that someone took their gifts seriously at an early age. Bloom's (1985) study of the development of eminent people showed that the early discovery of their talents by a mentor was critical to their achievement.

Boys with early-emerging gifts and specific interests often get the opposite of what they need. Instead of getting focused guidance and direction, they are encouraged to be well-rounded, to improve in the areas in which they do not shine, and to reduce the time they spend on their favorite talents. These well-meaning attempts to defuse the passion of the young gifted man are usually doomed, however. He will find ways to pursue his math or his music or whatever else has possessed him. However, without special instruction and the guidance of a mentor, he may never attain his full potential.

There are unique risks, as the Albert studies (1994) point out, for the boy with specific talents whose father has those same talents. The mathematically gifted boy with a scientist father, for example, or the musically gifted boy with a musician for a father, may never be able to differentiate his own interests and aspirations from those of his father. He may not mature fully in his own career or in other areas of his life unless he is able to liberate himself from his father's shadow. It is also possible that this overshadowing can happen with a mentor who is too possessive or controlling. Many eminent men have needed to break with their masters in order to flourish in their own right. Carl Jung, for example, had to break away from Sigmund Freud to become the great psychoanalyst of the Self; likewise, Frank Lloyd Wright had to leave the practice of his "beloved master," Louis Sullivan, to discover his own style. Often, such moves to liberation were emotionally tumultuous and troublesome, both for the student and the mentor.

Surviving the Peer Culture

"It's the way you're supposed to act to survive in our schools: make your whole life revolve around sports, walk tough—don't act too smart. Be a mean machine, and we'll let you get ahead."
                                              –Jello Biafra of the Dead Kennedys,
                                              quoted by Sam Claiborn (1999).

From earliest childhood, the gifted boy encounters relentless pressure to be a "real man"; and in most cases, that involves being athletic. Even if his parents have not fallen victim to the fear that his intelligence will feminize him, the gifted boy is surrounded by a peer culture in which the ideal boy is an athletic boy. By the time he enters middle school, Saturday soccer and Tee-ball have given way to football, baseball, hockey, and basketball. Now, not only must he be involved in a sport, he should play one of the high-status team sports such as football or basketball. In many schools, individual sports such as tennis, swimming, golf, skiing, and even track and wrestling are considered lower-status, though still marginally acceptable since they are better than no sport.

The school culture is predominantly a jock culture, so if a boy succeeds in athletics, it is almost certain that he will be popular and well liked. If he lives in an oppressed ethnic community or a small town, he may even become lionized as a scholar athlete, the boy upon whom all the hopes of the community are pinned. There are only a few starting positions in some sports, though, and the gifted boy, with his intense aspirations, usually feels that he must get one of them. But here, unlike in the classroom, he finds himself competing against guys who often are less intelligent, but perhaps bigger, stronger, and better coordinated than he is. He may resent having to compete in an area in which, no matter how bright he is, he may still be defeated by strength and speed. So because of the odds against him, he uses his intelligence to increase his athletic prowess. He reads about nutrition, exercise, and weightlifting, and he follows the procedures necessary to be at his physical best. He becomes obsessed with working out—going to the gym as often as he can and striving for ever higher goals. He may become very interested in diet supplements and might even secretly begin to participate in the culture of young men who use steroids.

Too often, this intense, high-achieving gifted boy puts impossible pressure upon himself to succeed athletically. The men in our study either talked of their athletic successes in adolescence or told of the humiliation of failing in sports. Many gifted male adults tell stories of miserable hours spent in the outfield and long, hot days of summer and early fall bumbling through football practice in a uniform, sweaty pads, and a helmet. If the boy does not prove himself on the athletic field or has the misfortune of being clumsy or overweight, then he opens himself to being called a geek.

Certainly, some gifted boys do succeed in athletics, and with significant enjoyment and benefit. Some, such as Bill Bradley or Tiger Woods, attend academically prestigious universities and still make a name for themselves in sports. And athletic activities undoubtedly promote health while simultaneously helping boys learn valuable personal, social, and emotional life skills—teamwork, taking turns, persistence, defeat, success—all of which nurture the confidence and skill development needed in everyday life. But pressure to be athletic can also be destructive to gifted boys in a number of ways. For some boys, it can create a distrust and even fear of his own feminine self, while at the same time creating an impossibly magnified masculine self. Many boys find that they must deny, or at least downplay, their intellectual giftedness to survive on the playing field with others who may be envious or contemptuous of their academic accomplishments. At the least, the culture often requires that boys participate in a lifestyle of intense competition that contains violence to such a degree that other human values are minimized.

Hazing as a way of producing conformity to peer pressure has long been a rite of passage for high school athletes—and it often leads to pain, humiliation, and injury. For example, the first author's gifted son, Sam Claiborn, received national notoriety when he published an article in his high school newspaper decrying the violence inherent in the game of football. He was subsequently and promptly physically beaten up for his words by a member of his school's football team.

In Sam's editorial, he writes, "Football itself is an activity that is based on violence and thrives not on reason but on so-called hormone-induced behavior. Unfortunately, society has made it seem like such organized athletic behavior is beneficial to all of us by making it a competitor to education in terms of recognition, emphasis and value. Scholarships, awards, and prestige are all offered to kids who have not learned a thing since eighth grade and who have nothing constructive to contribute to society.... The heroes of today might be the spouse abusers, drunks, and hamburger flippers of tomorrow" (1999, 2).

As with almost all adolescents, particularly gifted ones, Sam stated his case with great intensity and drama, and in ways that would provoke reaction from others. To some, his comments might be seen as merely inflammatory. But embedded within them was an important challenge to school officials—to take a critical look at where their priorities lie and at whether those priorities are appropriate to the school's mission. Sam's words must have struck a chord, at least in verbally gifted journalists, because his words were quoted in over 40 newspapers as well as on radio stations and television news. He was even given a "Dubious Achievement Award" by *Esquire* magazine for being beaten up (see story next page).

This is not to say that there aren't gifted boys who enjoy and do very well at athletic activities without becoming the stereotypical jock. Many gifted boys who have a true interest in their sport successfully and gracefully negotiate the sports culture; they avoid the most obnoxious activities but participate as friendly, yet highly competitive, members, even leaders, of the team. These boys are the most fortunate; they are able to achieve their intellectual promise shielded from "nerdhood" scorn through their athletic accomplishments.

Sam Claiborn, a bright high school senior who is now a college student, writes of his brush with fame when he spoke out against violence in high school sports and the culture of bullying.

By the time I reached my senior year in high school I was really tired of bullies. In the books and movies of my younger years, bullies had always been the bad guys, but in my high school they were often the heroes. To this day, I do not quite understand that.

You see, my high school life was pretty much a cliché; I was a punk rocker, and I was picked on by bullies. These bullies had pretty much been making my life horrible for years, and I was really getting tired of it. Perhaps the biggest problem I had with these guys is that they couldn't express their feelings in any way other than pushing me around and calling me names. It's not that I wanted them to express their negative feelings towards me at all, but I would have liked them to understand why I am different from them, rather than have them push me in the halls or call me a "fag." The thing is, my "politics," if you will, lead me to dress differently and to not be interested in playing football. And they had a problem with that.

All across our nation, parents and children watch football and boxing and wrestling and other violent sports, cheering on the violence and encouraging fighting, while not thinking of what might come of this. Boys and men are supposed to be tough; there is simply no exception to this. American families seem to be content with the fact that being tough—not necessarily violent, but tough—is the only way a boy can get respect. Much more important qualities, such as being able to communicate well with other beings, are often disregarded as being useless to boys.

I, however, have always liked to write, and during my senior year at Saguaro High School in Scottsdale, Arizona, I worked on the staff of the school newspaper, the Saguaro Sabercat. *Somehow, I got away with never writing a "news" story the whole year. Instead, I seized the much desired movie reviews position, and I wrote comics on the side. The only other contribution I made to that paper all year long came in January, when I wrote a full-length editorial stating that schools should not glorify violence—namely by focusing so much on football—and that teaching kids is more important. I quoted Jello Biafra, a social activist and ex-lead singer of the punk band Dead Kennedys, who once said: "Let kids learn communication instead of...competition. How about more art and theater instead of sports?"*

It didn't occur to me until the morning the paper came out that it might make some people angry. It did.

I was sitting on a short wall outside the school during a break between classes that day, when a member of the football team came up to me and asked me if my name was Sam. I told him it was, and then he punched me, hard, quite a few times in the jaw. Then he tried to get me to stand up and fight him, but he was already being restrained by several of the people around me. So he ripped a patch off of my jacket, swore, and then stomped away to rejoin his group of football buddies. In defending myself, I remember telling him that if he disagreed with my article, he could write a letter to the editor or something; needless to say, this came off sounding pretty lame. And there were no cops around, no security, no teachers, nothing. They were usually out monitoring the crowd, but not that day. Several of my friends who were girls (proving to be much braver than the boys) marched straight over to the players and yelled at them. I, however, just went to class.

To tell the truth, I was scared. I was afraid these kids were going to kill me. But still I didn't tell anyone of authority about it. My face was fine—no bruising or anything—so I suppose the punches hadn't been all that hard after all. But they still hurt. I had never been punched before.

That incident, though, only served to substantiate the position I had taken in my editorial. Here was a young person (the guy who punched me) who spent a major part of every week engaged in a school-sponsored, violent activity— football—and when he found himself disagreeing with someone (me), the only way he knew to communicate was by being violent. As far as I was concerned, the case was closed.

But then I became famous.

The editor of the Sabercat *had called the local city newspaper to report what had happened, and a few days later the story appeared on the second page of the* Scottsdale Tribune, *complete with a picture of me in my yard wearing a Dead Kennedys t-shirt. Later that day, people started telling me that they had heard about me on the radio on the way to school. Then, I heard that on several morning television talk shows the hosts had been talking about "Sam Claiborn at Saguaro High." By noon, there were four news vans outside my school, with reporters interviewing kids, and later, when I got home, there were vans lining the street, with reporters interviewing my neighbors and waiting for me to get home.*

One van, I noticed, was from a Colorado station, and another was all the way from Pennsylvania.

I had been asked by my high school principal not to talk to the news people yet—I might be able to do so at a press conference later—so I didn't. Then the next day the high school held a press conference, but I was not invited. This made me angry. The issues had already grown to encompass much more than just school priorities, football, and school violence. Now this was about free speech, as well.

Eventually, the story was carried by the Arizona Republic, CNN, Sports Illustrated, Esquire, *and even* Teen Magazine. *Syndicated newspapers everywhere had picked up the story, and in some editorials I was compared to other writers and advocates for change, such as Voltaire and Martin Luther King, Jr. The exposure turned out to be a good thing, in that it was prompting people to think about and discuss these issues. In thinking about all the publicity, I was reminded of something Jello Biafra once said— that it is important "not to be angry with the media, but to become the media."*

In that original editorial, I thought I was going out on a limb by telling people that what we're doing with high school is all wrong, and that many problems in America begin with boys not learning how to communicate, but then everything I said turned out to be so absolutely true. All of it demonstrated by one lunch-time assault.

This whole experience also showed me something else—something more positive. And that is that one's voice can still be heard, an idea that may seem contrary to the disillusionment people often sense in me and others in the subculture we call punk.

> *I feel that perhaps I scored one for the little guy that year, and I will never give up that fight as long as I live. I am in college now, and am planning a career as a physics teacher, but I will always write and create, and compose, and let my ideas be known.*
>
> *Two months after I demanded an end to the bullying in my high school, two youths in Colorado demanded an end to the bullying in theirs. They shot and burned the bullies who had tormented them so much. Perhaps if they had been able to communicate their rage, and had had someone listen to them, they wouldn't have destroyed Columbine High. I think we're damn lucky more massacres like Columbine haven't happened in our country. The social divisions in our schools have got to be healed, and we must teach people how to get along—not just how to battle on the football field.*

Disengagement

What about the gifted boy who doesn't make it onto the football team or basketball team? At one time, there were many options open to him. He could go in for another sport—it still is respectable to excel in any athletic activity. Or he could become involved in student leadership activities. But curiously, gifted boys seem to perceive that those options are closing as well.

A recent nationwide study by the National Association of Secondary School Principals shows that girls now dominate in school leadership activities (Fiscus, 1997). In positions ranging from student body president to yearbook editor, females are now much more likely to hold office. Student advisers interviewed in the study believed that girls are more effective in relationships with the administration and that the faculty is more responsive to the female leaders. When faculty and students in the study were questioned in detail, faculty gave a number of reasons why they believed that girls were leading and boys were disengaging.

Some cited female leaders' greater effectiveness. They claimed that females attended to details, while males wanted to govern in broad strokes. In addition, they said that females attended to emotional issues while males ignored them, and females were willing to compromise when males tended to just tell others how to act. Others cited males' unwillingness to engage in student leadership positions because too many of the school activities were social rather than political—the males did not want to plan dances; they preferred to work for greater power.

Only a few faculty focused on the issue of student leadership being a "girl thing." For many decades, boys dominated student leadership. But schools have increased their emphasis on raising girls' aspirations and assertiveness, and the result has been a flood of girls into student government. For male students in the study, this feminization of student leadership was highlighted as their predominant concern (Fiscus, 1997). That is, student leadership is now seen as just a "girl thing."

Why would this be the case? When did school involvement become a "girl thing" that boys shun? It is true that faculty enjoy working with the girls and that they may encourage them more. However, the study suggests that boys themselves are making the choice to leave the arena of campus leadership. The reason may be based on the tendency for any activity that is primarily engaged in by females to have lower status (Kerr, 1999). Boys are often encouraged by parents, grandparents, neighbors, and teachers from the earliest age to avoid any female activity; masculinity is defined as "not female."

From kindergarten through the professions, as females enter an activity in greater numbers, the status of that activity has gone down. Interestingly, it is not a gradual process. Once the ratio of females to males approaches one-half, the men suddenly exit the field in large numbers. This is happening across the country in college majors such as biology, in professions such as law and psychology, and in many leadership activities after college (Koerner, 1999). Although women are entering business and politics more than ever before, these two fields continue for the present to attract males—possibly because of their continued majority status in these fields.

For gifted boys, the dominance of girls in student leadership poses a dilemma. Gifted boys have usually been socialized to be extremely conscious of being high achievers and in charge. They have often attended the best preschools, the most prestigious summer camps, programs for the gifted, and have received coveted awards. By this time, they may, in fact, be addicted to high-prestige activities. They are aware that the best colleges look closely for leadership and service activities along with academic excellence. Despite this awareness, many choose to disengage anyhow. Thus, it appears that they are willing to jeopardize their chances for a high quality education to avoid being involved in a "girl thing." As a result, gifted young women are now in the majority in freshman classes at many prestigious colleges and universities (Koerner, 1999), and gifted young men may be more likely to be consigned to second-tier colleges. Disengagement and the abdication from school leadership and service positions seem a high price to pay to maintain one's masculinity.

Depression and Suicide

One particularly striking form of disengagement linked to some traits of giftedness is depression. The boy who is depressed by the world around him narrows his focus as his interests become subdued and turns his thoughts and concerns inward. In some gifted boys, the depression may be obvious; others may mask their feelings so that on the surface, it appears as if all is well. Gifted boys are skilled at hiding feelings from parents and teachers.

Sometimes depression results in suicide. News of a suicide is always disturbing, and the suicide of a gifted young person strikes us as particularly tragic and senseless. Because suicide victims are nearly always people who have been suffering from depression, counselors of the gifted and talented must also be deeply concerned about the life-threatening depression that seems to assail so many gifted young men, and they must educate themselves to the causes and intervention strategies.

Though most studies of academically gifted students do not show higher rates of depression and suicide for gifted boys than for boys in general (Gust-Brey & Cross, 1999), there are particular subgroups within the population of gifted boys whose members are indeed at much higher risk for various self-destructive behaviors, including suicide. Highly creative, highly gifted boys comprise one of the at-risk groups because these boys appear to possess certain personality traits that do indeed put them at higher risk for depression and suicide (Delisle, 1986; Lester, 1999). One of these traits is perfectionism. Perfectionism, with its self-criticism, pessimism, and obsession, is almost indistinguishable from depression on personality inventories. Perfectionists perceive failure as so humiliating that it is not worth enduring. Situations in which, for example, a perfectionistic gifted boy suddenly receives low grades or a lonely adolescent suddenly loses an intimate relationship may incline these boys toward depression and self-destructive behavior.

Another characteristic predisposing highly gifted boys to depression is their sensitivity and intensity. Emotional sensitivity causes adolescent gifted boys to feel particularly strongly about relationship problems and to become very upset over problems in the world around them. Their intensity causes them to feel a great urgency or pressure within themselves that they should be able to do something about their situation.

Yet another characteristic of highly creative, highly gifted boys that may put them at risk of depression and suicide is social isolation. Whenever a person is creative, he is being non-traditional because he is doing something in a way that is different than it is ordinarily done. Such non-traditional behaviors, though, often make others uncomfortable because they see the creative person as being different or even peculiar, and their reaction is to withdraw from that person. Gifted creative boys may experience loneliness and unwanted isolation that can lead them to serious depression as they become lost in their own black and despairing reality.

Lastly, highly creative people are also much more likely—

perhaps even genetically—to be predisposed to bipolar disorder. About 30 percent of highly creative people are manic-depressive, compared to only about one percent of the general population (Jamison, 1993). The presence of high rates of bipolar disorder in creative writers is very well documented, and strong evidence exists that visual artists and musicians are also at great risk (Piirto, 1998). Bipolar adolescents will show wild, prolonged rushes of euphoria and creativity followed by rapid decline into soul-crushing depression. These adolescents are at higher-than-average risk for both intentional and accidental death. Deaths among this group can occur not only following bouts of depression, but also during times when the boys are experiencing a state of manic frenzy.

Another subgroup of gifted boys that may also be at greater risk for depression and suicide is that of gay and bisexual boys. The extreme cruelty, taunting, bullying, and rejection experienced by these boys may make them give up on life. In addition, the confusion of identity that occurs for most adolescents is likely to be overwhelmingly greater for these gifted boys. There is evidence that among eminent men, those who committed suicide are more likely to have been gay or bisexual (Lester, 1999).

Boys who are involved in the use of narcotics comprise another high-risk group. It is not uncommon for gifted adolescent boys to experiment with various drugs, and they may feel "smart enough" to know what they are doing. Some gifted boys use street drugs in their attempts to numb their feelings of isolation and depression or to make themselves more acceptable to their peers. It is important to realize, however, that substance abuse can act not only to lower social inhibitions, but it also can lower inhibitions about an all-too-convenient method of committing suicide, the intentional overdosing.

Having been sexually or physically abused also increases the chances of a boy's contemplating and carrying out suicidal thoughts and actions. Among boys in general, those *most* at risk for suicidal thoughts and actions are boys who have been abused. Thus it is reasonable to assume that the sensitivity and intensity of gifted boys might make them even more at risk. In one study, it was shown that abuse tripled the risk of depression and eating disorders, and doubled the likelihood of smoking, drinking, and drug abuse (Schoen, Davis, DesRoches, & Shekhdar, 1998). Of the boys in that study, 13 percent had been abused, and of these, 40 percent later became depressed, and 15 percent attempted suicide. This, incidentally, is double the rate of that among girls who have suffered similar abuse—a fact consistent with the research showing that boys are more likely than girls to manifest their depression in lethal, and more often violent, acts of self-destruction.

Another trait found disproportionately more often among boys—and which works against them—is their reluctance to seek help. In the study mentioned above, the vast majority of the boys had sought no treatment for stress or depressive symptoms. The boys reported that they were more likely to exercise or use computers when they felt stressed than to talk to friends or family. In general, boys are much more likely than girls to believe that they have no one to turn to; one out of five of the boys in that study said they had no support system.

Given all of the above, it would seem best to direct prevention efforts toward those boys who are highly verbally, artistically, or musically gifted, those who have suffered abuse, those who are isolated by their giftedness and other factors, those who are gay or bisexual, and those who have mood disorders. This does not mean singling them out. Rather, it means that these boys need meaningful relationships with others in which they feel understood, accepted, and valued. Creative boys may need organizations or clubs that are devoted to their talent area or that otherwise provide emotional support as well as intellectual nourishment. Gay and bisexual boys, in particular, may need support groups and organizations, as well as rules to protect them from abuse and harassment.

Furthermore, parents, teachers, and counselors need to acquaint themselves with the signs of both bipolar disorder (manic-depression) and simple clinical depression. Perhaps the most obvious sign of the onset of mania is the sleeplessness and frenetic activity that precedes psychosis. It is difficult at first to distinguish mania from the intense creative productivity and all-nighters of the gifted boy in the midst of a project. However, mania lacks the focus of creative productivity and tends to degenerate into grandiose, illogical schemes and theories. The depression of bipolar disorder, which usually follows on the heels of mania, is extremely dangerous in that it is relentless and seemingly untouchable. Boys who show signs of bipolar disorder (onset is often in late adolescence) need immediate treatment with medication and supportive therapy. Most people with these disorders are very responsive to treatment.

Simple depression, unlike bipolar depression, is not subject to mood swings, but is often characterized by a long-term, pessimistic, critical, unhappy mood. Perfectionistic gifted boys may be particularly susceptible to this kind of depression, even though they may be highly achieving academically. This depression is exacerbated by the boredom of the regular classroom environment, as well as by the continual disappointment with school and friends that is so often the situation of the gifted boy in an average community.

Existential depression can be the culmination of deep disappointment and a poignant sense of alienation. Boys who are highly gifted are particularly likely to experience a depression where they feel alone in a world that seems shallow and often absurd, and to question whether life has meaning. More than one such gifted boy has committed suicide rather than continue to endure a life in which he feels powerless and alienated from others.

Depression is to some degree preventable—through relationships, honest conversations, and finding environments where the boy feels accepted. Depression is also very curable, particularly with a combination of medication and psychotherapy. Although many boys and their parents may initially be opposed to treatment with medication, there is very strong evidence that a combination of antidepressants and psychotherapy is a powerful antidote to depression. To those of us who have witnessed the profound improvements in the lives of adolescents and young adults made possible by such treatment, it seems cruel to deny gifted boys this avenue of hope.

This does not mean, of course, that we should not work to change family, school, and social environments that trigger the adolescent gifted boy's depression. Even though his mood may be prolonged and irrational, the triggering event is often quite justifiably appalling—a terrible conflict with parents, an irretrievably broken relationship, or a humiliating failure. Helping the depressed gifted boy means guiding him toward a new understanding of the triggering event, providing caring and support, and helping him re-build his life around goals he can control and realize.

Pursuit of the Perfect 10

Many gifted boys attempt to attain happiness through the "Pursuit of the Perfect 10." This was how James Alvino (1990) labeled the tendency of some gifted boys to believe it absolutely necessary to have a perfect girlfriend. Men and boys are persuaded by the media that a beautiful woman is the key to happiness and high status. The term "trophy wife" is common parlance for the reward a man gets for being rich and powerful. For gifted boys who are often already intensely achievement-oriented, a relationship with a girl becomes one more achievement. The perfect girlfriend should, or course, be slender, beautiful, pleasing, friendly, a good listener, and not too much of an achiever in her own right.

In our society, women generally marry their intellectual superiors or their intellectual equals. Men tend to marry their intellectual equals or their intellectual inferiors (Kerr, 1985). Many gifted men seem convinced that a woman's attractiveness can make up for her lack of intellectual ability. Not only is the lack of intellectual ability in a woman not seen as a liability by gifted boys and men, it is sometimes seen as an asset by men who are threatened by competition with a female. In high school, the achievement-oriented gifted boy may try very hard to attract a girl just because she is pretty, particularly if she is also sought after by other boys.

Nevertheless, there are many high-school boys who don't want to play the game of the Perfect 10. They would like the company of a girl, but they don't know how to find a girl who is an equal, a girl with whom they can have serious conversations. In addition, they may be puzzled or intimidated by the newly assertive, powerful young women in their class.

Another problem looms for the sensitive young gifted man who has hopes of finding true love. Increasingly, young men have been raised by single mothers or have witnessed the destruction of their parents' relationships. They have no model for a healthy relationship between equals, and they have no wish to participate in the bitterness and conflict that they believe characterize male-female relationships. These young men often hover around the edges of social groups, not wishing to engage with females, but being just as unhappy about being alone.

For gay gifted high school boys, there is an additional overwhelming problem—homophobia and gay-bashing (NAGC Task Force, 2000). In homophobic, conservative communities, gay boys know that their lives are literally in danger if they are discovered. They not only stay in the closet most of the time, but they also may go through the painful process of dating girls and pretending to want a girlfriend. They, too, are victims of the cult of the Perfect 10—the prettier the girl they are able to date, the safer they are from suspicion and attack.

Gay gifted boys will struggle with dual problems of being gifted and gay, perhaps trying to hide both, and losing themselves in the process. Those who suspect that they are gay, but who do not know yet, will defer that knowledge as long as possible, fearing that if it is true, then they must live life with the double stigma of being gay and gifted. And others who are simply gifted but not gay may fear that their sensitivity, unusual interests, and cultural concerns are signs that they are gay.

Gifted young men, heterosexual or homosexual, need relationship education that centers on finding love that is an experience in communication and intimacy rather than an achievement like a grade or a score. They need to learn to see girls and women as people who are more like they are in intellect, values and interests, rather than seeing them as different. They need help learning to love and to live with their intellectual equals, since there are few models for this in our culture. There is much emphasis in schools on sex education, but little on relationship education. Sadly, although there are marriage and family courses, there are no curriculum models for teaching gender relations—the art of getting along in both love and work. It is up to parents and mentors to help gifted boys learn how to have satisfying, mutually respectful relationships.

A Healthy Adolescence

Gifted adolescent boys, deprived of rites of passage and meaningful transitions to manhood, may become confused about their life's direction and purpose; many of them then disengage from their education and social involvements. Parents and teachers can prepare adolescent gifted boys for manhood by creating rites of passage that are meaningful and that introduce them to the privileges and responsibilities of adulthood. Parents might choose to focus their efforts on the responsibilities of the young man in the family; educators will more likely focus on the young man's vocation and sense of the future.

As mentioned above, gifted boys also are likely to struggle with relationships, trying to learn and appreciate in their associations with others the distinctions between achievement, possessiveness, friendship, and intimacy. Although confusion is part of the adolescent experience for all young people, and diffuse identity is part of normal development, these experiences can be complicated by gifted boys' heightened sensitivities and intense desire to be the best in whatever they do. The small failures of adolescence—such as not being invited to a party or the cold shoulder by a desired young woman—may be magnified by the gifted young man's emotional sensitivity and need to achieve.

Although little exists in the way of relationship education, parents and schools can, and should, collaborate to create programs that are broader than the usual sex education classes. Boys who are taught to respect girls as human equals, to enjoy their company, and to be interested in experiences of women as related in books and art are likely to make excellent partners later in work and relationships.

Finally, parents and teachers must stand ready to provide a safe haven from the turmoil of adolescent life. It may be that the peer pressure and humiliations suffered by gifted male adolescents lead them, even more than average boys, to avoid academic, vocational, and social risks at all costs. These conflicts encountered by gifted boys in adolescence are far less likely to be played out in adulthood if a safe haven is provided.

Key Points:

1. Gifted adolescent boys have few rites of passage to help them in the process of becoming a man.

2. Choosing a vocation can be difficult, both for the boy who has too many abilities and the boy who has just one extraordinary ability; both need help choosing a career based on deeply held values.

3. Peer culture relentlessly pushes gifted young men toward athletics. Those who enjoy sports discover that they are free to also be gifted. Those who don't may suffer non-acceptance, both on the playing field and off.

4. The increasing leadership of girls in high-school extracurricular activities has led to a corresponding flight of boys from those activities. Such disengagement alienates the gifted boy from his community even further and prevents him from learning to work as an equal with girls.

5. Gifted young men may see a relationship as an achievement rather than an opportunity for friendship and intimacy; they need guidance forming authentic relationships.

6. Adolescent gifted boys are at risk for depression, particularly if they are biologically predisposed, if they are perfectionists, if they are gay, or if they have many stressors.

7. Parents and educators can help a gifted boy through adolescence by providing passages that acknowledge his transition to manhood, providing relationship education, and creating a safe haven in class and at home.

References

Albert, R. S. (1994). The achievement of eminence: A longitudinal study of exceptionally gifted boys and their families. In R. Subotnik & K. D. Arnold, (Eds.), *Beyond Terman: Giftedness across the lifespan* (pp. 282– 315). Norwood, NJ: Ablex.

Alvino, J. (1991). An investigation into the needs of gifted boys. *Roeper Review*, 13 (4), 174-180.

Bloom, B. S. (1985). *Developing talent in young people*. New York: Ballantine.

Colangelo, N. & Kerr, B. A. (1991). Extreme academic talent: Profiles of perfect scorers. *Journal of Educational Psychology*, 82, 404-410.

Delisle, J. R. (1986). Death with honors. *Journal of Counseling and Development*, 64, 558-560.

Fiscus, L. (1997). Survey says: Gender issues survey. *Leadership*, 7, 17-21.

Gilmore, D. (1990). *Manhood in the making*. New Haven, CT: Yale University Press.

Jamison, K. R. (1993). *Touched with fire*. New York: The Free Press.

Kerr, B. A. (1998, March). When dreams differ: Gender relations on the college campus. *Chronicle of Higher Education*, Washington, DC.

Kerr, B. A. (1991). *A handbook for counseling gifted and talented.* Reston, VA: American Counseling Association.

Koerner, B. I. (1999, February 8). Where the boys aren't. *U.S. News and World Report Online*, 1-8.

Lester, D. (1999). Suicide. In M. Runco & S. Pritzker (Eds.), *Encyclopedia of creativity.* San Diego: Academic Press. pp. 585-589.

Milgram, R. & Hong, E. (1999). Multipotential abilities and vocational interests in gifted adolescents: Fact or fiction? *International Journal of Psychology*, 34 (2), 81-93.

NAGC Task Force on Social and Emotional Needs (2000). Washington, DC: National Association for Gifted Children.

Piirto, J. (1998). *Understanding those who create, 2nd ed.* Scottsdale, AZ: Gifted Psychology Press.

Pittman, F. (1993). *Man enough: Fathers, sons, and the search for masculinity.* New York: Perigee.

Pollack, W. (1998). *Real boys: Rescuing our sons from the myths of boyhood.* New York: Holt Publishing.

Schoen, D., Davis, K., DesRoches, C., & Shekhdar, A. (1998). *The health of adolescent boys: Commonwealth Fund survey findings.* New York: Commonwealth Fund.

Torrance, P. (1962). *Guiding creative talent.* Englewood Cliffs: Prentice Hall.

Webb, J. T. (1993). Nurturing social-emotional development of gifted children. In K. A. Heller, F. J. Monks, & A. H. Passow (Eds.), *International Handbook of Research and Development of Giftedness and Talent.* Oxford: Pergamon Press.

Webb, J. T., Meckstroth, E. A., & Tolan, S. S. (1982). *Guiding the gifted child.* Scottsdale, AZ: Gifted Psychology Press.

6

The Adult Gifted Male

Steve went to medical school, just as he had planned since he was young. Both his father and his grandfather were physicians, and as the oldest boy, it was always assumed that Steve would be one, too. Now, however, at 45, he finds that managed care has made his work as a family practitioner less and less rewarding. Surprisingly, the real joy he has in life is in photography. He spends his weekends wandering around the city at dawn, taking pictures.

Mark is a writer who has published two successful novels. He teaches in a creative writing program at a prestigious liberal arts college. He has an alcohol problem—something he has gotten away with partly because his readers and students expect him to live on the edge. But now his second wife is leaving him, and he is beginning to wonder if he still wants this role he has adopted. He has always felt like an outsider, and as he gets older and college students seem younger, he feels lonely.

Clement, president of his tribal council, has pushed hard for a new school and mental health center on the reservation. He is an accomplished musician and respected ceremonial leader. He grew up poor, but was fortunate in that his great basketball skills led him to a college scholarship, and his jazz talent landed him jobs that helped with his family's finances. His college education and the years he spent off the reservation were hard for him because he felt alone and apart from his people. But he has transcended the poverty and pain of those earlier years and now wants to make life better for kids growing up on the "rez."

The gifted adult male, like those in the above examples, is likely to be a success in the eyes of society. Gifted men are much more likely than average men to go to college and graduate school, enter a profession, and achieve within that profession. Most of them marry, have children, and contribute to their communities—though privately they find personal relationships and inner satisfaction to be the most difficult areas in which to "achieve."

Eighty-five percent of Terman's (1947) gifted men entered college, and 70 percent graduated—and this was during the Great Depression, when few were able to fulfill their educational goals. Nearly 35 percent won initiation into Phi Beta Kappa, having graduated at the top of their classes. As adults, 86 percent of the Terman men had careers in two highly regarded occupational categories— the professions, and business management. Terman called them men of "distinction and versatility."

Arnold's valedictorians (1994) and the former participants in the Talent Search programs (Albert, 1994) had similar histories. Success followed upon success for these men, and accomplishment led to further accomplishment. They became physicians, lawyers, engineers, and college professors. Most of Arnold's scientifically talented young people grew to become successful scientists and engineers. Male participants in the Talent Search programs also became high achieving college students, early graduates, and young recipients of higher degrees.

Interestingly, however, the results of more recent studies have painted a picture that is more complex and not quite so uniformly rosy. Later, more thorough studies often show that the linear progression of gifted males comes with some costs. In Albert's studies (1994), young men who followed a straight path from mathematically precocious youth to mathematically achieving professional often seemed not to have developed personalities that were as complex and mature as those of people who had changed their goals away from expectations of others. It is almost as if those who followed the direct path were handicapped in their personal and social/emotional development by the high academic expectations of their fathers, teachers, and mentors.

Even Arnold was alarmed at the later cynicism and regret among some of the young gifted men, whose success did not seem to be as satisfying as they had imagined it would be. It may be that these valedictorians, who had spent their lives "making the grade," were tired of living with external evaluations and were now yearning for inner satisfaction.

As these studies show, not all gifted boys grow up to be the American masculine ideal. Apparently, some bright men turn their backs on the expectations of others and willfully walk away. In our own study (2000) of gifted scholars from St. Louis, there were two who walked away. One was Donny, probably the most creative member of our class, who later became on different occasions a musician, artist, poet, and philosopher. When the Vietnam War was at its peak, Donny was the first to grow his hair long. He wrote essays criticizing the war in a high school where blue-collar conservatism was strong and where few dared to speak out "against America." He attended teach-ins at Washington University, and he became contemptuous of authority in all its forms. One day, our most terrifying teacher, a woman who ruled with an iron hand, told him to march right up to her desk and turn in his paper. He quietly said, "If I wanted to march, I'd be in Vietnam." He was expelled from school that afternoon, just a few months short of graduation. As it turned out, Donny had enough credits to graduate anyway and was allowed to receive his diploma after all.

Donny later went to a small liberal arts college where he majored in philosophy and continued his creative work. He became involved in the counterculture of the time. He experienced a long period of depression, dropping in and out of college for a number of years. He eventually earned enough graduate credits to teach philosophy. Twenty-five years after high school, he was living with a female friend and teaching. Then, his classmates lost track of him. Where he is now or what he is doing, we don't know.

Another man in our study, Paul, also dropped out of the conventional life expected of him. He traveled, worked at odd jobs, was in and out of college, was a Conscientious Objector during the

Vietnam War, and worked for many political causes. Today, he continues to be a social activist and writer.

Similarly, in Terman's studies and among Albert's young men, there were men who simply walked away. Terman's participants included men who became depressed and committed suicide, but also men who transcended emotional difficulties to go on to creative work or activism. Some of Albert's most mathematically gifted young men, who seemed predestined for careers as scientists, instead opted out and followed their true passions in literature and the humanities, proving that one's talent is not necessarily one's destiny.

Poverty and deprivation are not destiny, either, as the young men in Hebert's (2000) study proved. It is interesting to us to note that many of the most accomplished gifted men are those who had to overcome adversity to fulfill their gifts. Perhaps extraordinary accomplishment requires both resilience and talent, or at least uncommon persistence and talent.

The lives of gifted men—just like the lives of everyone else— are a complex mix of both accomplishment and disappointment. The ease with which gifted men attain apparent success is too often taken by others to mean that gifted men lead charmed lives. Gifted men are usually rather casual about their accomplishments and are careful not to outshine others too much—behaviors left over from a childhood where they learned to camouflage their talents behind a "regular-guy" front. Nevertheless, those closest to these bright men—wives and colleagues—often sense a discontent and constant restlessness that seem not to be assuaged by the comfortable lives they lead.

As the studies and the literature on masculinity show, all gifted males must find a way to negotiate the dilemma of being both gifted and masculine. After considering all of the published studies, we have tried to devise some prototype portraits of gifted adult men that seem to capture the essence of different kinds of male adaptations to giftedness or advanced development. Of course, these prototypes are less complex than in real life since most gifted men demonstrate a combination of these adaptations at various times in their lives. And as is true for all personalities, each type has both a bright side and a shadow. In what follows, we have tried to show both sides.

The Straight Arrow

Most gifted boys try to fit in with the traditional expectations of their families and society, and in fact continue to do so throughout their lives. The men from the Accelerated Learners Program in our study, the valedictorians, and the men in Albert's study who were "father-identified" were all "straight arrow" types.

These well-adjusted boys excelled in school, chose a college major in keeping with their parents' and teachers' expectations, married and had families, were good providers, and had successful careers. However, they did not strive to be outstanding or influential leaders in their fields. Their life paths were linear and generally conservative, or at least traditional, with few detours for self-discovery.

Although outwardly content, some of these straight arrows have constrained and troubled inner lives, resulting in problems with intimate relationships as well as in a vague sense of having missed out on something. Many of these young men are intrigued by others who are not as "straight arrow" as they are. Some are drawn toward the complexity around others' lives. But overall, they prefer the security and predictability of fitting in rather than the unsettling angst that so often comes from challenging traditions or being on the "cutting edge."

Out of Bounds

A few gifted men cross the line and do the unexpected. These men may be more creative than others, or they may simply never fit with the crowd. These were the minority of the Accelerated Learners and were represented by the "crossovers" in Albert's study and a few of Terman's "deviates" and eccentrics. A far more colorful group than any of the others, these men were literally "out of bounds" as younger boys; they had little interest in group sports or traditional boys' culture. They were too independent and self-directed to join the boys' peer group. Sometimes they could not join because they were different in some socially lethal way—i.e., too feminine, too fat, too short, or too geeky.

They chose not to follow in their fathers' footsteps. In fact, they were often alienated from their fathers and were closer to their mothers. These young men were likely to achieve only in areas of interest to them, and were more likely to be interested in creative occupations, enjoying the divergent thinking involved in making things or solving problems. Men in this category who were fortunate enough to find both a mentor and a passion often thrived and achieved recognition for their creative work; those who were not often became "lost boys" or "drifters" who lived on the margins of society rather than in the mainstream.

The Player

There are some gifted boys who want to fit in as kids, but who are too smart, too creative, or too different. Unlike the "Out of Bounds" gifted males who don't even try, these boys *want* to fit in but can't. So individuals in this group of boys become "players." This type of gifted man was represented by just a few of the Accelerated Learners, a few Terman men, and by those mathematically precocious boys in Albert's study who pursued careers in areas such as software development, Internet-based businesses, and law. These men learned to play the system and even to manipulate it. They often began as social outsiders or nerds who observed others and then figured out the rules. They used their intelligence to assess the system of rewards and payoffs, and then learned to work it so they could receive those rewards.

Players usually become wealthy and successful. However, they never forget what it was like to be an outsider. Because they remember being rejected, they retain a wariness, sometimes a shyness, and an underlying anger that fuels their accomplishments—but that also interferes with close relationships. These men typically have few close friends, maybe just one or two. In short, players are nerds who have decided that living well is their best revenge. Some of them become addicted to achievement. But under their smooth exterior, they may have some sharp edges. Strosser's (2000) account of the growth of Internet businesses gives many examples of players he calls "E-boys."

The Fragmented Man

Some gifted boys don't want anyone to know that they are different. They hide their giftedness behind a mask of conventionality. As boys, they are athletic, conscious of their social position, humorous, and easygoing. They get B's in high school and college and date pleasant, popular girls. By the time they grow up, they are almost aggressively ordinary. Despite how well they hide their giftedness, it often manifests itself in unusual and various hobbies or in avid reading in a field completely unrelated to the one they have chosen.

The boys in the Alvino study (1991) who worried about the acceptability of being gifted were at high risk of becoming fragmented men. The fragmented man is the man who is secretly gifted; he is intensely uncomfortable being open with his abilities and talents. In our St. Louis study, there was one businessman who loved to play the piano. Nobody knew the joy that his music brought him except his wife and the audiences in the clubs where he occasionally played. He dreamed of retiring and having more time to devote to composing and playing. A group of men that Terman and Oden (1947) characterized as having very active avocations fit this pattern as well; they were men who earned money in one occupation but gave their heart and soul to another.

A fragmented man can have two or more fragmented selves. He is a regular guy by day, just moderately achieving at an appropriately masculine occupation such as business, engineering, or law. But at night or on weekends, he is an artist, poet, or spiritual seeker. He sees his regular occupation as his more acceptable self; he sees his artistic, intellectual, or spiritual life as less acceptable and so keeps it hidden from those at work. He may have several sets of friends who do not know each other and that he keeps separate. He may have more than one intimate partner—for example, a traditional wife and then, in addition, a lover who shares his more creative, intellectual, or spiritual life. Maintaining these separate personas takes significant psychological energy, however, and often causes the fragmented man great distress. Though he compartmentalizes his life on the one hand, on the other hand he must also work to hold all of his fragments together. He may rely on alcohol or drugs in his attempt to cope with the discomfort that this causes him.

The Leader

These are gifted boys who are comfortable with both their giftedness and their masculinity. Their parents have encouraged them to seek their own vision and have provided the necessary education, emotional support, and resources to do so. These young men are neither bland nor ordinary, and they usually get quite involved in their academic and interpersonal activities.

Often, an accident of life or an unforeseen circumstance during a deliberate quest for the truth leads them to a crisis. Surviving a crisis seems to impart a richness of spirit and a sense of purpose to these young men. A young athlete who loses an athletic scholarship due to a career-ending injury, or a pre-med student who is rejected by every medical school to which he applies, must re-evaluate his purpose and direction in life. An affluent and beloved young man who meets poverty and injustice for the first time in the course of his travels or volunteer work may be sent into a tailspin of self-doubt and examination of values by the experience. A broken heart or a loss of religious faith can have the same effect. In any case, these men emerge from the crisis with a new wholeness and readiness for action, and they become so-called "Leaders."

Leaders are rare in the literature of giftedness, though they are undoubtedly present in society. Each of the studies of gifted boys and men yielded only a few of these men. Only Hebert's study of exceptional young men growing up in a hostile urban environment seemed to be primarily focused on leaders.

The leader is usually the gifted man who, as a boy, was fortunate enough to excel at both academics and sports, as well as to be comfortable with both his giftedness and his masculinity. Like the "Straight Arrow," the leader is both achieving and goal-oriented. Unlike the "Straight Arrow," he has suffered setbacks or has experienced crises that have led him to re-evaluate his life and to make his own choices. Like the "Out of Bounds" youth, he is creative and visionary; but unlike the outlaw, he chooses to stay within the system. He is committed to his vocation and to authentic relationships, even though they may be difficult for him because of his idealism, high expectations, commitment, and intensity. He is resilient in the face of challenges and setbacks. These are his bright side behavior characteristics. His shadow side trait is overwork—his intense idealism and commitment can be all-consuming. In addition, his optimism, idealism, and intensity will lead him to expect too much of others.

Gifted Men Who Become Eminent

What about men who do become eminent in their domains? As the previous short summaries suggest, men most likely to become eminent are those who are "Out of Bounds" or "Leader" types. In addition to the previous studies mentioned in this book, several other sources provide us with further insight into the lives of successful, creative, gifted men. Jane Piirto, in *Understanding Those Who Create* (1998), supplies an excellent guide to understanding the lives of gifted men who are considered by society to be leaders in the various domains of creative writing, science, music, and performance. Although there are personal development and career issues that are common to adult talent development across domains, Piirto also notes issues that are unique to each domain. In an article, *The Career Development of Creatively Gifted Adults* (Kerr, 1986), some of the critical events in the lives of creative adults are examined. In addition, the journal *Advanced Development*, founded by Linda Silverman, offers frequent updates on research on the lives of highly gifted, eminent men. Gleaned from these sources, here are some of the frequent concerns in the lives of these most productive men.

Seeking Advanced Training and Mentors

We noted in the previous chapter that the gifted adolescent who can resolve multipotentiality, stay engaged in learning, and find his passion is on the path to adult realization of his potential. However, in young adulthood, gifted men face the formidable task of seeking advanced training and finding a mentor. Bloom (1985) showed that in every domain, the gifted man must find a "master teacher"—a teacher who will bring out the genius within by constantly challenging the student to achieve his best. Master teachers in the lives of gifted men are not always friendly, supportive, or loving. They can be demanding taskmasters who place challenges before the gifted individual, but do so at precisely the right points. Examples of such notoriously exacting teachers include the great method acting coach Lee Strasberg, who taught Marlon Brando and many others; composer Aaron Copeland, who taught Leonard Bernstein; and Paul Engle, who was master teacher to an entire generation of great writers at the Iowa Writers Workshop.

The master teacher may or may not also be a mentor to the gifted man, but many gifted men have both—that is, they have one or more master teachers and at least one great mentor. The word "mentor" comes from the Greek myth in which Odysseus' son Telemachus is, in his father's absence, guided by a wise spirit named Mentor. Mentor turns out to actually be the goddess of wisdom, Athena, in disguise; she takes this role to encourage him to find his father, and at the same time to find his own destiny.

Much has been written about mentoring, and unfortunately, the term's meaning today has become rather clouded. It now refers to almost any informal, helpful relationship between a more experienced and a less experienced person. However, here we use the term "mentor" in its strictest sense—one who guides the young man into the very center of his profession by advising, guiding, modeling, and creating networks and openings needed for eminence. We should note that mentors for gifted men can be male or female. Ernest Hemingway and Pablo Picasso were both mentored by Gertrude Stein, and a little known fact about the life of eminent psychotherapist Carl Rogers was that Leta Hollingworth, educational psychologist and "mother of gifted education," was his clinical supervisor and mentor at Columbia University.

An interesting characteristic of mentoring relationships is their reciprocity. Studies of Nobel Prize winners have shown how frequently scientists not only made an excellent choice of protégés, but that many protégés also made excellent choices of mentors. That is, mentors seemed to have an intuitive sense of which of the bright students in their fields had potential for eminence, and protégés had an uncanny ability to find precisely the mentor who could take them where they wanted to go. This underlines one of the mysteries of mentoring; it cannot be deliberately planned by others, but like marriage, must be created through a special chemistry or reciprocal bond between two people.

Also like marriage, mentorship is fraught with interpersonal ambiguities and difficulties. A mentoring relationship between gifted individuals features the blending of two strong egos and two brilliant minds. In a worst-case scenario, the mentor is so overpowering that the protégé lives forever in the mentor's shadow. We know of many scholars who were crippled by mentors who used their considerable power to keep protégés as perpetual apprentices and who seemed to actually sabotage the protégé's capacity to separate and create his own career. There are also mentors who engage in inappropriate intimate and sexual relationships with protégés, creating dual roles that are confusing and often devastating. Although it is more rare for men than women to be victimized in this way, it does happen. Nijinsky, the great dancer, for example, was taught and promoted by Diaghilev, but was also kept in childlike dependence and in sexual thrall. Still other mentors end up competing with protégés or abandoning them altogether because of grave differences in doctrine or methods; the great "divorce" of Freud and Jung and the great conflict between Hemingway and Stein are examples.

In the best cases—we hope in most cases—the mentoring relationship goes through a series of predictable stages in which the student moves from initial imitation and dependence to differentiation (a stage which is sometimes tumultuous), and finally to mutual respect and mature collegiality. Leonard Bernstein and Aaron Copeland are good examples of a mentor and protégé pair who later became respectful colleagues.

Shamanic apprenticeships within American Indian traditions have culturally defined stages that include the separation of mentor and apprentice. A shaman's apprentice is often forcefully separated from his master at an appropriate time to seek his own vision and to develop his own "voice" as a healer. The joys and sorrows of such a mentorship are depicted in *Letters to the Medicine Man: The Shaping of Spiritual Intelligence* (Kerr & McAlister, 2001).

In any case, the seeking of a mentor, the development of the relationship, the differentiation, and the reconciliation are all critical events for the development of the talent of the gifted man. Men who find strong and productive mentor relationships are fortunate. Kaufmann (1986) showed how mentors had made the crucial difference for Presidential Scholars, and many other studies have illustrated the importance of this life-changing relationship.

Genius, Madness, and Substance Abuse

Perhaps no other topic in gifted education has such mystique as the fascinating relationship between mental illness and genius. Unfortunately, the stereotype of the mad genius is almost as prevalent and virulent as the "early ripe, early rot" stereotype once was. However, there is no denying that a great many eminent men have suffered from either mental illness or substance abuse or both. Kay Jamison (1993), in her research on creative people, and Nancy Andreason (1987), in her studies of eminent writers of the Iowa

Writers Workshop, found surprisingly similar and very high rates of manic-depressive illness among these populations. As stated in the earlier section on depression, most studies show that about 30 percent of highly creative people are afflicted with manic-depressive illness (also called bipolar disorder)—about 35 times higher than the incidence rate found in the general population, which is less than one percent. Why is this the case?

As with most research findings, there are multiple causes. First, it may be that the intensity and overexcitability of the gifted child develops later in life into manic behavior when other chemical imbalances or environmental stressors are present. Second, it may be that people with a predisposition to bipolar disorder are drawn to creative professions, where their eccentricities and flights of imagination are accepted. When the first author was a therapist for writers in Iowa, one writer with a mild bipolar disorder told her that his illness actually worked in his favor; when he was manic, he felt expansive, perceptive, and intuitive, and was able to stay up all night writing his grand visions. When he was depressed, he was able to look over these same writings with a critical, perfectionist eye, editing away the excesses and keeping the insights. Third, the lives of artists, writers, and musicians are generally full of stress; they never seem to have enough money, and recognition for their art is scarce. Personal relationships suffer tremendously from this impoverished and uncertain lifestyle. Certainly, it is to be expected that a personality already fragile can be destabilized further by the privations, rejections, and losses of the creative life.

Substance abuse is also the bane of many talented adults. Some familiar stories include Dylan Thomas' death by alcohol intoxication, Charlie Parker's overdose on heroin, and Sigmund Freud's struggle to overcome his addiction to cocaine. Sometimes, the substance abuse of creative people is romanticized and they become martyrs—this has been the case with many rock stars and actors lost to the needle. But the truth of substance abuse is sadder and shabbier. These people did not create *because* of the inspiration of alcohol, narcotics, or stimulants. They created *in spite of* their addictions and their constant attempts to self-medicate in the face of depression or sorrow.

In fact, a study conducted by the first author and her colleagues of substance use patterns in artists, writers, and musicians (Kerr, et al., 1991) showed an interesting division between those creative individuals who made their living entirely through their creative work and those who were "wannabes" or who were unable to survive financially with their work. Those people who were productive and who supported themselves with their work actually had very low incidence of substance abuse, whereas the other group had much higher rates of abuse. In addition, there was a tendency for younger creative people to use more substances than middle-aged artists. One writer told us that after recovering from alcohol and substance abuse, he now used two "crutches" when he worked—soda crackers and water!

For those creative adults who suffer from mental illness or substance abuse, there is really only one solution—treatment. Although many gifted men are very reluctant to seek psychotherapy and medical treatment for their disorders, those that eventually "hit bottom" or otherwise become convinced that there is a problem and go into treatment are the lucky ones. Some creative people actually fear that without their illness or addiction, they will lose their creative edge. And quite truthfully, the initial stages of medication may be accompanied by a loss in productivity. It often takes several months or even up to a year for an individual to be properly stabilized on psychotropic mood-disorder drugs or antidepressants. However, in the long run, most creative people who receive treatment for these disorders can gain tremendous relief from their suffering and also discover that they have an improved focus, increased productivity, and attained more balanced lives.

As for substance abuse treatment, the course is long and hard, and many do not succeed. Gifted men may have a better chance than most at overcoming addiction to alcohol and narcotics because of their capacity to read and learn about their illness, to be resourceful in seeking help, and to channel their intensity and achievement orientation into the fight against the substance (or substances). The moving story of Bill W., the founder of Alcoholics Anonymous, for example, is but one example of the successful struggle of a gifted man against substance abuse (Hartigan, 2000).

Blocks in Productivity

Writer's block and creative block is a nightmare, too, for many creative people. The sources of the block are many, and treatment must be tailored to the type, intensity, and duration of the stoppage. Two reasons for block have already been covered here: mental illness and substance abuse. But there are other, subtler reasons why sometimes a productive, creative man just stops. One of them is the natural result of "mining" an idea. Often, a scientist will follow the same line of research throughout most of his career. But occasionally, it happens that a lode of the particular element is essentially mined out—there are no further questions needing to be answered, or the ideas that the scientist was pursuing came to a dead end, or younger scientists have now taken over and have carried the work beyond his paradigm. A dead end can be a depressing and even frightening experience for a gifted man, and surprisingly, many of them do not hit upon the obvious solution, which is to find a new problem to solve. Those who do start over again, such as a painter who turns to sculpture or an entrepreneur who begins to explore spirituality, find themselves blossoming anew.

Sometimes, the field itself is essentially "landmined"—that is, there are fields of endeavor that hold within them their own destruction. The craze of deconstruction in the 1980s destroyed many original, passionate voices in literature, art, music, and architecture. The writer who creates lean, stark fiction in an effort to dispense with sentiment that is anathema to critics or the minimalist painter who paints more and more monochromatically or upon tinier and tinier spaces in an attempt to fulfill the current fashion may find himself written out of existence or painted into a corner, with nothing left to create. The first author worked with one artist in therapy who had simply lost confidence in his own vision after many drubbings by reviewers; in therapy, he learned to separate himself from the art circles that were silencing him, and to work independently toward his own vision of truth.

Conclusion

This chapter, and the studies upon which it is based, is meant to serve as a cautionary tale for gifted boys. The lives of grown-up gifted boys have much to teach those whose lives are still before them.

First, it is clear that there is a danger in attaining too fully the goals set by others, particularly fathers. Men who simply live up to their parents' or society's expectations may seem outwardly content, but they may also be wistful for a life with more action or personal or spiritual fulfillment. They may fragment themselves by trying to secretly fulfill their own personal dreams while at the same time doing what is expected of them. Those who are leaders may passionately involve themselves in causes and concerns for a better world, but may not realize until too late the cost of alienating close friends and family members who fail to appreciate their all-consuming mission.

Second, there is some danger in moving too far away from society. Without a cause to believe in or a mentor or significant other who believes in them, gifted men can easily drift into cynicism and despair. Creative men often forget that being creative inherently implies being non-traditional, that people are often uncomfortable with and critical of someone whom they see as non-traditional. Other people are likely to see him as a loose cannon, an unrealistic flake, etc. Even a player—one who learns how to play the game—can move too far away from society. If he does not have a social conscience, for instance, he can use his wealth and power for negative purposes. Consider a developer who buys large swaths of land and scrapes them clean for high-density housing, the new Internet entrepreneur who employs people at low wages with big promises of stock options only to callously abandon them when the bubble bursts, the politician who can be bought by any special interest entity with enough cash, or the hermit who avoids society altogether. If these men do not experience the sort of accident of fate that cause them to reevaluate their place in society, it may be necessary for them to be brought to terms with their disengagement from society by deliberate confrontation.

Of all the types of gifted men, the ones who seem to have the greatest life satisfaction are those who have had a childhood that prepared them to be comfortable with both their own masculinity as well as their own unique talents and abilities, including their differences from others. These men usually had to overcome some kind of adversity or loss at some point, but they later returned to a life of achievement—with a new commitment, a stronger identity, and a clear sense of meaning. Some of these men clearly experienced what is called a "positive disintegration" (Dabrowski, 1967). That is, the emotional and philosophical base underlying their lives seemed to disintegrate for a period of time, often leaving them shaken and distraught, but then, in the rebuilding, these men found that their morals, values, and achievements were now at a much higher level than ever before.

In the next few chapters, we will concentrate on those special issues that may be roadblocks for gifted boys on their way to becoming men. Parental misunderstanding, poor educational climate, underachievement, antisocial behavior, victimization, poverty, and minority status can all put the gifted boy at risk. Each of these will be taken up before we return to the question of how we can help gifted men fulfill their own dreams and contribute meaningfully to society.

Key Points:

1. Most gifted men grow up as "Straight Arrows" and follow a linear path toward their goals.
2. Some gifted men go "Out of Bounds" and turn their backs on the expectations of others.
3. "Players" work the system and use their intelligence to gain money and power.
4. "Fragmented Men" compartmentalize into multiple lives—one in which they follow an acceptable masculine path, and at least one other in which they express a creative, intellectual, or spiritual gift.

5. A small group of gifted men achieve both a secure masculine identity and a strong identity as gifted men; they suffer adversity, but transcend it to become leaders.
6. Mental illness is not a result of giftedness, but is sometimes an aspect of creative people's lives.
7. Substance abuse blocks the creativity of many gifted men, and treatment is the only option.
8. Blocks in productivity can occur for many reasons; they often require a change of vocational direction.
9. Mentors and advanced training are important, particularly in helping gifted young men reach eminence.

References

Albert, R. S. (1994). A longitudinal study of gifted boys. In R. E. Subotnik & K. D. Arnold, *Beyond Terman: Contemporary longitudinal studies of giftedness and talent.* Norwood, NJ: Ablex.

Alvino, J. (1991). An investigation into the needs of gifted boys. *Roeper Review,* 13 (4), 174 –180.

Arnold, K. (1994). *Valedictorians beyond Terman: Contemporary longitudinal studies of giftedness and talent.* Norwood, NJ: Ablex.

Bloom, B. S. (1985). *Developing talent in young people.* New York: Ballantine.

Dabrowski, K. (1967). *Personality shaping through positive disintegration.* Boston: Little, Brown & Co.

Hartigan, F. (2000). *Bill W: A biography of Alcoholics Anonymous cofounder Bill Wilson.* New York: St. Martin's Press.

Hebert, T. (2000). Defining belief in self: Intelligent young men in an urban high school. *Gifted Child Quarterly,* 44 (2), 91-115.

Kaufmann, F. (1986). The nature, role, and influence of mentors in the lives of gifted adults. *Journal of Counseling and Development*, 64 (9), 576-578.

Kerr, B. A. & McAlister, J. C. (2001). *Letters to the Medicine Man: An apprenticeship in spiritual intelligence.* Cresskill, NJ: Hampton Press.

Kerr, B. A., Shaffer, J., Chambers, C. & Hallowell, K. (1991). Substance use patterns of talented adults. *Journal of Creative Behavior*, 25, 145-154.

Piirto, J. (1998). *Understanding those who create.* Scottsdale, AZ: Gifted Psychology Press.

Strosser, R. E. (2000). *E-boys: The first inside account of venture capitalists at work.* New York: Crown Publishers.

Terman, L. M. & Oden, M. (1947). *The gifted group at midlife.* Stanford, CA: Stanford University Press.

Section III:
Special Challenges
for Gifted Boys

7

Underachievement

Why don't some gifted boys live up to their academic potential? Why do some gifted boys refuse to participate in class?

When a boy's academic performance is much lower than past academic performance or than would have been predicted by achievement test or IQ scores, teachers and parents often turn to the school's counselor for an explanation. Underachieving gifted students have been a source of much controversy for educational researchers and have long generated many practical difficulties for the counselor and classroom teacher.

Surprisingly, some education researchers disagree about whether underachievement actually exists. One leading psychologist, Anastasi (1998), contends that underachievement is not a legitimate category of academic behavior, because the label is often based on comparisons of intelligence tests to achievement tests, and this is inappropriate. Anastasi sees most underachievement as simply test error—a statistical artifact of imperfect methods of measurement.

Other authors (Reis & McCoach, 2000; Dowdall & Colangelo, 1982) are concerned that there are too many definitions of the underachieving gifted. Dowdall and Colangelo find three different measures of underachievement in their review of the literature—the difference between two standardized measures, the difference between a standardized measure and performance on some nonstandardized measures, and the difference between two non-standardized measures. And within these categories, there are scores of definitions. The authors conclude that "the variability of definitions is of a magnitude that makes the concept of under-achieving gifted almost meaningless" (p. 179).

Nevertheless, most educators, at least at the elementary and secondary levels of schooling, recognize that many very smart children function far below their academic potential, and these educators have continued to attempt to identify the underachieving gifted, to draw conclusions about their behavior, and to develop remedial interventions (Kerr, 1991; Rimm, 1995; Whitmore, 1980). And one of the most important facts that emerges from every study done with underachievers has great significance for this book—and that is that the vast majority of child and adolescent underachievers, by any definition, are male.

Common Issues for Underachievers

Despite the wide variability in definitions, there *is* some agreement among researchers who have observed and measured students who are not performing as expected. Dowdall and Colangelo (1982) found that underachieving gifted students resemble underachievers in general more than they resemble gifted students in general. In fact, they resemble gifted students only in their high scores on IQ tests or achievement tests or in their success in earlier grades.

Compared to achievers, underachieving gifted students seem to have four distinct and significant characteristics. They generally are more socially immature (Hecht, 1975), have more emotional problems (Pringle, 1970), engage in more antisocial behavior (Bricklin & Bricklin, 1967), and have lower self-concepts (Colangelo & Pfleger, 1979; Whitmore, 1980). We will describe each of these characteristics of underachievers in more detail and will then propose strategies to end the underachieving cycle.

Social Immaturity

For many gifted children, their social and emotional judgment tends to lag behind their intellect (Webb, et al., 1982). However, underachieving gifted boys may be less well adjusted socially than gifted students in general. Their social immaturity is expressed in many ways. They may have difficulty making friends, and when they do establish friendships, they may not be able to sustain them. Underachieving gifted students may have difficulty cooperating in a group, often either participating too much or not participating enough. They may either dominate the group or be too unassertive. They may show off, or engage in other behaviors that block the group's progress.

In their elementary school years, underachieving gifted boys may have problems separating from their parents during school hours. They may be overly dependent on teachers or behave inappropriately toward adults. In games and athletics, underachieving gifted students may be poor sports, finding it difficult to play by the rules or to accept loss and failure in competition.

Emotional Problems

Underachieving gifted children's emotional problems include crying too easily and getting angry too easily. These children tend to be oversensitive or overly aggressive. On personality tests, they, as a group, show a wide variety of personalities, but also some commonalities, including emotional problems such as depression or anger. Personal problems may also be manifested in extreme moodiness. In addition, the emotional problems of an underachieving gifted boy tend to be long-term rather than situational (Dowdall & Colangelo, 1982).

Antisocial Behavior

One of the most common findings about underachieving gifted boys is their tendency toward antisocial characteristics and behavior. In fact, on most personality tests, these boys' scores are somewhat similar to those of sociopathic individuals (see Chapter 8). Sociopathic people have poorly developed consciences, are impulsive in their behavior, are angry and act out their anger by being aggressive toward people or by destroying things, and tend to use their intelligence to deceive or "con" others.

Gifted underachieving students often are angry and sometimes engage in antisocial behavior such as cheating on tests or stealing school property. They may even hurt other children or take or destroy other children's toys or belongings. As adolescents, antisocial underachieving gifted students may engage in illegal activities such as selling drugs, shoplifting, or creating computer viruses. Nevertheless, their personalities are seldom entirely sociopathic or antisocial. A study by Arcenaux (1990) shows that although underachieving gifted students do possess such antisocial personality characteristics as impulsivity, need for play, and a self-centered orientation, these characteristics are uniquely combined with a need for understanding and knowledge. Although they engage in behaviors that are not socially accepted, underachieving gifted boys seem to have a longing to understand their own behavior and the world around them. In contrast to the unthinking and unfeeling sociopath, they usually feel the need for profound thought and for expressing intense feelings.

Low Self-Concept

The majority of studies of underachieving gifted students have also found that most students classified in this way have very low self-concepts. They are negative about themselves in many ways. They see themselves as unattractive, unlovable, and unintelligent. Despite high intelligence test scores or achievement test scores, many underachieving gifted boys are convinced of their own inability to succeed. Some of these boys have hidden learning disabilities or have Attention Deficit Disorder without hyperactivity. Without diagnosis as learning disabled gifted, they may simply come to believe that they are unworthy of the gifted label. Many feel that they do not deserve to succeed. Although low self-esteem always has many causes, persistent low grades may be a major contributing factor in underachieving gifted boys. For these boys, negative academic feedback creates a vicious cycle. Poor grades lead to low expectations of self, which lead to even lower performance. Many underachieving gifted students see no way out of this cycle.

We are convinced that there is a "true" group of underachieving gifted students—one that is not made up of people who simply represent measurement error. With this conviction, in this chapter we will examine the various kinds of underachievement this group exhibits, explore the causes of that behavior, and suggest strategies that parents and teachers can use to redirect the academic behavior of members of this population.

Varieties of Underachievement

Probably the most disturbing pattern of underachievement behavior is that in which a student's classroom performance does not match that student's scores on IQ tests, achievement tests, or other aptitude tests. It is important to explore the possible meanings of these discrepancies and to describe behaviors associated with each of these types of underachievement.

Discrepancies Between IQ Score and Classroom Performance

Observed discrepancies between intelligence test scores and academic performance are perhaps the most common instances of underachievement. What are the possible explanations for these discrepancies? The following lists some explanations for this form of underachievement.

Hypothesis 1: The Test Score Is Wrong

In some cases, when a single high IQ score conflicts with all other measures and when classroom behavior is consistently average or below average, the intelligence test score may very simply be wrong. There is, after all, a margin of error for every intelligence test. Scores can vary widely around the point that was chosen as the cutoff for the gifted label. A student, for instance, who scores 130 on the *WISC-III*, the *Wechsler Intelligence Scale for Children— Third Edition*, may actually have a "true score" of 115, which is within the average range.

In addition, some group tests of intelligence over-identify when selection is being done for gifted classes. This is because these group tests often have a low ceiling—that is, the test is simply not difficult enough for brighter-than-average students. In particular, tests that were developed primarily to identify developmental disabilities will often identify students as gifted who are simply high average.

In fairness, it must be said that it is rather uncommon for test scores to be a notable overestimate—at least for individual tests. Individual tests of intelligence are almost never multiple-choice types allowing one to guess the correct answer. And usually, the person administering the test knows whether or not the student solved the problems by trial and error. Consequently, it is typical to administer more than one test of ability to a child, allowing the examiner to compare the results of the various tests.

Hypothesis 2: Classroom Activities Do Not Tap the Student's Specific Intelligence

Although intelligence tests such as the *Stanford-Binet* and the *Wechsler Intelligence Scale for Children, Third Edition (WISC-III)* are good long-term predictors of academic success, the kinds of abilities intelligence instruments measure do not necessarily correspond to those that are needed in each particular classroom. Some of the most confusing cases of discrepancies between IQ and classroom grades are the result of comparing the student's high verbal test scores with his quite low academic performance in tasks that are non-verbal. Or sometimes the student will obtain very high visual-spatial or overall performance test scores, but will function poorly in classroom activities that require verbal performance only. For example, a student who scores very high on the *Stanford-Binet* is likely to be a student with excellent verbal and abstract reasoning abilities. However, there is little on the *Stanford-Binet* that can be helpful in predicting a student's mathematical reasoning ability, artistic ability, social studies skills, or fine- or gross-motor skills.

Certainly, it is possible for a student to be verbally gifted but to perform poorly in situations that do not call for excellent verbal expertise. This kind of underachievement is most likely to be seen in kindergarten or the very early grades, during which a student's verbal precocity may not be recognized in his classroom evaluations as much as his social, physical, artistic, and musical skills will. In these cases, it cannot be said that the child is not "truly" gifted; it is more accurate to say that the child's giftedness has not yet had an opportunity to manifest itself. It is also important to bear in mind that gifted children do show asynchronous development—that is, they do not develop smoothly in all areas of ability even within the intellect. And like all other children, gifted children will show developmental spurts and lags, particularly in their younger years prior to age eight.

A much more common form of behavior labeled as underachievement is associated with situations in which gifted students with very high scores on tests of spatial-visual abilities, such as the

WISC-III Performance Scale or the *Raven Progressive Matrices*, fail to perform well in a gifted education class. Most school activities, particularly activities for gifted children and especially for those in middle school and high school, are highly verbal in nature. And it is quite possible for a child to have achieved high scores on spatial-visual tests and yet be only within the average range on verbal abilities.

Another of the most common scenarios for this kind of underachievement is a situation in which a child scores 140 on the *WISC-III* on the overall Performance Scale and a 110 on the overall Verbal Scale. The Full Scale score will then be well within the gifted range, obscuring the fact that the child has only average verbal abilities. It is for this reason that school psychologists who have worked closely with the gifted recommend that counselors and teachers go well beyond the full scale score in making decisions about student placement (Hollinger & Kosek, 1986). The regular classroom—even the gifted education classroom—often has little to offer the child of extraordinary spatial-visual ability. Beyond geography, geometry, art, and technical classes such as mechanical drawing and shop, the regular curriculum is oriented mostly toward the verbally gifted child. It is common that a child with advanced spatial-visual abilities will not be noticed, understood, or allowed to develop in a talent area until adolescence or young adulthood. Albert Einstein and Thomas Edison are known to have done poorly in elementary school. Today, we can make an educated guess that Einstein and Edison were probably spatial-visual geniuses whose abilities were not tapped by normal schoolwork.

Counselors need to be aware that parents and teachers may have unrealistic expectations of classroom performance from children with high IQ scores that are based on high spatial-visual abilities or other nonverbal measures of performance. Counselors also need to help the students themselves reach a better understanding of the specific nature of their talents. Students with spatial-visual skills need to be guided into classes in which their talents can be expressed. Too often, test results are tucked away in a file, without a counselor ever interpreting them or connecting them to the student's course of study.

Hypothesis 3: The Student Has Decided to Camouflage his Abilities

There are a wide variety of reasons a boy might wish to hide his intelligence. In our earlier chapter on young gifted boys, we explained the "Bartleby Syndrome"—the case in which a boy simply stops performing in the classroom as a way to establish his masculinity and to assure his peers that he is not a nerd or a brown-noser. Or he may stop achieving in class because the classroom activities simply do not seem interesting, important, or relevant to his life. For example, learning grammar rules or spelling may seem unimportant to a young computer whiz who relies on software programs to check his skills in those areas.

However, intelligence tests such as the *WISC-III* and the *Stanford-Binet* can be particularly helpful because they are individually administered and because the test administrator is usually warm, supportive, and engaging. A child who might otherwise be cautious about showing his abilities in a group situation might, with the appropriate test administrator, show skills that are normally hidden from the classroom teacher. Similarly, teachers, counselors, or parents will often seen flashes of exceptional ability in gifted children who are normally camouflaging their abilities—brief periods during which the child's demonstrated abilities are far greater than usual.

Members of particular minority groups may believe that there are important reasons for them to hide ability in the classroom (Colangelo & LaFrenz, 1981). A boy with a strong African American identity, for example, may attempt to camouflage his abilities so as not to be perceived by peers as a teacher's pet, particularly if the teacher is white; among his peers, high achievement may be regarded as "acting white." American Indian boys and those from some Asian groups may simply be embarrassed by the competitiveness of the classroom and may not wish to humiliate others, particularly if their cultural values stress humility—i.e., not standing out or seeming to show off.

Perhaps most commonly, a gifted boy camouflages his abilities as an expression of a power struggle. By underachieving, he can push his parents' buttons or "get back" at teachers, failing to realize that he is only hurting himself. He then feels that he is at least somewhat in control of his own destiny, while at the same time hoping that his parents and teachers will reduce their expectations.

For most of these boys, the camouflage stems from a fear. Counselors and teachers need to help the child who is hiding his abilities find ways to "come out of hiding." Group counseling in all-male groups or groups of gifted children from the same minority group may be useful.

High Achievement Test Scores, Low Classroom Performance

Underachievement that involves high achievement test scores and poor classroom performance differs from underachievement associated with a high IQ and low classroom performance because achievement tests are tests of specific knowledge and are often closely tied to curriculum. IQ tests are more broad measures of reasoning, memory, and general knowledge. Therefore, a boy who scores high on achievement tests is likely to possess the precise knowledge that is linked to work in school.

It is difficult to explain how a child can seem indifferent or unmotivated in class and yet can apparently have the knowledge necessary to score high on an achievement test. Where did the knowledge come from? Why isn't it possible for the child to show what he knows in class? Here are some possible answers.

Hypothesis 1: The Test Score Is Wrong

Again, it is possible, given measurement error, that in rare cases, achievement test scores can simply be wrong. This is likely to be the case when the achievement test scores are not extraordinarily high, but merely above average. Occasionally, lucky guessing on a multiple-choice achievement test may give an unrealistic score. However, if high achievement test scores have been achieved more than once and there is a consistent pattern, this hypothesis is unlikely to be true.

Hypothesis 2: The Child Is Learning at Home

Apparently, there exists a group of boys who are essentially "closet learners." These are students who seem highly motivated to read at home and practice school-related skills such as solving math problems. Why these boys learn at home but seem uninterested in work at school can be related to a wide variety of psychological or cultural factors. Some gifted students have difficulty with authoritarian classrooms or schools and seem to underachieve in the classroom deliberately.

Gowan, one of the many guidance specialists whose clinical observations support the concept of the underachieving gifted student, describes a "kind of intellectual delinquent who withdraws from goals, activities, and active social participation" (1957, p. 101). Although little has been written about this kind of student at the elementary and secondary levels, the "intellectual delinquent" appears often in the literature of college student development. Psychologists who work with college students have long recognized the existence of a group of students who seem uncommitted or unconnected to campus life (Colangelo, Kerr, Christensen, & Maxey, 1993; Katchadourian & Boli, 1985; Keniston, 1960). These students are troubling to college educators because of their apparent failure to succeed within the structure of the college environment despite their high aptitude. These students do not lack academic ability, although they may lack study skills. In many cases, the underachieving gifted student seems to be deliberately choosing to fail. This kind of underachievement represents one of the greatest challenges to the counselor.

It should also be noted that many students who earn high achievement test scores might be similar to those who achieve high IQ scores and do not perform in the classroom. That is, they may be avoiding competitiveness or attempting to avoid peer group disapproval.

Hypothesis 3: The Student Is Bored

Students who have long ago learned the material being presented in a class may be too bored to perform well in that class. Gifted students who have been grouped all of their academic lives in the regular classroom may have simply given up on the possibility of being stimulated and challenged. They know the material on achievement tests and may be willing to show their knowledge on them, but they are too angry or depressed about the repetition and dullness of classroom work to feign interest there.

Some of these students may actually try very hard to attain high scores on achievement tests purely for the surprise value. They may enjoy puzzling teachers and counselors with their high scores. Whereas the "intellectual delinquents" mentioned in the second hypothesis are rebelling against authority, these underachievers are rebelling against boredom. Despite the fact that these students seem beyond the reach of counselors or teachers, their kind of underachievement may be the most easily cured. Extraordinary academic challenge seems to be the treatment of choice. Often, these students are hungry for any teacher or class that will provide them with new knowledge, new skills, and the opportunity to work hard at learning.

Hypothesis 4: The Student Is an "Early Emerger"

An early emerger is a gifted student whose interest in one area is so intense and so focused that he has little interest in any other subject. Some gifted boys *know* that they are going to be writers or artists or scientists and therefore believe that all other learning is irrelevant. It is a case of career maturity outstripping emotional maturity, because his neglect of other subjects may be shortsighted. In fact, he may close the door on the very goal he loves the most by earning poor grades in other areas. However, his profound interest in language, math, science, or computers may earn him very high scores on tests in these specific areas.

Previous High Grade Point Average, Low Classroom Performance

This kind of underachievement, which is based on a difference between a cumulative, unstandardized measure of ability and performance at a particular point in time, is often observed during transitional periods from elementary to junior high, from junior high to senior high, or from senior high to college. A student who previously had an unblemished record of A's suddenly seems to be unable to do better than C work, for example. Teachers are often particularly alarmed by students with this pattern because of their seemingly precipitous decline in abilities. Here are some possible explanations for this phenomenon.

Hypothesis 1: Standards Have Been Lower in Previous Schooling

Gifted boys who change schools or who are making transitions in school from one level to another may show this pattern if the expectations of the previous school were simply not as high as those of the present school. There is a certain momentum that gathers behind the student who receives excellent marks in the early grades. Teachers in each consecutive grade, having spoken with previous teachers, may assume that the child is bright and highly achieving and mark that child accordingly even when the abilities may not be as high as presumed. Only when the student encounters a teacher who does not have access to previous records or to former teachers do the grades decline.

It should also be no surprise that grades may decline when a student moves from a regular classroom to a gifted classroom or changes from a regular school or a magnet school to a school for the gifted. Faced with much greater competition, many students will no longer earn straight A's. Unless the child is experiencing debilitating anxiety about the change, this is not a true case of underachievement, but is simply a case of students performing at their true ability level in an environment of students with similar and greater abilities.

Hypothesis 2: Situational Factors Are Interfering with Academic Performance

As with all children, a gifted boy's academic performance can be affected by trouble at home. Family conflict or divorce, substance abuse in the home, spouse and child abuse, a move to another city or school, or illness or death of a family member are all possible causes of a decline in academic performance. Webb, Meckstroth, and Tolan (1982) observed that gifted children seem to be much more sensitive than average children to conflict and loss. Therefore, any of these situations may cause drastic changes in the gifted child's behavior at school. Although many gifted children continue to do well in school despite crises in the home, for many of them, school becomes just one more source of stress.

Poor classroom performance may actually be a cry for help. The gifted student, aware of his reputation as an excellent scholar, may be counting on the teacher or counselor to notice the change in his grades, to comment upon them, and to offer help and support.

High Classroom Performance, Low Achievement Test or IQ Scores

Although sometimes labeled as underachievement, this is more often called overachievement, since the actual academic performance is higher than that predicted by psychological tests. There are several reasons why boys' actual academic performance may be better than what was predicted by IQ or achievement test scores.

Hypothesis 1: The Student Has Test Anxiety

There are students who, under individual or group testing conditions, become so anxious that they cannot perform up to their true ability levels. Students may be test anxious because they feel the pressure of others' overly high expectations of them, because they have learning disabilities that interfere with performance on particular types of tests, or because they have had frightening past experiences with test taking. True test anxiety goes far beyond simple nervousness or heightened arousal before the test. Test anxious individuals may become physically ill, lose all capacity to remember information, and experience extreme symptoms of stress such as trembling, sweating, dryness of the mouth, and lack of concentration.

It is likely that test anxiety not only affects the performance of test-anxious students on standardized intelligence or achievement tests, but it also affects their performance on tests in the classroom. Therefore, the discrepancy between high classroom performance and low test scores should occur only among students who have been educated in schools or classrooms in which performance is largely measured in ways other than in-class testing.

Because past grades generally are the best predictors of future grades, it is probably best simply to ignore the test scores when grades are high and test scores are low. However, in cases in which it is apparent that low achievement test scores will significantly interfere with a student's chances of entering a gifted program or a particular college, it may be necessary for a counselor to help the gifted boy alleviate test anxiety through relaxation training or desensitization procedures.

Hypothesis 2: The Student Is Benefiting from a Reputation or Halo Effect

Occasionally, when a student's grades are much better than his achievement test scores, the student is benefiting from either his family's reputation or his personal reputation. It is a common complaint of younger brothers and sisters that teachers are constantly comparing them to their older siblings. In many cases, however, these comparisons can be advantageous. When an older sibling or whole line of siblings has been highly achieving in school, teachers come to have extremely high expectations of any family member. Sometimes such students are graded somewhat leniently and given the benefit of the doubt because it is simply assumed that, being from the same family of high achievers, this student, too, is one of unusual ability. Only when the student goes to a school where his siblings or family are not known will grades begin to match achievement test scores more closely.

One of the most common patterns that we have observed when presented with an otherwise inexplicable case of low test scores is that of the boy with high interpersonal intelligence. A student may have extraordinary social skills that allow him to build a reputation as a high achiever not in keeping with his actual accumulation of knowledge and skills in the classroom. A student who is personable, lively, and an active participant in class may be perceived as intelligent and knowledgeable, even when his actual recall and understanding of curriculum materials are no better than average. Achievement tests will nearly always show a discrepancy between what the student seems to know and what the student actually knows. This kind of overachievement can be particularly frustrating to teachers and counselors whose liking for an interpersonally skilled student causes them to be unhappy with the results of achievement tests. When low test scores prevent the student from access to a gifted program or a chosen college, it is a particularly sore point with those teachers and counselors who support the student's abilities. In these cases, retesting is always a good policy to reduce the likelihood of error. When tests consistently show that the student is average or less than average in his understanding of particular curriculum materials, though, it is probably not a good idea to expect that student to be able to succeed in more challenging work.

Interventions for Underachievement

Clearly, there are many causes of underachievement and many cases in which classroom behavior does not match test results. It is important, then, to understand that there must be as many types of interventions as there are types of discrepancies. What follows are strategies ranging from the simplest to the most complex.

Retesting or Reinterpreting Test Results

In several cases described above, discrepancies were considered as possibly due to test error. When this hypothesis is a possibility, it is important that the boy be retested, preferably with a parallel form of the same test. Also, when it is likely that the test has been misinterpreted, counselors should seek an expert opinion concerning complex results. Sometimes simply consulting the test manual will allow one to determine how the test could have been misinterpreted. Occasionally, though, it may be necessary to call a school psychologist, clinical psychologist, or counseling psychologist with expertise in measurement to understand particularly puzzling results. It is important to remember that most psychologists do not have training in interpreting the results of intelligence or achievement tests for gifted students. The psychologist consulted should have some course work and/or practice in gifted education.

Occasionally, it is the policy of a school district to provide only a limited amount of testing and no re-testing. In such cases, it may be necessary for parents to seek testing and interpretation from a private psychologist. Though this can be expensive and time-consuming for the parents and the student, the benefits are often well worth the cost if the student can then be appropriately placed in the academic program that best meets his needs.

Appropriate Academic Placement

Many problems related to underachievement and so-called overachievement can be solved simply by changing a child's academic placement so that it is more appropriately challenging. Unfortunately, more elaborate interventions such as personal counseling or time management and study-skills training are frequently tried before attempting the rather simpler solution of appropriate academic placement. An underachieving gifted boy's behavior often appears to be markedly similar to the behaviors of students who are having trouble with work habits or whose personal problems are interfering with academic work. But a great many gifted underachievers will promptly begin to achieve once they are placed in a more challenging environment. Bored, restless, and resentful, many underachieving gifted students are simply turned off by classroom activities.

Robert Sawyer, former director of the Talent Identification Program at Duke University, observed that intellectual challenge was often the treatment of choice for students who had been identified by talent search procedures as highly gifted but who were not highly achieving in their home school. Often, these students were being schooled at a level of instruction that was four or five years behind their actual abilities, and they were extremely frustrated and bored. It should be kept in mind, however, that a student who has been inappropriately placed in a regular classroom might also need counseling or help with study skills in addition to proper placement. Many years of boredom can create a wide variety of emotional and behavioral problems.

Different combinations of placement and counseling should probably be tried at different school levels. For example, a gifted boy in early primary school who is showing signs of underachievement may benefit simply from being advanced in the appropriate academic areas, whether this involves being moved to a higher reading group or allowed to skip a grade. In later primary grades, it may become necessary to combine some helping interventions with appropriate placement. Joanne Whitmore's (1980) Underachieving Gifted program in the Cupertino Public Schools provided a proper degree of challenge for students while at the same time making available support groups and counseling for students with low self-esteem, depression, and school-related difficulties.

At the Guidance Laboratory for Gifted and Talented at the University of Nebraska, one successful technique used was to radically accelerate gifted but underachieving junior high students into college courses (Kerr, 1991). Middle school seems to be a critical time for highly gifted students who, if given appropriate challenge, are able to advance rapidly in their learning and development, but who, if they lack challenge, may become rebellious or withdrawn. Enrolling junior high students in upper-level high school courses or even college courses may give the underachieving gifted students a new start. For the underachieving gifted high school student who seems to be increasingly cynical and bored, early admission to college may be the best option.

Frequently, it is sufficient for students to graduate with a minimum number of credits or even to complete a high school graduation equivalency exam to move on to college. Although it seems paradoxical to accelerate a student who is doing poorly, adding challenge to the student's life may be more effective than any number of counseling interventions.

Counseling Interventions

Despite the success of appropriate academic placement as an intervention for underachieving gifted students, some will still require short-term or long-term counseling to improve their academic performance. Sometimes, these are underachieving boys who have personality disorders above and beyond the realm of boredom and lack of a challenge. Students whose underachievement involves depression, substance abuse, family difficulties, or other conflicts are also likely to need more than just appropriate academic challenge.

Some underachieving students who need counseling are simply students who have been frustrated for so long by the lack of challenge in their education that they have become embittered and pessimistic about the possibility of ever loving learning again. Many of these students can be considered to be suffering from existential depression, which is characterized by alienation and a sense of meaninglessness. Attentive, short-term counseling interventions aimed at the development of purpose and meaning is particularly effective with this latter group.

A counseling intervention designed to help underachieving high school and college students discover a sense of meaning and purpose was developed at the University of Iowa's Counseling Laboratory for Talent Development (Kerr, 1991). Underachieving gifted students were referred to the program by their school's academic probation office. In groups of eight to ten, these students took vocational and personality assessments, experienced group counseling that focused on their dreams and wishes for the future, and individually saw counselors who interpreted the results of the tests and encouraged students to choose career and life goals in keeping with their interests, personality traits, and most deeply held values.

In many cases, these were college students enrolled in majors that were greatly out of sync with their personalities and values; a subsequent change of majors brought relief and new motivation. In some cases, the student did not want to be in college at all and had an avid interest in pursuing some other goal. One student, for instance, wanted to go back and help save his family farm from foreclosure, using his intelligence to help get his family out of debt and the farm back into production. Another young man was the leader of a rock band that was inventing a new form of multimedia production; for him, time spent in class was precious time away from the creative work that thrilled him. In both cases, the counselors in this study encouraged the young men to "stop out" or drop out of college to pursue their goals, because if they didn't, their continued unmotivated performance in school was likely to jeopardize their future opportunities for education.

Finally, many of the students in this study who suffered from depression and alienation required long-term counseling to allow them to discuss issues of meaning and purpose that had been accumulating in intensity since childhood. One young man had suffered from his pessimism about the world situation from the time he had read about nuclear winter as a child; he therefore found it absurd to be in class learning about the history of a planet he believed was soon to go up in smoke. A psychologist, whose own background as a theology student prepared him for sophisticated discussions of the problems of evil, empathized with this depressed and lonely student and eventually helped turn his despair into hope.

Many stories of well-known famous men tell of a time of darkness, despair, and underachievement prior to their rise to leadership or greatness. In some cases, it was the reading of a philosophical or spiritual text that changed their lives; in others, it was their meeting with a wise teacher. Sometimes it was a near-death experience or a great adventure that provoked self-examination and a search for meaning. In any case, a crisis of meaning cannot be resolved by standard academic interventions. Some exceptional experience is needed, and in many cases, it involves a relationship such as that found in either counseling or mentorship. Counseling to help a person discover meaning and purpose is extremely important, whether done formally with a licensed professional or with an understanding mentor, teacher, or friend. Only sensitive, intelligent discussion that explores meaning and that leads to a challenge in the face of despair can heal the wounds of the alienated gifted boy

Key Points:

1. Although underachieving gifted students seem to have more in common with underachievers in general than with other gifted students, there are important differences.
2. Underachieving gifted boys may be socially immature, may experience more emotional problems, may engage in antisocial behavior, and may have low self-concepts.
3. However, it is also likely that they have a deep need for understanding the world and themselves, a thirst for knowledge, and the capacity to change negative behaviors when intellectually challenged.

4. It is necessary to consider the full range of hypotheses about underachieving behavior before choosing an intervention.

5. Interventions for underachievement include re-testing or reinterpretation of the test by someone trained in understanding traits of gifted individuals, proper academic placement, and counseling or mentoring.

6. Existential counseling focused on the discovery of meaning and purpose is often helpful.

References

Anastasi, A. (1998). *Psychological testing*. New York: Macmillan.

Arcenaux, C. (1990). *Personality characteristics, interests, and values of differentially achieving able college students*. Unpublished doctoral dissertation, The University of Iowa, Iowa City.

Arcenaux, C., & Kerr, B. A. (1989). *Intervention for underachievers*. Unpublished manuscript, Belin National Center for Gifted Education, Iowa City.

Bricklin, B., & Bricklin, P. (1967). *Bright child, poor grades*. New York: Delacorte Press.

Colangelo, N., Kerr, B. A., Christensen, P., & Maxey, J. (1993). A comparison of gifted underachievers and gifted high achievers. *Gifted Child Quarterly*, 37, 155-160.

Colangelo, N., & Lafrenz, N. (1981). Counseling the culturally diverse gifted. *Gifted Child Quarterly*, 25, 27-30.

Colangelo, N., & Pfleger, L. R. (1979). Academic self-concept of gifted high school students. In N. Colangelo & R. Zaffrann (Eds.), *New voices in counseling the gifted* (pp. 10-11). Dubuque, IA: Kendall-Hunt.

Dowdall, C. B., & Colangelo, N. (1982). Underachieving gifted students: Review and implications. *Gifted Child Quarterly*, 24, 51-55.

Hecht, K. A (1975). Teacher ratings of potential dropouts and academically gifted children: Are they related? *Journal of Teacher Education*, 26, 172-175.

Hollinger, C. L., & Kosek, S. (1986). Beyond the use of full-scale IQ scores. *Gifted Child Quarterly*, 30 (2), 74-77.

Katchadourian, H. A., & Boli, J (1985). *Careerism and intellectualism among college students*. San Francisco: Jossey-Bass.

Keniston, K. (1960). *The uncommitted: Alienated youth in American society*. New York: Harcourt, Brace, Jovanovich.

Kerr, B. A. (1991). *A handbook for counseling gifted and talented*. Reston, VA: American Counseling Association.

Pringle, M. L. (1970). *Able misfits*. London: Longman Group.

Reis, S. M. & McCoach, D. B. (2000). The underachievement of gifted students: What do we know and where do we go? *Gifted Child Quarterly*, 44 (3), 152-171.

Rimm, S. B. (1995). *Why bright kids get poor grades, and what you can do about it*. New York: Crown.

Webb, J. T., Meckstroth, E. A., & Tolan, S. S. (1982). *Guiding the gifted child*. Scottsdale, AZ: Gifted Psychology Press (Formerly Ohio Psychology Press).

Whitmore, J. R. (1980). *Giftedness, conflict and underachievement*. Boston: Allyn & Bacon.

8

Gifted Sociopaths, Redeemable Rebels, and How to Tell the Difference

One would have to work hard to ignore reports from newspapers and news broadcasts about the persistent recurrence of violence committed by schoolboys against their classmates and teachers in America over the past several years. The boys who perpetrate these acts suggest to most of us the notion of someone mentally ill—a psychopath or sociopath. These crimes do not fit our image of middle-class life in America; they shock us because they are occurring not in the dangerous neighborhoods of big cities, but in the small towns, in the heartland, in the suburbs, and in our children's schools—places we always assumed were safe from the kind of violence found in other areas of society.

In nearly every instance of recent extreme violence in schools, the perpetrators are adolescent white boys, most often described as smart. Are these boys sociopaths, or are they suffering from some other types of problems? Why are so many of them described as smart or gifted? Are smart or gifted boys and men more likely to be sociopaths? Are they more likely to be violent?

In this chapter, we are attempting a difficult task. We do not in any way condone violence in society, nor do we believe that acts of violence by any individuals should go unpunished. However, we do believe that the reasons for violence can be discussed and understood, and that in many cases, the violent acting out by gifted boys could be prevented if parents, educators, and counselors understood the issues involved. These boys, who engage in violent, cruel, selfish behaviors, are most often, we believe, nonetheless redeemable.

Very likely, there is a small percentage of gifted boys who are truly sociopaths or psychopaths. But most gifted boys who become aggressive are not actually psychopaths, in our opinion. Instead, we believe that some gifted boys have adopted a survival strategy similar to that of certain species of butterfly, which have evolved the appearance of other species that are toxic to birds that prey upon them, and so are avoided by predators. In an analogous manner, some redeemable gifted boys may take on some of the characteristics of sociopathic behavior to defend themselves from those who would humiliate and hurt them. When gifted boys have been subjected to bullying, scorn, and ridicule; when gifted boys have so many models for aggressive behavior; when they are impaired by substance abuse; or when they are isolated from normal peer relationships, they may choose psychopathic-like behaviors or even choose true psychopaths for their role models or companions. In fact, books such as *On the Road* by Jack Kerouac and *The Electric Kool Aid Acid Test* by Ken Kesey could be considered examples of gifted men hanging out with sociopaths in order to participate in the excitement. Truman Capote's fascination with the murderers in his book *In Cold Blood* may be another example.

What do the terms "psychopath" or "sociopath" mean? Though widely used by the public, *psychopath* and *sociopath* are no longer used by mental health professionals. Instead, the *Diagnostic and Statistical Manual of the American Psychiatric Association, Fourth Edition* (DSM IV) (1994) defines the psychopath and sociopath as belonging to the diagnostic category of Individuals with Antisocial Personality Disorder, and it estimates that about three percent of adult males and one percent of adult females suffer from this disorder.

These individuals, according to the American Psychiatric Association, have longstanding personality and behavior patterns in which they characteristically lack empathy and are generally callous, cynical, and contemptuous of the feelings, rights, and sufferings of others. They have little or no conscience, are deceitful and manipulative, often have inflated and arrogant self-appraisals (e.g., they may feel that ordinary work is beneath them or may lack a realistic concern about their current problems or future), and they may be excessively opinionated, self-assured, or cocky. They may display a glib, superficial charm and can be quite voluble and verbally facile (e.g., using technical terms or jargon that might impress someone who is unfamiliar with such terms). These attributes may be particularly apparent in persons with Antisocial Personality Disorder who are in prisons or other legal settings, and the criminal, delinquent, or aggressive acts committed by such people are likely to be quite varied.

Individuals with this disorder may also be irresponsible and exploitative in their sexual relationships. They often have a history of having had many sexual partners and may never have sustained a monogamous relationship. They are likely to be irresponsible as parents, not providing proper nutrition or hygiene for their children or failing to arrange proper childcare, meanwhile squandering on themselves money necessary for household essentials.

These individuals may receive dishonorable discharges from the armed services, fail to be self-supporting, become impoverished or even homeless, or spend many years in penal institutions. As a result of their behaviors, individuals with Antisocial Personality Disorder are more likely than people in the general population to die prematurely by violent means (e.g., accidents, homicide, and suicide).

There is a debate among professionals over the extent to which the behavior of persons with Antisocial Personality Disorder is a result of their environment, and the extent to which it is the result of an inborn predisposition. Certainly, much has been written about the anger, deceit, protective withdrawal, and manipulative behavior shown by persons who lived in environments in which they were abused as children. Furthermore, it is not difficult to understand how disadvantaged or minority children might turn against a society if it disenfranchises them from full participation. The behaviors of someone with an Antisocial Personality Disorder can easily, then, in certain settings, be seen as a reaction by that person to his environment and as simply an attempt to survive.

But it is difficult for us to imagine how advantaged children of mainstream, middle-class American society could behave in the same way. Our society relies on people being basically respectful, honest, and non-violent toward one another, and we work diligently to make sure that our children learn these values. So when we read of deviant behavior being committed by people who live in mainstream society, we rush to label those perpetrators as psychotic or as having Antisocial Personality Disorder—terms that separate them from healthy people, thereby reassuring ourselves that we—and those around us—could not possibly behave that way.

In his book *Savage Spawn* (1999), Jonathan Kellerman argues that the children who commit the violent crimes that we read about need to be locked up forever. In his opinion, they suffer from a disorder that is a fundamental flaw in their nature—one that does not respond to treatment.

There are indeed such youths who seem from very early childhood to be so lacking in the capacity for empathy and conscience and so filled with anger that environment can have little positive influence on them. However, it is an inappropriate, knee-jerk reaction to conclude that all, or even most, of the violence in today's youth is because of a genetic predisposition or other "fundamental flaw" in their psychological makeup. A more thoughtful consideration of the underlying reasons for the increase of schoolboy violence must consider the manner by which we, as a society, may be shaping sociopathic behavior in otherwise normal boys—particularly gifted boys. Perhaps this is why the American Psychiatric Association has not allowed the term Antisocial Personality Disorder to be used with children and instead has developed at least three other diagnostic categories to describe them: Oppositional Defiant Disorder, Intermittent Explosive Disorder, and Conduct Disorder. For simplicity, in this chapter, we will talk about psychopathic or sociopathic boys as a way of referring to behavior and personality patterns, but we do not imply that this would actually be a formal diagnosis.

It is our belief that, although truly sociopathic gifted boys do exist, there are many more gifted boys whose sociopathic-like behaviors of self-centeredness, manipulation, rebelliousness, aggression, and self-destructiveness are learned behaviors that can be unlearned.

The rest of this chapter is devoted to distinguishing true sociopaths from sociopathic "mimics"—i.e., gifted boys who in some ways have come to resemble sociopaths, but who can be redeemed.

Smart Boys Who Become Violent

People who commit violence have biological, psychological, and social causes for their behaviors. Certain kinds of genetic backgrounds predispose individuals to aggression. Lists of psychological characteristics have also been generated to explain violence. In addition, particular environments and experiences seem to prepare a child for a life of violence.

The Biological Bases of Violent Behavior

In the last decade, neuroscience has given us a far greater awareness of the underlying biochemical bases of our emotional states and the behaviors they arouse in us. People differ greatly, not only in the expression of these states and behaviors, but also in the balance of a variety of neurotransmitters in the brain. When certain neurotransmitters are out of balance in an individual's central nervous system, that person can become hypersensitive to life's tribulations and can react in unpredictable and dramatic ways.

In addition, it seems that true psychopaths habituate so quickly to situations that they are forever bored and restless. Nothing can arouse them much, so they seek greater and greater stimulation to achieve some measure of arousal—some thrill that will make them feel alive. Finally, there are conditions in which brain damage has destroyed those parts of the brain that inhibit aggression or allow for the development of empathy. True psychopaths, also called sociopaths, suffer from such conditions.

These are the ones that Kellerman suggests must be locked up forever, as their disorder is a fundamental flaw in their natures and does not respond to treatment. In fact, the experience of decades of treatment of violent offenders of this sort has given little hope that their behavior can be substantially altered, though they can learn some self-control, and their behaviors do improve as they get beyond the age of 40 (American Psychiatric Association, 1994).

The Psychological Bases of Violent Behavior

Though obvious, it is important to remember that the reasons for human behaviors are complex. Usually, people who are biologically predisposed to violent behavior also have psychological precursors for violence as well. In fact, some researchers are now suggesting that early childhood experiences cause physical biological changes in the brain that are semi-permanent.

Violent behavior does not always have to stem from biological predispositions, however. It is also true that a naturally unaggressive gifted boy can learn such aggressive behaviors.

Hurt, frustration, and anger are part of everyone's daily life, but individuals differ in how they react when they experience these emotions. When angry withdrawal or violent behavior occurs as a response among smart boys, it occurs for the same reasons that it occurs within anyone else: they feel hurt, frustrated, or angry. The hurt can be physical or can come in the form of psychological injury, such as humiliation in front of a group. Frustration can result in an explosive attempt to break down the real or perceived barriers to one's desired progress. Violence in response to a threat of bodily injury is a long-identified expression of a fight-or-flight reaction to danger. In fact, one of the best-documented findings of studies of juvenile delinquents and adult violent offenders is that, as children, they experienced harsh, inconsistent punishment on repeated occasions. Most of them also suffered from a lack of emotional acceptance from members of their families. In short, they lacked a "safe haven" in a world that was, to them, both dangerous and unpredictable. They had no place where they were simply accepted.

Not every boy reacts to frustration with open violence. Some try desperately to hide their frustration and simply do not show their emotions, especially to their adversaries. They shove their feelings down inside of themselves and may even attempt to cut off their own awareness of such feelings. This coping mechanism can work for quite a while. When it fails, however, a forceful explosion of violence or tears can erupt. Any time feelings are kept in a pressure cooker, there is a risk that a violent outburst will occur. Often, someone gets hurt or something gets broken.

At the other end of the continuum is the person for whom hurt, frustration, and anger can trigger immediate and catastrophic episodes of violent acting out. There is no pressure cooker of time with these individuals. The angry expression is immediate.

The intensity with which we experience our feelings and the nature and sensitivity of our emotional triggers to violence represent two fundamental variables in our understanding of violent behavior. And of course, gifted boys are more sensitive and intense in their feelings. Their reactions to hurtful situations—at least their reactions within themselves—will be more intense than those of boys in general. Whether their reactions become manifest in overt behavior will depend on how well they have learned to understand themselves and their feelings, as well as on the extent to which their environment provides them with support and, conversely, the extent to which the people around them are confrontational or bullying.

Characteristics of Violence-Prone Teenagers

If we are going to help boys learn to manage their anger and prevent violence, it is necessary to know which children—gifted or not—are prone to violence. A recent report released by the Federal Bureau of Investigation (2000) indicated four categories of psychological risk factors found among youths who attempted to murder their classmates or teachers: 1) personality traits and behavior patterns, 2) patterns of family dynamics, 3) patterns of school dynamics, and 4) patterns of social dynamics.

Among the profile of personality traits (fairly stable and long-lasting characteristics of a person) and behavior patterns were the following:

1. Alienation
2. Depression
3. Intolerance
4. Narcissism
5. Lack of trust
6. Low tolerance for frustration
7. Poor coping skills
8. Inability to bounce back from a frustrating or disappointing experience
9. Failed love relationship
10. Resentment over real or perceived injustices
11. Inappropriate humor
12. Unusual interest in sensational violence
13. Fascination with violence-filled entertainment
14. Identification with negative role models, such as Hitler or Satan
15. Drawn to inappropriate role models associated with violence and destruction
16. Intentional or unintentional expression of clues to feelings, thoughts, fantasies, or attitudes that may suggest interest in committing a violent act (e.g., writings, drawings, verbal references)

Family patterns and family dynamics were important, too, and the FBI suggests several that merit our attention. These include:

1. Turbulent parent-child relationship(s)
2. Parents' refusal to recognize or acknowledge that their child is having problems
3. Lack of closeness among members of the family

4. Parents always giving in to the child's demands
5. No limits or monitoring of television or Internet use
6. Access to weapons

The personality characteristics and the family patterns, of course, interact with each other. And since a great part of a child's day is spent in school, it is important to look at behavior patterns there as well. The FBI cites the following patterns of school dynamics that should be of concern and which may signal possible acts of violence:

1. Detachment from school, other students, and teachers
2. Unyielding and insensitive behavior toward others
3. Commitment to a "Code of Silence"
4. Unsupervised computer access

And finally, two patterns of social dynamics that should arouse concern are:

1. Participation in a peer group that is fascinated with violent or extremist beliefs
2. Use of illegal drugs or alcohol

Shaping Boys for Violence

Where do boys learn how to commit acts of violence? Some leaders have observed that in today's society, we are far more likely personally to experience crime and violence than in the days of the supposedly turbulent and dangerous "Wild West," and almost three-fourths of middle schools and high schools report one or more violent incidents each year (U. S. Department of Education, 1998).

Although the leaders of our society repeatedly emphasize their opposition to violence, in fact, our society in many ways shapes boys to be violent. The information explosion has brought into our homes sensationalistic news of violent murders, beatings, torture, and other acts so cruel that virtually no behavior is unthinkable any longer. Furthermore, television, movies, music, and computer games—as enjoyable as they are—are often full of violence. And consider the "gangsta" rap lyrics that talk about murder, mayhem, and rape; the TV shows that feature ridicule, sarcasm, and self-centeredness; the murders that are often graphically portrayed as part of a game. Although these media do not *cause* violence, they do reinforce the idea that violence is fun and that it has few consequences. And they provide models of behavior that often are not only selfish and psychopathic-like, but which are also anti-intellectual. Media portrayals of gifted boys, in particular, show them as inept nerds and geeks who are to be ridiculed almost for sport.

Violence is even used to sell things in our culture. In his book *Jack and Jill Why They Kill* (2000), James Shaw points out the subtle connection between enjoyment of fast food and toy weaponry, for example. The pleasure that children take in a kid's meal is intensely associated with the excitement they feel for a free toy. When that free toy is a weapon or an action figure with violent characteristics, a connection between violence and pleasure is made that is unconscious but powerful.

Through all these ways, we have inadvertently produced a generation that has become emotionally calloused to violence, and the boys of this generation may even suffer additional, unique influences. As William Pollack (1999) points out in *Real Boys,* people who say that "boys will be boys" are suggesting that thoughtlessness, aggression, and recklessness are all right for boys because "that's just the way they are." It is this kind of thinking from the beginning of a boy's life that can lead to acting out later. Although boys may be born with more testosterone and less serotonin than girls—both conditions that can be precursors of aggression—it is more likely that the constant reinforcement of aggressive acts creates the violent boy. Examples are the infant who is handled too roughly and who is punished for crying, the little boy who is encouraged to fight other boys, the boy who is allowed to play with real and toy weapons and to play video games that feature bloody killings—all are being shaped, unfortunately and perhaps without realization of it, for violence.

When the intensity of giftedness and a feeling of angry alienation are combined with such shaping for violence, a volatile condition is created. Eric Harris, who with Dylan Klebold shot and killed teachers and students at Columbine High School on April 20, 1999 in Colorado, was an honors calculus student. Like most high schools, the social pressure to fit in at Columbine was strong. He was known as a geek, and he hated his reputation. He was exposed to violence in the media, and he began to spend large amounts of his time focusing on violence. He became fascinated with white supremacist literature, and he used his considerable intelligence to research everything he could about this philosophy, as well as about how to create instruments of killing.

Similarly, Ted Kaczynski, the Unabomber, was a mathematical genius who developed a warped moral intelligence. It is probable that he was born with a strong proclivity for paranoia. At an early age, he was exposed to severe and sweeping punishment and criticism from the adults around him and was exhorted to make changes in the world. This increased his paranoid ideation. Soon, his interest in violent methods of achieving social change was fueled by ample exposure to the literature of radical violence. He was able to find and use all the information he needed to create the mail bombs that killed three people and injured 23 others during a span of almost two decades.

Both of these examples are of people who might not have committed acts of violence if they had grown up in an environment that shaped them away from violence rather than toward it. A boy is less likely to harm others if he is never taught that violence is fun, that aggression pays, or that you can control others by inflicting pain upon them.

Three Patterns of Angry Gifted Boys

One way of understanding the development of sociopathic-like behavior is to examine the ways in which people think of brilliant, cruel people collectively—in other words, the archetypes that are used to describe these people. We can think of three popular examples—one from comic books, one from literature, and one from musical theater. By looking at these three popular examples from our cultural milieu, we may see patterns that help us understand some of the angry reactions of gifted boys.

Lex Luthor, Superman's nemesis, is indeed brilliant. He constantly invents machines to subvert society for his own gain. He also exists to subvert Superman's wholesome goodness and to mock his application of manly strength to the benefit of social good in Metropolis. How did Lex Luthor become evil? He was the brightest boy in his school until the young Superman appeared. Of course, no human being could compete with the latter's powers. The more Lex tried to exceed Superman's accomplishments, the more frustrated and self-absorbed he became. The result was that he focused his brilliant mental energy on accumulating wealth and power and on destroying Superman.

Many gifted boys find themselves facing the same problem Lex Luthor did. They are bright—but not as bright as an older brother, or the top honor student in their school, or someone else who seems perfect. Often, the gifted boy who comes in second or who loses his princedom to another boy feels resentment and humiliation. If parents and teachers increase that humiliation by criticizing and comparing him constantly to the superstar, he may decide that he will use his gifts in another arena besides the classroom. If he is athletically or musically inclined, for instance, he can turn his brilliance in those directions. However, if his special talent is intellectual and he cannot excel academically because another gifted boy has "taken" that position, he may find that illegal activities, such as building explosives or hacking into computers, not only fulfill his intellectual curiosity and drive, but also win him angry friends like himself. In these cases, it is important to salvage the gifted boy's lost self-esteem by helping him to excel in a unique area and to curtail the comparisons to others. Sometimes parents need to insist that teachers and other adults stop measuring a boy by what his brother or a "super" peer can do.

Another highly visible archetype is embodied in the story of Dr. Jeckyl and Mr. Hyde, the mad scientist with two personalities.

Unlike Lex Luthor, this complex being has a proper face during the day, but at night he transforms into an explosive expression of blood lust. He became this way because of an experiment gone awry. The theory behind the experiment was remarkably sound and of good intention, but the release of the highly repressed shadow being resulted in a force that overwhelmed the ordinary and conforming persona.

Parents or other adults who savagely suppress any opposition or outbreak with bizarre punishments can also create two-faced monsters. As therapists of gifted boys, we have heard of outlandish teaching and parenting techniques that created seemingly angelic little boys who just "happen" to set fires or hurt other children. One gifted man we know tells of how he was put in a closet by his teacher day after day because he was hyperactive and refused to speak English (Spanish was his native language). This young boy was terrified of the dark, but he had a hard time containing his jumpiness. Through sheer force of will, he eventually learned to sit quietly, speak English quietly, and act like a perfectly good quiet little boy. But when nobody was looking, he liked to torment small children, tying them up or putting them in closets as the teacher had done to him.

Of course, there are much less extreme cases that still reflect our tendency as educators to try to force bright little boys to sit still and speak quietly and in turn. Not only are gifted boys discouraged from expressing their boredom, they are told to help the other children if they are bored. Any approaches to parenting or educating gifted boys that require that they repress their "shadow"—all of their active, wild, aggressive tendencies—may lead to an explosion of the shadow later in life. Instead, we need to encourage boys to channel these potentially negative aspects into creativity, appropriate competition, and humor (Kindlon, 2000).

Yet another archetype of evil brilliance is the Phantom of the Opera. Here, pathos is mixed with terror in a tale of tragic love and desire. Born deformed and paraded as a freak in a sideshow during much of his childhood, the Phantom suffers daily because of his ugliness, which he hides behind a mask, eventually taking up residence in the tunnels of the opera house. Only upon discovering a beautiful woman, whom he recognizes could bring his musical compositions to the heights of expression to which he aspires, does he re-appear as her behind-the-scenes mentor. He falls in love with her and takes her to his secret lair beneath the opera house. There, she insists on seeing the face behind the mask. This he cannot allow, though, perceiving himself to be a monster. When a former suitor of the woman later begins to compete for the attention of the Phantom's new protégé, the Phantom becomes mad with jealousy and conspires to kill the other man. Unlike Lex Luthor and Dr. Jeckyl, however, the Phantom is later transformed by love and is, in the end, redeemed.

Much like the Phantom, many gifted boys think of themselves as freaks. Some of them actually do have a physical characteristic that makes them different in the eyes of society. Perhaps the boy is too short compared to his classmates, or perhaps he has terrible acne or a physical or learning disability.

Many gifted boys, however, have no visible disfigurement, but instead see their very giftedness as the cause of their deviance. Highly gifted boys whose talent for math or music or languages is so extreme as to propel them into the top ranks of students nationally may truly see their talent as a dark gift that they wish they could hide, because it makes them so different at a time when fitting in is so important. The boy who is too curious about school subjects, the boy who feels the tragic nature of the world around him, or the boy who finds the behaviors of his peers to be senseless, inane, petty and hypocritical—all of them find themselves wondering whether they are different, strange, or weird.

If a gifted boy is totally rejected by his peers, he may close down his emotions entirely. These boys develop a mask of uncaring and unfeeling, and as adults, they may engage in activities that are indifferent or even harmful to other people because they claim not to care about other people. For example, they may withdraw—angrily and full of hurt—choosing to isolate themselves rather than take any responsibility for the society around them. As adults, they may run scams or fraudulent business schemes, or they may work in weapons development or in highly polluting industries because they really don't care how the products of their brilliance are used.

In adulthood, many highly gifted boys do discover a mask that they can hide behind—the mask of normality, or even of obscurity. We know many highly gifted males who work in low-pressure jobs—in a bike shop, for example, or selling comic books, or working as an office assistant for their parents' business. Often, however, there is an anger in these men that breaks forth in psychotherapy, particularly when they speak of their lack of fulfillment, their aloneness, and their lack of love.

In extreme cases, the man "behind the mask" acts out against those people who have rejected him. The gifted man who has been humiliated because of his own clumsiness or because of the rejection of a young woman might engage in date rape. Or the boy who has suffered too much bullying might bring a gun to school.

In all of these examples, it is clear that the boy behind the mask should be encouraged to talk through his anger and despair. He needs the encouragement that will help him understand that his giftedness is not a flaw. Like the Phantom, he needs something to live for—a cause or a relationship that will help him transcend his mask.

The three "evil genius" archetypes discussed above give us some insight into the factors that may cause otherwise normal gifted boys to act in sociopathic ways. They also offer us hints as to how society might respond in ways that allow the gifts to emerge without the attendant destructive forces.

Lex Luthor is the archetype that underlies the Hitlers, the Milosevics, and the Ted Bundys. They spend their lives demonstrating their superiority by inflicting pain and death upon those they hold as inferior. The only cure for this affliction is prevention. But by the time the Hitler type emerges, it is usually too late.

We recognize that the real-life examples we have given are of people who differ vastly from most other people in their psychological makeup. And these extremely violent people probably have biological predispositions that prompt them to lack empathy, to dominate, and to find pleasure in violence. When these tendencies are combined with the intensity and intellect of giftedness, the results are sometimes disastrous. Society's only option is to contain or combat the perpetrator of the evil.

From this realization, however, arise several difficult dilemmas. First, preventive detention is not allowed in our society, even
if we were able to reliably say which children are biologically predisposed to violence. And despite the best efforts of psychologists
and psychiatrists, it is certainly difficult to accurately predict which
children—even if they do show violent behavior—will become
sociopaths as adults. Children, by their nature, do not have the personal and social judgment of adults, and their emotions can get out
of hand.

How does one know whether a child is likely to become a
sociopath or psychopath? Parents and teachers should watch for children who show a strange lack of feeling, who lie constantly to get
what they want, who enjoy acts of cruelty toward animals and smaller children, who act out sexually, who steal, set fires, and demonstrate no remorse for any of their actions. These children may be
showing early signs of becoming true sociopaths. However, children
who have suffered severe emotional traumas may temporarily show
one or more of these characteristics and, though these behaviors
clearly would suggest significant personal problems, they are not
indicators of true psychopaths. Personality tests and clinical interviews with trained psychologists or psychiatrists are needed to identify whether such behaviors appear to be those of a true sociopath.

Many gifted children, with their intensity and creativity, will
challenge traditions and authority, and will drift into power struggles with adults. Ironically, the more an adult cares about the future
of the child, the more likely a power struggle is to occur. That is,
the adult who wants the best for a child often tries to push the child
into doing things a certain way or into certain activities or criticizes
or punishes the child in order to help the child reach his potential.
However, the relationship with the child is often a casualty in this
kind of power struggle. Next, the adult may take the gifted boy to a
psychologist or psychiatrist to "get him straightened out."
Unfortunately, unless the counseling professional understands the
characteristics of gifted boys, a misdiagnosis of Oppositional
Defiant Disorder is likely to be made (Webb, 2001), with the result
being inappropriate treatment that is likely to make the situation
worse rather than better. Sometimes, for example, the professional

will recommend that the parent do whatever it takes to win the power struggle by taking away things that the child cares about whenever the child is oppositional. One gifted boy told us that he learned from that approach that he could win his power struggle by simply not caring about anything at all.

A diagnosis of Conduct Disorder—the prelude to Antisocial Personality Disorder—must be made thoughtfully, carefully, and over a period of time. Despite the difficulties involved, gifted boys who are headed down the road to becoming true sociopaths must be identified and, to the extent possible, should be contained in an environment that will at least not worsen their characteristics. A special class or school for troubled boys, special camps, or foster homes are possibilities. Though there is little hope that these people can be changed in any fundamental sense to help them develop a strong conscience and sense of empathy, it does seem possible to help them become more thoughtful and less impulsive. Character education programs (Davis, 1996a, 1996b) beginning in the first or second grade can be helpful in stressing the social consequences of certain behaviors. School, home, or camp situations can be structured so that there are clear, frequent, and consistent connections between a child's behaviors and consequences—both positive and negative. With these youngsters, it also must be recognized that situations in which they are humiliated or overwhelmed by others' superiority may lead to outbreaks of antisocial behavior such as violent retaliation.

For the gifted redeemable rebel—the male with sociopathic-like behaviors who suffers from the Jekyll-and-Hyde type of divided self—there is more hope. If the division—two disparate aspects of the self—can be brought into an integrated wholeness, the need for aggressive expression disappears into creative achievement. The compartmentalized thinking can be reduced by helping this smart boy learn to value himself in ways other than those reflected in the opinions of others. A gifted boy who is angry about racism, for example, can be encouraged to write about racism as a journalist rather than physically lashing out.

A sympathetic counselor who helps the gifted boy reveal his true, vulnerable self can redeem the rebel. In this redemption, the gifted boy may become immune to the failure of others to recognize and value his genius. To change a gifted boy's life, it often takes just one trusted adult who recognizes the boy's giftedness and who values the boy unconditionally. Gifted boys who have become divided need help expressing the "shadow" side of themselves—the side that they keep hidden from others because they feel it will not be accepted or will even be ridiculed. They will, of course, feel irritation on occasion and will need to learn skills for expressing their anger verbally rather than physically. They need to know how to talk about their fears rather than ignoring and repressing them. In this way, the negative aspects of the self become integrated, and the need for a "good boy" and "bad boy" disappears.

The smart boy who is afflicted with a potentially isolating defect, such as, say, a large nose or a scar or a speech impediment, can also avoid reacting to his situation in sociopathic-like ways. By bringing the defect into the light of day—by removing the mask created to hide the real or imagined defect—and by permitting and nurturing the love of another, he will lose the impetus for violent acting out. It is not only by recognizing and nurturing the gift that we redeem the Phantom, it is accomplished by accepting him as a person and recognizing the beauty of his true self.

It can be difficult to reach out to such smart boys. Some of these boys seem to initially put their worst foot forward to see if you can tolerate them, and only then will they attempt to be open with you. Other gifted boys who are disappointed with themselves will project this disappointment onto the world around them. They are disgusted simultaneously with the world and with themselves. As one colleague said, "Those boys that are the hardest to love are the ones that need our love the most."

Gifted boys with real or imagined defects need help overcoming their self-disgust. Several strategies can help these boys overcome their feelings that they are unacceptable because of disfigurement or disability. It is important for them to learn social skills that will dispose others to like and accept them, such as how to reach out to others, give to others, point out similarities, indicate liking, and offer to share or help. It is also important for them to learn to do things that will garner respect from others, including techniques such as showing confidence, quietly giving needed knowledge, and sharing opinions in an interesting and humorous way. Goldstein, Harootunian, and Conoley (1994) have developed role-play techniques that can help adolescents learn these skills.

For the gifted boy who believes that his giftedness is itself a handicap, the task of the helper is to teach the boy a new way of seeing giftedness. Although it is important to avoid being too super-ficially positive, it is also necessary to point out various ways in which gifted people have changed the world. In our psychotherapy with gifted boys, we show them examples of adult eminent people who had childhoods similar to their own and whose personalities were similar as well. "Carl Sagan, the great astronomer, had a per-sonality just like yours!" "You know, the great writer Isaac Asimov was a gifted kid who felt like a freak when he was growing up, too. Educators studied his giftedness and made him feel that he was really different. But he went on to become a great science fiction writer that millions of people liked." When boys can accept their own talents, they can step from behind the mask—and can be freed from the anger of being hidden from others and from themselves.

Taking Steps

In the case of sociopaths, we must recognize that the progno-sis is not good. However, we believe that the vast majority of gift-ed boys who are acting out with violence and aggression are not true sociopaths, but instead are boys whose behavior can be modi-fied if the right steps are taken at the right times. Regardless of the causes, however, acting-out behaviors of various kinds are disturb-ing to others, and to modify these behaviors, it is first important to try to ascertain whether the child is indeed a redeemable rebel or is developing into a sociopath.

In either case, parents or educators of children who show angry, acting-out behaviors should seek professional help immedi-ately. Extremely structured environments with consistent conse-quences can reduce the delinquent behavior of sociopathic young people, particularly when combined with Reality Therapy (Glasser, 1999; 2000). Reality therapy emphasizes a person's responsibility for his own behavior, highlights that one can control only oneself, and focuses on current and future behavior rather than on the past. This approach is even more effective when used with children who are younger and when parents and educators are able to join together in the use of consistent consequences.

Gifted boys who are redeemable rebels typically respond much better to psychological intervention than to the structured consequences described above, particularly with the use of approaches that try to promote understanding and relationships. Remember, these gifted boys often take on the characteristics of sociopathic behavior to defend themselves from those who would humiliate and hurt them. If they are taught to understand that the world is not always dangerous and that at least some other people value their sensitivity, intensity, and interests, then they can come to appreciate the value of relationships in which there is give-and-take and mutual consideration.

How do we prevent gifted boys from adopting sociopathic-like behaviors in the first place? It has been our experience in treating gifted boys with Oppositional Defiant Disorders—the precursor of conduct disorder and antisocial behavior—that they feel they have been forced to increase the volume and intensity of their communication to their parents and teachers simply because no one hears them. No one is listening. So how do we hear these boys better? They often use their bodies and loud voices to express their feelings. If our only response is to shut them up and make them behave, then they may perceive that their only choice is to become even more disruptive in order to be heard. We need to listen to their words and to their behaviors: "You are acting like you feel bored. It must be time to change what we are doing." "You must be feeling put down. What can I do to make you feel better?"

We have also found that gifted boys need more honesty about the realities of their lives, their talents, and the prejudices of others toward them. One of the first and most important things about which to speak to them honestly is their intelligence. Gifted boys need to be told, in very specific terms, the type, extent, and implications of their talents. For example, a verbally gifted 5th grade boy might be told, "On all of these tests, you are scoring above the 95th percentile on verbal abilities. That means that most of your life, you will be able to read better and faster, to understand language better, and to write and express yourself better than most others in your class. All of your life, it will probably seem as if other people are thinking slower than you or are not really trying hard enough. They really are trying hard; it's just difficult for them to keep up with you. Being gifted or having this high ability doesn't mean you are a better person than others, but it means in this case—in verbal tasks—that you learn faster and differently than others."

Failure to discuss the child's abilities or to provide him with books about giftedness (e.g., Galbraith, 1998; Galbraith & Delisle, 1996) often results in a smart boy's growing up with contempt for other children who he thinks are simply lazy. At the same time, it is helpful to discuss areas in which the child is weaker: "Your math scores are not quite as high as your verbal, so you may have to work harder in math. And your physical coordination is a little behind other kids your age, which is why you have trouble in physical education. But you'll get better as you practice." Knowing that you score differently and have different abilities in different areas leads one to have more realistic expectations for others' performance, rather than continually being disappointed in them. And so, with better and more specific information about his gifts as well as his weaknesses, a boy develops compassion instead of arrogance and contempt.

Another kind of honesty centers on the burden of being gifted. The anti-intellectualism that characterizes today's American society is hard for all gifted kids, but it particularly stigmatizes gifted boys (Schroeder-Davis, 1998). In movies and television, gifted boys are regularly portrayed in quite negative ways as dorks, nerds, and geeks. The contempt of the average citizen for the life of the mind makes gifted boys who truly love learning feel like freaks. In the same way that Jewish children need to understand anti-Semitism so that they can make the proper attribution when someone attempts to humiliate them, gifted children need to know about anti-intellectualism so that when they are taunted, they can make the proper attribution. Bright boys need help in understanding that it is not the bright boy who is the freak; it is the culture that demeans the intellect that is freakish.

There is a controversy about limiting viewing of violent television or movies. The research does show that such media do prompt aggressive behaviors. On the other hand, however, censorship does not sit well with gifted boys who are curious. Perhaps a balanced approach is best. For young gifted boys, limiting shows and viewing would certainly seem appropriate. For older boys, the limiting should be less, but when shows are viewed, it should be done in the presence of parents so that there can be discussion that puts the violence into proper perspective.

Gifted boys also need honesty and open-mindedness with regard to their emerging needs for independence and adult interests. Because of their intellectual curiosity, they may want to watch films and read books that have adult themes. For example, one 13-year-old we know loved the movie "Pulp Fiction," not because of the sex and violence, but because he was delighted with Quentin Tarantino's complex cinematic structure. Parents need to listen to their son's interests and sometimes decide in favor of his curiosity.

Intellectual precocity and curiosity extends beyond academic interests into more advanced and diverse areas. Advanced skills in reading and with technology bring smart boys into contact with information other kids don't have. Gifted boys can find wonderful sources of knowledge on the Internet, for example—but they may also come into contact with tainted sources such as racist Web sites and those that demean women. These boys need guidance in choosing not only what they want to know, but also how they want to go about knowing it. That means critical evaluation, with the help of an adult, of the sources of knowledge that are available, friendly assistance with technology, and frank discussions of values and moral issues.

Gifted boys also need honest information about their own roles in the family. If a boy is the family superstar, he needs honesty regarding whether or not he will be getting more, or at least different, resources in the family than his siblings. Occasionally, highly gifted children need special coaching or tutoring that the other children do not (Bloom, 1985). Even in healthy families, sibling resentment occurs if one child gets more resources than another, but this tends to fade after about a year if it is treated as no big deal and if it is explained to the children that the resources are being allocated on the basis of need, not on the basis of favoritism. Sibling rivalry becomes a big deal if, in response to taunts and teasing, smart boys remind others of their princely status. If a gifted boy is the sibling of a family superstar, then he may feel that he is the second most talented in a family, or perhaps that he is not talented at all. He will need loving help in finding his own arenas of excellence, as well as steadfast refusals by parents to compare the two siblings. It is always important to give special time to each child and to convey that you value each not for what he can do, but rather simply because he is a member of the family and is important to you. Many practical techniques that can help parents can be found in parenting books such as *Guiding the Gifted Child* (Webb, et al., 1982).

Gifted boys need instruction and guidance in emotional, moral, and spiritual intelligence. This kind of guidance may be the best protection against the shaping of violence in our society.

Within the field of gifted education, one of the major voices calling for morality education and character education has been Abraham Tannenbaum. In *Gifted Children: Psychological and Educational Perspectives* (1983), he suggests a curriculum for gifted children that can help ensure that they use their gifts in ethical ways. The first element of the curriculum is self-knowledge. Here, gifted children learn to take pride in specific accomplishments, to know what it is that makes them unique, to choose a hero, and to understand their deepest commitments. The second element is learning that life can be a challenge. In this section of the curriculum, they learn how to engage in conflict resolution, how to survive frustration, and how to overcome temporary failures. They also discuss delayed gratification and the importance of risk-taking. In a third section, they consider those processes that have caused misery and destruction—dehumanization and misogyny. Here, they learn about the "rogues gallery" of gifted people—such as Adolf Hitler, Leni Riefenstahl, and Ezra Pound—who used their intelligence to destroy or torment others or, in the case of Pound, to engage in vicious propaganda. The students read Henrik Ibsen's *A Doll's House* to see how women have been robbed of their power and to understand oppression. Finally, they learn how to use language, art, science, and political skills in responsible ways.

This sort of curriculum has great promise for the prevention of gifted sociopaths and for the redeeming of rebels. Gifted boys are hungry to hear about values and eager to engage in debate about right and wrong. A curriculum such as this helps them discover themselves and teaches them to value others and to take responsibility for their gifts.

Conclusion

Gifted sociopath or redeemable rebel? Certainly, boredom, lack of honest information, ridicule, and lack of acceptance of the gifted boy's true self can lead him to behave like a sociopath. True sociopaths, however, are people without conscience, empathy, or the capacity for serving others; these kinds of people can be identified only by professionals and then carefully guided or contained. Redeemable rebels, on the other hand, need permission to live according to their own masculine identity, and not according to the "Boy Code." They need honesty and openness about their gifts. And they need to be helped to believe that there is a place for them in society and that their gifts can be used in service and leadership in such a way as to make the world better for all of us.

Key Points:

1. There are some true sociopaths who are also gifted. There are biological causes that predispose them to their dishonesty, cruelty, and violence, and they respond only very modestly to counseling.

2. There are certain environments, such as abusive and punitive families, that interact with the biological predispositions and make violent anti-social behaviors more likely.

3. There are many gifted students who "mimic" sociopaths in their behavior; these students are not true sociopaths, but are redeemable.

4. The archetypes of the evil genius, the divided self, and the disfigured genius help us understand sociopaths and also gifted boys who mimic sociopathic behaviors.

5. Although the prognosis for true sociopaths is a poor one, their behaviors can be controlled somewhat through highly structured programs with consistent feedback, particularly if such a program is begun early in childhood.

6. For gifted boys who are the redeemable rebels, a quite different approach to promote insight and understanding works well, particularly in the context of establishing a relationship with the boy— something that is extremely difficult for a true psychopath to do.

7. For gifted boys who mimic sociopaths, instruction in emotional, moral, and spiritual intelligence may be helpful.

References

ABC News (1999, September 24). An explosion of violence. ABCNews.go.com.

American Psychiatric Association (1994). *Diagnostic and statistical manual of mental disorders, 4th ed.* Washington, DC: American Psychiatric Association.

Bloom, B. S. (Ed.) (1985). *Developing talent in young people.* New York: Ballantine.

Capote, T. (1994 reprint). *In cold blood.* New York: Vintage.

Davis, G. A. (1996a). *Teaching values: An idea book for teachers (and parents).* Cross Plains, WI: Westwood Publishing Co.

Davis, G. A. (1996b). *Values are forever: Becoming more caring and responsible.* Cross Plains, WI: Westwood Publishing Co.

Galbraith, J. (1998). *The gifted kids' survival guide for ages 10 and under.* Minneapolis: Free Spirit Publishing.

Galbraith, J. & Delisle, J. R. (1996) *The gifted kids' survival guide: A teen handbook.* Minneapolis: Free Spirit.

Glasser, W. (2000). *Reality therapy in action.* New York: Harper Collins.

Glasser, W. (1999). *Choice theory.* New York: Harper Collins.

Goldstein, A., Harootunian, B., & Conoley, J. C. (1994). *Student aggression: Prevention, management, and replacement training.* New York: Guilford Press.

Kellerman, J. (1999). *Savage spawn: Reflections on violent children.* New York: Ballantine.

Kerouac, J. (1991 reprint). *On the road.* New York: Penguin.

Kindlon, D. J. (2000). *Raising Cain: Protecting the emotional life of boys.* New York: Ballantine.

McQueen, A. (2000, September 7). FBI lists characteristics of violence prone teens. *Arizona Republic,* p. A5.

Pollack, W. (1999). *Real boys: Rescuing our sons from the myths of boyhood.* New York: Holt.

Schroeder-Davis, S. (1998). Parenting high achievers: Swimming upstream against the cultural current. *Parenting for High Potential* (Dec.).

Shaw, J. E. (2000). *Jack and Jill why they kill: Saving our children, saving ourselves.* Seattle: Onjinjinkta Press.

Tannenbaum, A. J. (1983). *Gifted children: Psychological and educational perspectives.* New York: Macmillan.

U. S. Department of Education (1998). *Violence and discipline problems in the U.S. public schools: 1996-97.* Washington, DC: National Center for Education Statistics.

Webb, J. T. (2001). Mis-diagnosis and dual diagnosis of gifted children: Gifted and LD, ADHD, OCD, Oppositional Defiant Disorder. *Gifted Education Press Quarterly,* 15 (1), 9-13.

9

They're Called Sissies, Fat Boys, and Nerds

There are three groups of gifted boys who are consistently marked by their peers for rejection and cruelty—the boys who are called "Sissy," "Fat Boy," and "Nerd." We have devoted a special chapter to these boys for several reasons. First of all, parents and teachers are often frustrated by their attempts to protect these boys from bullies who are remarkably persistent in their attacks against them. Sometimes it almost seems as if the defenses of the obese, effeminate, or overly intellectual boy are so ineffectual that they actually encourage more bullying. Naturally, many parents and teachers want to know how they can help these boys. What follows is an examination of the origins of the roles of obesity, of "sissy" behavior, and of nerdiness, and then some suggestions on how these boys might accept themselves and thereby transcend the rejection of their peers.

A second reason for including a special chapter on this topic in this book stems from the fact that an unusual number of eminent men suffered such rejection as children (Goertzel & Goertzel, 1962). This has led us to wonder whether these individuals' rejection by traditional male culture may have somehow actually contributed to their capacity for creative accomplishment. Could it be that the rejection allowed such smart boys to break free from the intense pressures toward conformity, thereby promoting independent, creative thinking and behaviors? Perhaps the rejection by others caused them to reject the values displayed by those who rejected them.

There is terrible pain that can come from being labeled a "sissy" or a "nerd," or from being an obese child. However, we want to recognize that there are ways to transcend that pain. The pleasures and comfort of learning and achievement can be a powerful salve, so valuing creative productivity is one of the strategies for teaching boys to cope with needless cruelty. Another way of transcending the pain of these negative stereotypes is to re-invent oneself as a positive, beloved type that others will value—for example, the generous and magnanimous leader; the gentle, sensitive, creative spirit; or the clever, indispensable genius.

It is certainly not the case that all smart boys are "feminine," "nerdy," or overweight. However, these stereotypes and the corresponding labels, unfortunately, are often associated with young gifted men who have a certain appearance or who choose to engage in activities that are not thought of as traditionally "masculine." And it is true that some gifted boys simply do not buy into the importance of developing rippling muscles, wearing the latest fashion styles, or participating in macho rituals. When they ignore these symbols of masculine brotherhood, they risk being called sissies or nerds. Some smart boys know this in advance and don't care. Others are unaware that they are being labeled until they have already been stereotyped by others.

Often considered "outsiders," these boys are easy targets for bullies, particularly during their school-age years. Fortunately, however, the bullying usually is time-limited. Once a boy graduates from high school, most often he finds that he is not exposed to bullying, or at least that it is far less severe and less frequent. Intellectual pursuits and abilities tend to be more valued by peers after the high school years. In colleges, there is much less bullying than in high school or middle school, and smart boys have more freedom to leave situations if bullying does occur. And though occasionally there may be bullying in job settings, there is generally far less tolerance for it and much more legal protection against it.

Boys who are identified with these stereotypes may be quite different from one another, but they are likely to share at least two experiences: (1) they have probably been bullied, and (2) they often later choose a nonconformist life path. If they are not too traumatized by their early marginalization, their nontraditional, nonconformist interests and lifestyle may lead them to fulfill their gifts in unexpected ways—in areas such as the arts, religion, or philosophy.

The Boy Code

As soon as kindergarten begins, so do the teasing, the peer and adult pressure, and the education about the Boy Code (see Chapter 3). The pressure for boys to conform to the Boy Code is particularly intense during the school-age years, K-12. William Pollack (1998), in his description of the Boy Code, lists four stereotypically male ideals (or models of behavior) that all children, but especially boys, encounter in virtually all settings outside of their homes. The code is taught by the boys' agemates, teachers, coaches, and practically everyone they know, and it is a widely accepted part of our culture. It is so imbedded within our culture that adults who contribute to it aren't aware that they are teaching "the code."

The "do-or-die" rules of the code were expressed directly by the boys who participated in the study that was the basis for Pollack's book, *Real Boys* (reviewed in Chapter 3). These boys of all ages, even those who were quite young, indicated that, according to the Boy Rules, they must "keep a stiff upper lip," act tough, not act "too nice," be cool, and "just laugh and brush it off when someone punches you or when you feel you'd like to cry."

The Boy Code that emerges from these imperatives can be summarized in four caricatures of highly valued masculine behavior:

1. "The Sturdy Oak." Men should be strong, silent, and self-reliant. Showing emotions and being kind are seen as breaking this rule.

2. "Give 'em Hell." The world of competitive sports and the on-screen conduct of such hypermasculine role models as John Wayne, Arnold Schwarzenegger, and Sylvester Stallone or virtually any professional wrestler promotes an enormity of daring, violent, and "over-the-top" attitudes and behaviors in boys. The assumption that boys are somehow hardwired to think and act in this manner allows parents and teachers to shrug their shoulders and accept risky and antisocial behaviors as "normal for boys."

3. "The Big Wheel." This ideal motivates boys (and men) to achieve status, power, and dominion over others, including an assumption of sovereignty over girls and all things feminine.

4. "No Sissy Stuff." Pollack identifies this "gender straitjacketing" imperative as the most traumatizing and dangerous part of the code, because it inhibits the expression of any feelings and desires that might be construed as feminine, such as dependence, warmth, and empathy.

According to this code, then, what gifted fat boys, sissies, and nerds have done is unforgivable. From the point of view of American male culture, they have disobeyed the Boy Code, either by choice or by chance.

Sissies

How do boys become sissies? Whatever the reasons, boys who are identified as "sissies" simply learn to interact with their world by modeling after their mothers and sisters, grandmothers, aunts, or other close females, particularly those who reflect traditionally feminine behaviors. Gifted boys simply tend to be more far-reaching and androgynous than boys in general; they enjoy all activities, whether they are traditionally "girl" activities or "boy" activities. The injunctions of the Boy Code fail to override these boys' expressions of feelings, their idealism, their sensitivity, their capacity for compassion and love, their creative urges, and their connection to heart, home, hearth, and even the earth itself.

Every individual, no matter which gender, has both feminine and masculine characteristics. Femininity and masculinity are not separate, distinct poles of a single dimension, and most people are at least somewhat androgynous. Sandra Bem (1993; 1995) conceptualized sexuality as having three components:

1. Sexual Identity. Our personal sexual identity relates to how closely our perceptions of ourselves match the stereotypes of our biological gender.
2. Gender Identity. This relates to how closely the perceptions others have of us match our own biological gender.
3. Sexual Orientation. Sexual orientation describes the gender to which we are attracted sexually.

Gifted boys—or anyone else—may have any combination of sexual identity, gender identity, and sexual orientation. However, when their behaviors and verbal expressions are perceived to be different from the stereotype of their biological gender, or when their sexual orientation is perceived to be toward others of the same sex, they are particularly likely to become targets of bullies and homophobic peers.

A study reported by the Gay, Lesbian, Straight Education Network (GLSEN) (1999) found that children in today's elementary schools hear the word "gay" used as a pejorative epithet 25 times a day on the average! It is considered the strongest and most hurtful epithet that one can hurl at another. It speaks of nothing other than the fact that its target is inferior. Young children often have no clue as to its referent behavior, but they know that to call someone "gay" or a "faggot" is a curse of potent magnitude and that to be called such is a crushing insult to their being, and even a threat to their lives. To be called a "sissy" is the precursor to the more street-wise term "gay."

Gay and gifted

When asked to name an eminent person who was gay and gifted, many people think of Oscar Wilde, the brilliant writer who struggled continually to define a lifestyle that included the love of other men. Although a model of affable genius and dramatic flair, he was eventually arrested and jailed because of his lifestyle and sexual orientation. Families continue to fear the ostracism that threatens every gifted gay boy, and every gay boy hopes that he will be able to avoid Oscar Wilde's fate—exile from society.

For those youths who face the reality of being both gifted *and* gay—or more inclusively, gay, lesbian, or bisexual (GLB)—or who are even just questioning, feelings of being marginalized are intensified substantially. Gifted youth, by definition, are a minority; they are in the top three percent of their age group in some intellectual capacity. Within this group, probably three to ten percent are GLB—a minority within a minority. So they find themselves dropping from one small peer group of three in a hundred to an even smaller group of one to three in a thousand. Even in a large urban comprehensive high school of 3,000 or so students, probably only three to nine students are both gifted and gay—a situation that can lead to particularly strong feelings of marginalization. Even across four grade levels, the likelihood of such individuals finding one another or even feeling safe seeking others like themselves is miniscule (Anderson, 2001).

Feelings of alienation, isolation, and overwhelming anxiety among these adolescents are often exacerbated as they become aware of a strong and outspoken political block of individuals in present-day society who argue that being gay is, at best, a sickness to be cured, or worse, that all gays should be exterminated. The sense of vulnerability among these youths is affected to the greatest degree, however, by a larger group—those mainstream adults in their lives who simply are silent and passive about acts of hate and intolerance, and who often fear that coming to the aid of the victim might somehow compromise their own positions in society.

It is this social context that appears to have inhibited behavioral and educational researchers from investigating the intersection of these two low-frequency individual differences. To date, only a handful of studies has examined possible relationships between sexual orientation and cognitive abilities.

Only three studies of gifted GLB youths report adolescents' experiences associated with being both gifted and gay (Friedrichs, 1997; Tolan, 1997; Peterson & Rischar, 2000). Each of these authors explored the influence of being gifted on being gay, as well as the influence of being gay on being gifted, and several themes emerge from these studies. First, the burden of being twice different did appear to create additional emotional burdens of depression and feelings of social isolation. Coming to terms with being different from the majority of their agemates in both ability and sexual orientation often resulted in attempts to deny one or the other of these significant aspects of one's identity, or more frequently, in social isolation and loss of self-esteem.

The school climate experienced by some of these teenagers seemed particularly unsafe because of both psychological and physical harassment. In some cases, individuals sought to handle their quandaries by academic or athletic overachievement, perfectionism, or over-involvement in extracurricular activities, or on the other hand, by self-destructive behaviors such as underachieving, dropping out of school, running away, abusing drugs or alcohol, or committing suicide.

Certainly, it seems essential for parents and teachers to become more alert to issues associated with being both gay and gifted. It is especially important to create for them a school climate in which students with all kinds of differences are safe and accepted and where adults are available to listen, support, and help solve problems.

Homophobia and the fear and distrust of all things feminine provide bullies with their most effective weapon of verbal abuse. Yet they also prevent both bully and victim from expressing talents that do not conform to the stereotype of masculinity. Not all boys who are identified as sissies in their youth grow up to be attracted sexually to members of their own gender. They do, however, bear the scars of being so cursed by their contemporaries. Some hide behind the Boy Code, doing so in a variety of ways.

Some overreact in a direction that is opposite to their own beliefs; they become aggressive and violent. Others refuse to seek help when they need it, preferring instead to "tough it out like a real man," because to ask for help would suggest that they really are sissies. Still others suffer the demise of their relationships; they would rather be accepted by the other boys than experience the criticism and rejection that might occur if they were to continue to be friends with the wrong sort of boy or if they are too closely aligned with girls. And still others seek to numb or fill the void in their internal lives with all sorts of addictive behaviors.

In short, boys who do not adhere to the Boy Code often come to believe that they are inferior. As a result, they approach everyone and every situation from a station lower than others. The prophecy all too often fulfills itself. These boys deprive themselves of opportunities to discover and honor who they really are. And they deprive us and the world of the contribution they would make if they pursued self-discovery, self-actualization, and self-expression.

What can we do for the gifted boys whose feminine behaviors, whether related to sexual orientation or not, cause them to be derided and ridiculed? What these boys crave more than anything else is simple acceptance for being who they really are. If a boy is called a sissy, he needs both of his parents, or a male figure as well as a female figure, to affirm him. It is not enough for his mother to reassure him; he needs a man to tell him that he is indeed a male and that there are many acceptable, even honorable, ways of being a man that don't correspond to the traditional Boy Code.

The gifted boy who is taunted as a sissy also needs protective strategies for dealing with bullies. He will need to learn to use humor to defuse tense situations, and he will need to learn assertiveness to state his rights.

For the gifted boy who is gay, GLSEN has provided a number of strategies for making schools safer. *The GLSEN Lunchbox: A Comprehensive Training Program for Ending Anti-Gay Bias in Schools* (2000) is a GLSEN publication that shows how gay boys, teachers and parents can use education about gay people and gay issues, discussion groups, and interpersonal exercises to diminish bias against gays. In addition, the gifted boy with feminine behaviors needs an environment in which he will not only be accepted, but in which his talents can be expressed and appreciated. The cultures of dance, theater, design, and art have always been open and accepting of boys and men who have talent in these areas, even those who display non-traditional gender behaviors or sexual orientation. And if the boy is nurturing and caring, he might explore a career in the "helping" professions, such as counseling, nursing, psychology, and social work. The gifted boy who participates in service projects will find that elders, children, and suffering people to whom he gives comfort will usually return his caring.

These comments are not meant to reinforce stereotypes. While it is true that the professions and cultures listed above are more open to boys with "feminine" interests and behaviors, many very masculine boys and men have pursued careers in these areas as well. On the other hand, many others have had the courage to express their "feminine" side while still doing "masculine" things. Dennis Rodman, for example, is known to dress in drag, color his hair, and wear lots of earrings. Alice Cooper and Marilyn Manson delight in using feminine names and wearing traditionally feminine hairstyles and makeup, while playing hard rock music for a predominantly male audience. While some parents may hesitate to consider these men role models for their sons, for those boys who are determined to be true to their feminine sides without restricting themselves to the helping or theatrical professions, these celebrities do serve as reassuring and trailblazing new paradigms for alternative conceptions of manhood.

Fat Boys

What does it mean to grow up fat, male, and gifted? The literature of obesity in children divides neatly into two categories: (1) those books that exhort the reader to do everything possible to prevent a child from being fat, and (2) those books that attack the American obsession with weight and focus on the improvement of the child's total body image.

In the first category are books by authors who assume that being overweight is dangerous to children's health and destructive to their social standing, and that the response must be to get rid of the fat. Although we agree that obesity carries health risks and is indeed a source of tremendous humiliation, we disagree that traditional weight-loss programs, such as crash dieting, are the answer. Such programs have in fact been shown to be dangerous (Krasnegor, Grave, & Kretchmer, 1988).

Recent reports show that a larger percentage of the current generation of youth is overweight compared to previous generations, probably because it is more sedentary. Even so, we are concerned that so many boys feel that they must buy into the current fad for physical perfection. Reasonable nutritional habits and body-image counseling may be helpful for overweight gifted boys, but more than that is needed if these boys are to be emotionally healthy.

How do gifted boys get fat? The origins of obesity in children in general are well spelled out in the book *Childhood Obesity: A Biobehavioral Perspective*, by Norman A. Krasnegor, Gilman D. Grave, and Norman Kretchmer (1988). Genetic predisposition, hormonal variations, brain chemistry, early nutrition, energy expenditure through exercise, attitudes toward the body, and parental reinforcement of eating habits all play a part in the creation of an overweight child. And of course, all of these factors are at play in the lives of fat gifted boys. But other complex issues contribute to a gifted boy's obesity as well.

First, according to Alice Miller (1996), the child's role in the family can certainly contribute to obesity. For example, a gifted boy may become his mother's companion and confidante if she is needy and has difficulty understanding boundaries. If the mother rewards her son with food, then food can become associated with love and safety. (We would add that if any adult who is the main caregiver of the boy does this, the result would be the same.) Second, a gifted boy may intentionally gain weight as a "protest" against enforced participation in athletic events. If being overweight puts him literally out of the running for school sports, then he may not be expected to excel in that area. Third, there is a certain stage for many gifted boys when they love nothing so much as sitting around the house all day reading. It is not that they lack friends or are uninterested in the out-of-doors; it is rather that they have discovered that whole exciting worlds can unfold before them in a book. Unfortunately, an entire summer of reading and little exercise will usually result in quite a few extra pounds on a prepubescent boy. And despite the joy that his summer love affair with reading may have brought him, his extra weight at the beginning of the new school year will put him at risk for continued weight gain if he is socially rejected at school— and goes back to his sedentary, bookish existence. Finally, and paradoxically, some gifted boys are fat because they diet. Gifted boys are smart enough to read about the calorie values and fat content of foods, so occasionally, the slightly chubby boy who is determined to be thin will use his considerable brains to become an expert in starving himself. Unfortunately, diets, particularly in children, affect metabolism and can lead to imbalances in the body that make it likely that the weight will be regained. The body prepares for future famines by increasing its fat storage capacity.

For the boy who already feels stigmatized by his giftedness, being fat is just one more strike against him. It may make him just want to give up. One boy described it this way: "By the time I entered school, I had been identified as extraordinarily smart. I had also injured my feet during a stint as a five-year-old mascot drum major for a competitive drum and bugle corps. Athletic and active prior to that injury, I suddenly became completely sedentary. Plus, my mother suffered from a rare and debilitating illness, and she taught me how to live life as an invalid."

Another boy said, "It seemed that I really didn't ever have much of a chance to live the life of a normal boy. My advanced facility with words, my insight and the way I expressed it, and then my poor physical condition made me completely out of sync with my classmates. Everyone called me a fat sissy. I prayed to be opposite—stupid and well-built."

What can parents and teachers do for the fat, gifted boy? One of the most important things a parent can do is resist panic. In our experience, the only thing that seems more frightening to American parents than effeminate behavior in their sons is obesity, and parents may begin to obsessively watch everything the boy eats. The parents may put the boy on a cruel regimen of exercise that teaches him to hate anything physical, as well as a diet that starves his spirit as well as his body. Carried to an extreme, this can lead to a negative cycle of abstinence, secretiveness, eating, fulfillment, punishment and guilt, and then abstinence again. This behavior separates the boy from his true self. Conversely, if parents can stay cool and relaxed about the boy's weight, this type of vicious cycle can be avoided.

Next, parents can examine the lifestyle of the whole family, not just the boy's. It is likely that if a boy has begun overeating and resists exercise, he has at least one role model in the family doing the same thing. If he is expected to lead a different existence from the rest of the family, any efforts to change his behavior are doomed. The family needs a life that does not center on food—or on the resistance of food. Fun activities together that involve some exercise, movement, and stretching are the best ways of ensuring that a food-oriented lifestyle does not evolve.

Family walks and easy hikes in interesting places are a wonderful way of keeping everybody fit. Gentle, consistent exercise is always better than periodic boot camp-like forays into the world of exercise. We know of one family that picked out two new places to walk every week, including museums, malls, caves, new subdivisions, and college campuses. Sometimes, music or a class of some sort motivates movement. Martial arts, various types of dance, gymnastics, tennis, swimming, and even aerobic exercise classes can offer incentive for these boys simply to keep moving, even after they think they want to stop.

Except when recommended by a physician because of health risks, severe dieting should not be attempted. It is far more dangerous than previously thought, and the increase of eating disorders in boys (once thought to be solely the domain of girls) seems to indicate a dangerous trend of ineffective dieting among males. The achievement drive of gifted boys, coupled with their intensity and passionate sensitivity, can make them brutal dieters. Instead, a family refrigerator that is full of healthful, tasty, low-fat foods, along with a reduction in high fat meats, high fat snacks, and highly sweetened drinks, can have a positive effect on a child's weight and overall health.

In addition, gifted boys and adolescents also need accurate information about the use of steroids, body building nutrients, and stimulants, including accurate information about the dangers inherent in their use. Too many gifted boys are exposed to anti-drug programs that are laughable in their exaggerations, as well as patronizing in their style. It is unfortunate how much credibility is lost when authorities present drug information in this way. Gifted boys can read scientific studies and professional reviews about these topics, so they can see for themselves, from credible sources, how dangerous the use of these substances can be; however, teachers and parents need to guide boys to this material. One excellent resource is *The Adonis Complex: The Secret Crisis of Male Body Obsession* by Pope, Phillips and Olivardia (2000).

Finally, models of masculine attractiveness that encompass various body types, shapes, and sizes can be introduced through film and literature. Not all male movie stars are gorgeous; in fact, some are actually short, some are plain, and some are overweight.

Adults should talk with gifted boys about the ways in which charisma, intensity, and feeling project beauty onto the man exhibiting these characteristics. A large, bright boy who accepts himself can help make others comfortable with themselves. In modern society, we see overweight men who are quite highly respected—Luciano Pavarotti, Peter Ustinoff, Tom Arnold, Al Roker, just to name a few. In literature, there are many other positive examples of the large man—for instance St. Nicholas, the great detective Nero Wolf, and John Kennedy Toole's hilarious Ignatius Reilly. These are men whose weight is a symbol of prosperity, plenty, and humor, and who often use their size to protect the weak. Even the boy who is very fat can learn to carry himself with dignity and behave with generosity and kindness toward others. It is the intelligence of the large gifted boy that can allow him to create a positive new image for himself. Self-acceptance is the first step for these boys, but transcendence is the second step to actualizing oneself as a large, gifted male.

Nerds

Smart boys who are seen by their age peers as nerds typically exhibit idiosyncratic talent in one area, such as chess, fencing, poetry, or computer programming, or show talent in areas that are different from the societally-valued skills of verbal expression and social interaction. These boys may tend to be gifted in their capacity to reason abstractly, mathematically, spatially, visually, and/or mechanically. However, these smart boys are not as interested in or facile at social or language customs, or even social contact. It is these boys in particular who often prompt comments such as, "His social skills lag far behind his intellect."

Why is it that these boys seem so interpersonally unsophisticated when they are so smart intellectually? In part, it is because the rules for social interaction, politeness, clothing styles, etc. are far more ambiguous, diffuse, and even illogical compared to the symbol systems and logical operations to which they gravitate in their thinking. As one boy said, "Social customs are an archaic mosaic."

Nerds are the boys who may be likely to take everything literally, so that if you ask them "How are you?" they will actually proceed to tell you in detail. Or they may explain other things far more extensively than you care to hear, being unaware that your eyes glazed over after the first sentence. As one mother said, "If I ask him what time it is, he first has to tell me how to make a clock!"

There is another reason for these boys' interpersonal ineptitude. Often, their interests are so intense that their passionate curiosity overrides whatever judgment they do have. For example, the gifted boy may insist on knowing the weight of everyone in the elevator—even of strangers—because he wants to see if the combined weights are approaching the maximum allowable limit posted on the wall. He knows that it is generally considered rude to ask such questions of strangers, but "inquiring minds want to know!"

Even though many of these boys read extensively, they may also tend to be shy and to stumble with words when speaking publicly, often because they are so concerned with finding just the precisely intended word. Sometimes they are physically clumsy, too, seemingly unable to walk and talk at the same time. (Ironically, their capacity to *intellectually* "multi-task" is often formidable.) Feelings can easily overwhelm them, so they simply cordon them off. As one young self-identified "geek" put it, "I became 'Spock' [the character from the original Star Trek series]. There was no place for feelings in my life. Everything had to be logical."

For "nerds," it isn't so much their expression of feminine behaviors that makes them targets of teasing and ridicule. Rather, it is more the absence of sexuality in any of its aspects (sexual identity, gender identity, or sexual orientation). Nerds appear to be gender-neutral; the objects of their attention and fascination frequently are technology and genderless robotics. Alternatively, some boy nerds might be very interested in females, but awkward and clueless about how to engage girls' attention.

As a result, such a smart boy is often seen as someone who is different, weird, bookish, and intellectual, and so he gets the label of nerd, dork, or geek—terms that we will use interchangeably, even though some adolescents make distinctions between them.

School culture often fails to engage these boys because, since social abilities are so strongly emphasized there, it almost solely explores their areas of least capacity. In the process, their brilliance all too often goes unnoticed, or even if it doesn't, teachers often know little about how to draw it out. These boys frequently, then, develop a sense of being "invisible." And because their teachers fail to "see" them, nerds tend to perceive the teachers, in turn, as either blind or stupid or both. This is especially the case if the teacher demonstrates that he or she feels threatened by the unconventional nature of the nerds' thought processes, sense of humor, and/or behavior. As for parents, they often perceive these boys only as puzzling, in that they don't seem to be willing or able to listen to "common sense."

A subset of these "nerdy" boys—those who are oriented toward precise, logical or technical areas—may sometimes be misdiagnosed as suffering from Asperger's Disorder. The actual disorder is a variant of autism, but one in which a child's intellectual abilities remain intact (Neihart, 2001). Children with Asperger's Disorder are lacking in so-called "emotional intelligence," have an intense fascination with a special interest, are more fascinated with machines, statistics, and ideas than they are with other people, and typically engage in compulsive rituals such as counting or having to touch objects in a certain sequence. Nerdy boys may seem to exhibit these same characteristics in many social situations, but their behavior changes dramatically when they are in a situation with intellectual peers who share a common interest or aptitude (Amend, 2001). In Asperger's Disorder, one is not likely to see reciprocal interaction about a topic, even if both children have an interest in the same topic. By contrast, gifted youngsters will engage in very intense and reciprocal conversations and play if both boys share the same interest in, say, Pokemon, Harry Potter, chess, or computer games.

This brings us to another subset of young nerds—a group we might refer to as the "gaming nerds" or "gamers." Gamers usually are clustered in small groups in corners of the school's campus during lunchtime or at class recess, or they can be found staying up all night on the weekends at one another's homes, immersed in some fantasy or role-playing game such as *Dungeons and Dragons* or *Risk*. It is difficult to say which came first for these boys—the interest in gaming or the isolation from mainstream peer culture. However, the two clearly seem to reinforce each other. The games provide a structured, competitive, and impersonal forum in which to interact—all characteristics that appeal to these smart boys—and it provides them with a subculture which is, in its own way, supportive and pleasurable. In this milieu, they are accepted and respected, and they can enjoy the human-to-human interaction that may be all too lacking at home or at school.

On the other hand, such activity, if taken too far, can exacerbate these boys' estrangement from the larger society, particularly from girls since the popularity of these games is vastly greater among boys. It does this in at least three ways: (1) by fostering the illusion that the "real world" operates on a system of similarly clear-cut rules; (2) by physically separating them on a regular basis from their classmates who do not share or comprehend their interests; and (3) by fostering a compartmentalization of sorts as the boy now maintains multiple identities throughout his week—as mystical sorcerer at lunchtime, as commander of vast armies on the weekends, but still as a neglected loner during school hours or at home. It is not hard to see why, for many of these boys, their "real" identity is their least favorite.

The creative imagination and keen aptitude for shrewd strategic planning that these games require and nurture are valuable and should not be discouraged. But parents and teachers should also try to ensure that, for balance, these gamers have ample opportunities for warm, meaningful, "real world" interactions with people—across generations, across genders, and across interest and ability levels. Encouraging this balance will help these boys in their transition later into more realistic adult relationships as they mature and—usually—outgrow these games.

Another type of nerd is the boy with a knack for remembering great amounts of very detailed information—a knack that often is combined with an intense and very specific interest in just one subject. It could be the U.S. Civil War or bridges or trains or birds. Whatever the area of interest, this boy can tell you names, locations, dates, and details. Boys with such interests and talents are often quickly labeled "nerd" by agemates who do not share a similar level of passion for *any* subject, and who are intimidated or confused by its appearance in the gifted boy.

These various types of nerds all pose a dilemma for parents and teachers. Though their technological prowess, boundless imagination, and encyclopedic knowledge are all impressive and valuable, it is important to help boys learn some basic social courtesies—not just for facilitating a happier adulthood in the future, but also for easing their acceptance into the school cultures of today. Learning such graces can lessen their vulnerability to bullying, as well as boost their confidence in interacting with girls and others. These skills might include learning to speak in "sound bites" rather than lectures, learning to ask others questions about themselves, learning to listen and follow others' conversations, and learning civilities and pleasantries such as expressions of gratitude.

Teachers often express concern to us about the nerds in their classrooms. We point out to them that being a nerd is not nearly as great a problem for adults as it is for children, and that the primary task of the teacher is to help that child grow to adulthood with the least amount of scarring from other children's taunts, insults, and injuries. The implication, then, is for teachers to create a classroom climate that minimizes ridicule and a setting in which boys' intellectual talents are valued.

It also can be helpful for teachers to recognize that some nerdy boys come from nerdy parents. As James Webb (2000) says, we need to worry less about those nerds who come from the "nerd families"—in which both parents are nerds, the grandparents were nerds, and where there is a longstanding family tradition of "nerdism." Why? Because these nerds have role models for how nerdism can work for you—at least as an adult—where one can live in a world of ideas in which you don't need to fret about clothing or hairstyles and other peer issues. These nerds have a safe haven and sanctuary in their own homes.

We have had some parents come to us and ask us to transform their nerds into socially graceful people. While we believe in the need for courtesy and basic social skills, it is not necessary to change the personality of the nerd to simply make him more attractive to girls. When a parent says, "My son doesn't date," we often tell him or her, "No, he doesn't, and he quite possibly won't throughout high school, and maybe not in college either. He will probably become a highly skilled, highly paid engineer. And during his senior year of college, he might go to a Star Trek convention and meet a girl engineer who knows the genetic code of the Tribbles as well as he does. They may date for some years, and then they will marry. They will have little engineers for children. They may start an Internet-based company. And they will be rich and live happily ever after, because out of all the professional groups, engineers have the lowest divorce rate."

This is actually a fairly accurate rendering of the situation of many gifted nerds today. So we encourage parents of nerds to accept the nerd behaviors as expressions of their child's talents and gifts and of his own special uniqueness.

An odd social life in adolescence is not too high a price to pay for the kind of happy, stable lives that most grown-up nerds live. Therefore, the problem for these kids is often learning how to manage their parents' anxiety rather than changing the behaviors they have that are comfortable for them and harmful to nobody. Unhappy nerds who want social skills need their parents' help and emotional support, and perhaps professional guidance as well. However, nerdy kids who are content with their lives as nerds need to let their parents know that they are happy with the few friends they have and happy with their special or technical amusements. And parents who have a genuinely happy, nerdy and unusual child need to relax.

How can we help the young boy nerd survive the peer pressure toward mediocrity and fitting in? Fortunately, there are now successful adult role models we can point to. The last quarter of the 20th century has seen the apotheosis of the adult nerd in the likes of Bill Gates, founder and CEO of Microsoft; Steve Jobs and Steve Wozniac, creators of the Apple computer; and others in the information technology and dot-com industries, some of whom now proudly call themselves "technogeeks." Many of them are among the world's richest men. Their professional and financial success has made being a nerd less of a liability than in decades past. These former nerds have established their status, power, and dominance— all traditional masculine ideals. The ruthlessness, however, with which some of these men conduct their business and personal lives makes one wonder whether their sense of ethics and compassion was injured by their early years in school.

More immediately, we can honor this boy's talent by helping him identify and nurture it, while providing a balanced social environment. Boys who demonstrate a facility with modern technology, for example, can be recognized by their teachers and classmates as highly valued participants in today's world. They can become their teachers' or neighbors' assistants in technology or other special areas. They can help their classmates learn additional skills they want to know. Those boys who are not technology nerds, but who are intellectuals, can also become highly valued by participating in quiz bowls, spelling or geography bees, and writing contests that bring honor to their school and community. They are still "nerds," but the label carries with it a tone of respect, sometimes even awe.

The evolution of complexity and increased technology in our society will continue to help many grown-up nerds achieve positions of responsibility, with lifestyles full of opportunity and comfort. The danger rests in the perpetuation of old Boy Code attitudes and behaviors that do not leave room for respecting boys whose focus is on the new technological world, the information age, or a future world that can now only be imagined. By helping these men recognize their gifts as children, and by helping them honor and express those gifts, teachers and parents can increase the possibility that they will use their talents for the benefit of humankind rather than as vehicles for the expression of their rage against a society that has long teased, ridiculed, and excluded them.

For children, school is the primary socializing agency outside of the family. And to be unrecognized in school, yet to know inside that one is indeed brilliant, often disenfranchises these capable youths. If school seems irrelevant to them, why should they invest in it and, in turn, in the society that created schools? When we give these young people the message that we don't care about them— about what they need or what they want—we plant the seeds of alienation and apathy. Sometimes, they simply turn off, as described in Chapter 4 as the Bartleby Syndrome ("I prefer not to"). Unfortunately, this is a best-case scenario. Those who turn off and refuse to invest in school fail to discover their true value and shut down. But no one is so dangerous as someone who thinks he has nothing to lose. And so at the other extreme is the young man who acts out his anger and aggression against the institution that denies him. He is angry enough to harm others that he sees as causing his pain. This is the prototypical brilliant rebel who may show sociopathic-like behaviors and whose creation we might in fact be fostering under the current systems described in the previous chapter. These rebellious boys must be noticed, accepted by caring adults, and shown how to redirect their energies to positive areas.

Dealing with Bullies

All of these boys—sissies, nerds, and fat boys—have in common the fact that they are frequently victims of bullies. To deal with this, parents and school personnel must work fervently to "bully-proof" their schools and playgrounds—an action that should involve everyone including custodians, cafeteria workers, administrators, faculty and parents. In addition, we have devised a number of interventions based on sources such as *Bullies and Victims* (Freid & Freid, 1996) and *Breaking the Cycle of Violence* (Hazler, 1996). We suggest teaching smart boys one or more of the following coping skills and strategies.

1. Do not give the bully what he or she wants—an expected emotional reaction. The bully is seeking the pleasure of dominance and of seeing another in pain. The less emotionally reactive a child is to bullying, the more quickly the bully loses interest and stops bullying, because there is no payoff. A bullied boy needs to react with very plain language and a quiet, firm tone, with as little apparent emotion as possible. We are not saying that the boy should suppress his emotions forever, but just in the presence of the bully. Once in a safe environment, the boy should be encouraged to talk about his fear and anger. The support and encouragement you give him can be invaluable.

2. Learn nonverbal ways of communicating assertiveness. Squared shoulders, direct eye contact, and relaxed arms all indicate that a boy is neither interested in submitting nor aggressing, but is holding firm to his rights.

3. Seek allies. Renew old friendships and seek new friends. It is a child's isolation, both social and physical, that tips off the bully that it is okay to intimidate him. Bullies are less likely to attack a child who is with a group of friends.

4. Do something unexpected when confronted by a bully. Speak in a loud voice to other people to draw attention to the situation, call out to a person at a distance and engage them in a conversation while ignoring the bully, or change the topic suddenly.

5. Make clear observations about what is happening in the present situation. This can be very effective in defusing, or at least confusing, the bully. For example, say in a puzzled tone, "You've pushed me out of line three times, and I've gotten back in line. I'm wondering if you are getting what you want by acting this way," or "You act like you want me to cry. Why would you want that?"

6. Ask for adult intervention when appropriate, and learn when it is appropriate to ask for adult help. If boys ask for help with every incident, they don't learn to be self-sufficient. If they never ask, they may not get the help they need and will suffer far too long. So once a boy asks for help, an adult needs to help him carefully assess when and how the adult should intervene.

Surviving into Adulthood—and into Eminence

We have read the biographies and autobiographies of eminent men and have found it rather surprising that most of these men describe childhoods full of rejection, bullying, and loneliness. Curious about this, we began to examine the lives of eminent men more closely to see if there was indeed a relationship between this kind of unhappy childhood and later eminence. There does seem to be a clear link between instability in childhood—particularly a loss of their father—and adult creativity in men (Kerr & Chopp, 2000). There are many examples of boys whose mothers nurtured their creativity while coping with ill, insane, or absent fathers. A great many of the geniuses of the 20th century—Sigmund Freud, Frank Lloyd Wright, Pablo Picasso, Charlie Chaplin, among others—had this kind of childhood. Although not all of these creative people were sissies, they were different or nerdy as children and were by no means typically masculine.

In addition, there are a notable number of creatively gifted men who were gay: Oscar Wilde, the playwright; Nijinski, the great dancer; and international pop music star Elton John, among others, suffered in adolescence as well as adulthood because they were exposed as homosexuals.

Finally, being a techno-nerd as a child seems to be very predictive of creativity and productivity in science, engineering, and technology as an adult. The biographies of Richard Feynman, Isaac Asimov, Bill Gates, Steve Wozniak, and Stephen Hawking are all illustrative of this.

Perhaps one of the best explanations of the role of nonconformity in gifted boys' lives comes from Sheldon (1999), who examines psychoanalyst Otto Rank's theory that exceptional creativity occurs only when individuals have succeeded in differentiating themselves from the crowd. He suggests that creatively productive individuals go through three stages of personality development. In the first stage, the conformist stage, the person takes his cues from those around him. In the second stage, the person breaks free of the norms, but is unhappy because he is in conflict. In the third stage, a person emerges who has gone through the other two stages to emerge with a powerful, creative voice of his own.

How do bullied and rejected boys break through their pain to become creative people? Eminent people often speak of one teacher or mentor who cared and who showed them the value of their own work and aspirations. In addition, creative people usually report that they looked for and found an environment in which they felt safe, an environment in which there were other nonconformists like themselves. Computer camps, special schools for the arts, and student organizations aimed at overcoming discrimination against gays or overweight people are all examples of safe havens for gifted young people who have been rejected. These environments provide friends with similar interests who are not concerned with the Boy Code or other stereotyped matters.

Engaging in social action and creative expression in opposition to discrimination or other social causes can be tremendously empowering and may offer the opportunity needed to transcend the pain of being different. The support of like-minded people working together for change can build resilience in a boy who has been beaten down by the cruelty of his peers.

It seems clear that if a gifted boy who is a sissy, a fat boy, or a nerd can survive childhood and adolescence without too much trauma, he has a good chance of applying his skills in nonconformity to the service of creativity and knowledge. In addition, being an outsider as a child forever endows these children with an understanding of the marginalized and rejected people of this world, and with good guidance, the gifted sissy, nerd, or fat boy may become a future champion of the rights of others who are left behind.

What can we do to help smart boys who are also sissies, fat, nerds, gays, physically challenged, or different in some other way that exacerbates an already overdeveloped feeling of isolation and alienation? The answer is fairly simple and direct. We need to include them—authentically—not just make them feel as if they are valued. We, ourselves, need to understand and help them understand the enormous contributions to our world that have been made by brilliant men who were also different from the masculine stereotype. We need to be their friends, their advocates, and their benevolent mentors. And we need to create learning environments that acknowledge and celebrate differences and diversity and that encourage self-knowledge and self-actualization.

Key Points:

1. Feminine boys, obese boys, and nerdy gifted boys have in common that they are the targets of bullying and rejection by other children.

2. Sissies may be boys who are simply feminine in behavior or who may later be gay men. Their inability to conform to masculine roles puts them at risk for being treated cruelly and even violently. Support groups are critical to their development.

3. Obese boys need help living active, healthy lives while accepting their body type. Models exist of large, gifted men that these boys can emulate.
4. Nerds, geeks, and dorks are gifted boys with special intellectual talents and few social or athletic skills. They will often do well if they have just one or two friends and if they are supported in their highly specialized interests.
5. Sissies, fat boys, and nerds all need strategies for dealing with bullies that defuse tension and deflect the bully's attention.

References

Amend, E. R. (2001). Misdiagnosis of Asperger's Disorder in gifted youth. *Gifted Education Press Quarterly*, 15 (2), 13-14.

Anderson, J. (2001). Number crunching, *Respect*, Issue 5 (Spring 2001), p.18. Washington, DC: GLSEN.

Bem, S. L. (1995). Dismantling gender polarization and compulsory heterosexuality: Should we turn the volume down or up? *Journal of Sex Research*, 32 (4), 329-334.

Bem, S. L. (1993). *The lenses of gender: Transforming the debate on sexual inequality*. New Haven: Yale University Press.

Fried, S. & Fried, P. (1996). *Bullies & victims: Helping your child survive the schoolyard battlefield*. New York: M. Evans and Co.

Friedrichs, T. (1997). Understanding the educational needs of gifted gay and bisexual males. *Counseling and Guidance*, 6 (3), 3, 8.

Gay, Lesbian, Straight Education Network (2000). *The GLSEN lunchbox: A comprehensive training program for ending anti-gay bias in schools*. Washington, DC: GLSEN.

Gay, Lesbian, Straight Education Network (1999). *Respect: Making schools safe for all kids*. Washington, DC: GLSEN.

Goertzel, V. & Goertzel, M. G. (1962). *Cradles of eminence.* Boston: Little, Brown.

Hazler, R. J. (1996). *Breaking the cycle of violence: Interventions for bullying and victimization.* Washington, DC: Accelerated Development.

Kerr, B. A. & Chopp, C. (1999). Families and creativity. In M. A. Runco & S. R. Pritzker (Eds.), *Encyclopedia of creativity* (pp. 709-715). San Diego: Academic Press.

Krasnegor, N. A., Grave, G. D., & Kretchmer, N. (1988). *Childhood obesity: A biobehavioral perspective.* Caldwell, NJ: Telford Press.

Miller, A. (1996). *The drama of the gifted child: The search for the true self.* Translated from German by Ruth Ward. New York: Basic Books.

Neihart, M. (2001). Drawing the line: The adjustment and maladjustment of gifted children. *TEMPO*, 21 (1), 10-16.

Peterson, J. & Rischar, H. (2000). Gifted and gay: A study of the adolescent experience. *Gifted Child Quarterly*, 44 (4), 231-246.

Pope, H. G., Phillips, K. A., & Olivardia, R. (2000). *The Adonis complex: The secret crisis of male body obsession.* New York: Free Press.

Sheldon, K. M. (1999). Conformity. In M. A. Runco & S. R. Pritzker (Eds.), *Encyclopedia of creativity* (pp. 341-346). San Diego: Academic Press.

Tolan, S. S. S. (1997). Sex and the highly gifted adolescent. *Counseling and Guidance*, 6 (3), 2, 5, 8.

Webb, J. T. (2001). Mis-diagnosis and dual diagnosis of gifted children: Gifted and LD, ADHD, OCD, Oppositional Defiant Disorder. *Gifted Education Press Quarterly,* 15 (1), 9-13.

Webb, J. T. (2000). *Do gifted children really have special needs?* (Video). Scottsdale, AZ: Gifted Psychology Press.

10

Gifted Minority Boys

There is much theory and little research to help us understand the needs of gifted boys who are American Indian, African American, Asian American, Hispanic, or from another minority group. And unfortunately, most of the research that is available centers around how to find and identify gifted minority students through testing, rather than focusing on how to help these children achieve their potential.

The research on testing deals with such things as creating new norms for intelligence tests by including minority students in the groups used to develop the tests, or by making the existing tests more useable by developing new techniques for interpreting the results. And some researchers have simply created entirely new methods of identification. However, the sad fact is that the gifted potential of many of our minority children has often been obscured both by the physical and psychological effects of poverty and by the inferior schooling available to poor students that is still so often the situation for minority families. No amount of re-configuring of tests can change the social conditions that prevent giftedness and talent from emerging.

In our work, we have tried to downplay issues of testing and identification; instead we have attempted to use definitions of giftedness that are more inclusive. It is our hope that in this way, children with great potential for achievement in any talent area will not be missed when selections are made for gifted programs and guidance. This means training teachers of minority students to identify those who have "that special spark," searching for students who have displayed leadership in their schools and neighborhoods, and asking students to identify their peers who have the greatest potential for excellence.

Through our counseling workshops and special projects, we have had the opportunity to meet and work with talented boys from many ethnic backgrounds—African American young men from inner-city St. Louis, Chicago, and Kansas City; American Indian young men from Pima, Navajo, and Apache tribes in Arizona; and Hispanic young men from migrant families and from urban Arizona. Some of these children experienced poverty and circumstances of deprivation; others did not.

One of the most striking things about these groups of boys is their absolute refusal to live according to white, middle-class stereotypes or expectations. As a result, we have had to give up our own preconceived notions about everything from gangs to girlfriends. For example, one Hispanic/Pima gifted boy, Luis, came to our career development workshop for talented at-risk boys and told us about his experience of being in a gang. Luis was a short, large-eyed boy with a thick shock of black hair, dressed in neat jeans and a white t-shirt. He told us that he had joined a gang because his brothers were members and because they had said that the gang would take care of him. So far, that had been true for Luis.

Luis' father was not a part of his life at all, and his mother was not home much because she worked long hours at a casino. Luis said, though, that he could go to his "homey's" mom's house and eat good food. He also had a "little homey brother," a younger gang member who admired him a lot and who liked to iron his clothes and keep his things neat! Luis knew some guys who did crystal meth, but he did not, because, as he said, "I don't want to mess up my head and be a slave all my life." Luis was doing very well in science and math, and he believed that college was a real possibility if he could find a scholarship. Imagine our surprise at our own unavoidable conclusion: that the gang, so far, had been a positive influence in Luis' life! Of course, we knew how quickly that could change, and we let him know the dangers of assuming that gang membership was safe. However, what we learned from that experience was that gifted boys will be resourceful with whatever is given to them, and the gang was the only support system that this boy had been given.

Another example of our changed expectations was our initial belief, based on meeting a number of pregnant, talented at-risk girls, that the boys in their lives were primarily interested in sexual conquest. We quickly learned that these boys were more thoughtful and appreciative of girls. Many of our talented at-risk boys spoke proudly of their girlfriends and their girlfriends' accomplishments. One young man, Tomas, told us that he was going to put off college for two years and work with his uncle repairing air conditioners. When the counselor asked him why he was making that decision, he said that his girlfriend had straight A's and lots of potential, but not much money to go to the university. He wanted to help her out financially so that she would have a chance to attend college.

We were also naïve about the living conditions faced by many of our gifted minority boys who lived in the inner city. We knew that life there was difficult, often frightening, and sometimes dangerous. But only when we read the statements of the gifted African American boys in our *Something to Prove* study (Kerr & Colangelo, 1994) did we understand how very desperate the situation was for many of these young men. When we asked the boys, "What is your greatest accomplishment?" we would never have guessed the responses most of them gave—"I survived," or "I am still alive."

The first author and her colleague, Nicholas Colangelo, did a long-term study of the minority students who scored in the 95th percentile and above on the American College Testing Assessment Program (Kerr, Colangelo, Maxey, & Christensen, 1992; Kerr & Colangelo, 1994). These students had received among the highest scores that year on their college admissions tests and had defied the stereotype that, as minority students, they could not score well on standardized tests. We found that these extraordinary boys were indeed mostly urban, mostly poor students. However, they were distinguished from other boys in their settings who had not done as well by having had at least one teacher or one mentor who believed in them, by having attended a parochial school or a special school or program for gifted students, and by having a profound belief that they had "something to prove." Our findings certainly support the value of a significant adult, a challenging education program, and high self-esteem.

Minority gifted boys are also faced, as are most adolescents, with the task of defining their own identities. Another erroneous notion we had about these boys was the idea that their identity is primarily based upon their skin color. As Hebert (2000) pointed out in his study of minority boys, racial and ethnic identity seems less important to them than are other identities—their family, their membership in youth groups, their church, their community. Racial and ethnic identities seem to be the primary concerns of scholars who study young people of color, but not of the young people themselves. According to Heath and McLaughlin (1993), only later, when such individuals are in college or at work, will their race become an issue of personal identity. In the meantime, it seems that young gifted boys of color are eagerly creating an identity based on their accomplishments, their memberships, and their deeply held values. And the more guidance and mentoring they receive from significant adults, the more likely they are to have a strong sense of self.

Gifted African American Boys

The poverty of the inner cities and all of the related problems that it creates affect many gifted African American boys and men (Staples, 1988). Other issues, such as low expectations of academic performance from teachers and other significant adults, and peer pressure from other African American students to not be too smart, often greatly discourage academic achievement.

Poverty can block all but the most fortunate African American gifted boys from the educations they deserve. Poorly funded schools of the inner city often struggle to provide special programming for gifted students. This is not to imply that all African American children are to be found in poverty, but rather simply to recognize the high proportion that are in dire economic circumstances.

In addition to these obstacles, in schools where counseling and guidance are considered unaffordable luxuries, it is unlikely that the boys will be made aware of such things as the availability of scholarships or of assistance with vocational school or college planning. And while the road to success for many talented but poor African Americans has in recent decades been through the armed services, which provide training and help pay for college, this option is not for everybody. Gifted boys need to be aware of all of their options.

Peer pressure to underachieve haunts many African American gifted boys. In a society still struggling against racism, African American boys who achieve high grades in school often find their peers accusing them of "going over to the white side" or collaborating with white people in putting down black people—especially when the teachers and administrators are white and the students are people of color. Many gifted African American young men have told us of the strong peer pressure to not do well academically, and that if they did get high grades, they were accused of "acting white." Gifted African American boys need to believe that academic achievement is good for them personally, good for their families, and good for their communities. It takes courage for bright African American boys to raise their hands in class, score a 100 on a test, and apply for college scholarships. And if they do achieve, they find themselves in a situation in which their peers will not accept their achievement and white people will not accept their blackness (Helms, 1990). Thus they are pressured into "racelessness"—a surrendering of any racial identity.

In addition, a profound misunderstanding of the meaning of achievement test scores among most Americans creates considerable resentment against blacks when they are admitted to prestigious programs with lower achievement test scores than whites. One purpose of achievement tests is to predict future achievement. When used for this purpose, achievement test scores typically under-predict black achievement—that is, lower scores predict the same level of achievement as higher scores for whites (Cleary,

Humphreys, Kendrick, & Wesman, 1976). For example, on a particular Reading Comprehension English achievement test, an African American student who scores in the 85th percentile is likely to achieve an A in Freshman English, whereas a white student might need to score in the 95th percentile in order to reliably predict an A in Freshman English. This misunderstanding of differential prediction curves—that lower achievement test scores predict higher grades for certain groups of students, in this case black students—has led to much controversy, and once again, it is African American gifted students who are hurt the most, because it is perceived that they are getting a "free ride."

Being identified as gifted can have a powerful effect on African American boys, according to Ford and Harris (1992). Boys who were so identified by these two researchers tended to be more optimistic about their educations and about their possibilities for achievement. They were less affected by what Ford and Harris call the "poverty of the spirit," which is caused by a paradox that African Americans often observe—that even though they are told that hard work pays off, sometimes, no matter how hard they work, they are not rewarded. This is a circumstance depicted frequently in African American literature—that of the black male who works hard and follows the rules, but ends up a victim of racism anyway. The archetypal character is Bigger, in Richard Wright's *Native Son*, whose conscientiousness could not overcome the racism of his community.

Gifted African American boys who succeed are usually not those who become "raceless," but rather those who take advantage of the strengths of the African American community (Kerr & Colangelo, 1994; Ford & Harris, 1992). There is clear evidence that African American parents of gifted children have high expectations of them (Ford, 1993; Van Tassel-Baska, 1984). Fortunately, the African American family is often an extended one composed of several households in which there are great resources for emotional support (Nobles, 1997). Sudarkarsa (1997) called these families "some of the most flexible, adaptive, and inclusive kinship institutions in America." Therefore, those gifted boys who rely upon their extended families for emotional support and mentoring are likely to be buffered from the stresses of poverty or of inner-city life.

African American churches are also a great source of strength and spiritual nourishment for gifted young black men. One gifted young man we know was involved in his church choir to the extent that he developed his *basso profundo* voice into a professional operatic bass. Later, he not only was able to get major singing roles in college operas, but also was invited to join a professional *a cappella* group that made frequent recordings and concert tours.

Finally, in recent years, an increasing interest among African American adult men in the lives of young boys has led to a variety of mentoring organizations and rites-of-passage ceremonies based on African-centered spirituality (Franklin, Franklin, & Toussaint, 2000). In these ceremonies, young men are escorted in a commencement-like procession, heralded by African drums and surrounded by all of their families and friends. They are introduced to the community and given words of wisdom based on African proverbs. These powerful rituals introduce boys to the privileges and responsibilities of adulthood and help them define their identities as men.

What does giftedness mean to African American men? An African American professor of counseling had this to say about his own giftedness:

> *I don't see myself as talented or gifted. When there's work to be done, you persevere and you pay the price and sometimes other things have to be reprioritized.*
>
> *I've been blessed with some very good teachers, mentors, and friends. My uncle, for instance, taught me to never get so full of myself that I start thinking someone's supposed to give me something. Or that I am to get something without earning it. Work, provide for your family. That's what's important.*
>
> *The bottom line of my work is about trying to help in some way. The operative question is: "What have you done for the cause today?" You're the only one who really knows whether or not you have done your share that day.*

This quote is illustrative of several ways in which African American men see their talents. First, there is a reluctance to label oneself gifted, for many reasons, including separating oneself out from one's brothers and sisters. Second, there is the belief that giftedness lies in one's connection to the community and in one's actions on behalf of that community. Finally, there is the belief that giftedness is an interaction of the individual with all of those who have helped, supported, and blessed the young man with their presence. This way of seeing giftedness may be helpful to educators who are trying to understand the achievement, or underachievement, of African American boys. (A moving portrayal of some of these dynamics at work can be found in the major film *Finding Forrester*.)

Asian American Gifted Boys

Asian American gifted boys and men come from many countries, with diverse cultures and languages. Asian Americans are frequently confused with Asian international students, and all Asians are often lumped together in the same category. A Japanese American student may be expected by white students and teachers to have much in common with a recent arrival from Cambodia, when all they may share are some Asiatic physical features. Asian Americans may be Muslims from Malaysia, Buddhists from Thailand, Shintos from Japan, Christians from Taiwan, or any of a dizzying combination of religions and countries. Or they may be the fifth generation descendants of Chinese railroad workers in America, third generation descendants of Japanese Americans who were interned during World War II, or newly arrived Hmong people from the hills of Cambodia.

Asian American gifted boys, therefore, may be much more different from each other than they are alike. However, there are some shared features that may be important for understanding them. A strong emphasis on family loyalty and respect for one's elders is a feature of most of these cultures—boys are expected to be loyal and obedient sons who maintain the family's traditions. A belief in the importance of honor means that Asian American gifted boys may be particularly sensitive to issues of "saving face"— that is, avoiding humiliation of any kind. Subjecting another to humiliation is considered despicable. In addition, cooperation for the good of the family and of the community is prized above individual competition; therefore, many gifted Asian American boys are high achievers, not for themselves, but for their families. Individual pride in accomplishment is often frowned upon.

These simple generalizations, however, can lead to harmful stereotypes when carried too far. Of greatest concern to educators is the increasing stereotype of Asian American students as overachieving, uncreative, and obsessed with math and science. In our 1994 ACT studies of the career interest areas of high-scoring students, we found Asian American students to be as interested in arts and humanities as they were in math and science. In addition, there is no evidence that the high academic achievement of this population is linked to a lack of creativity. This erroneous stereotyping may affect the choices and the opportunities for Asian American gifted boys in insidious ways. For example, because it is expected that someone else will let them in to engineering or medical school, the admissions committee of other graduate programs may decide against them (Kerr & Colangelo, 1994).

The surprising thing about the gifted Asian American boys in the ACT study (Kerr & Colangelo, 1994) was that they were attending the least prestigious group of colleges of any of the ethnic minority groups. Apparently, they either were not seeking or were not being offered scholarships to the high-status colleges. Although it was not clear from our study which of these was the case, we became concerned that there might be a new wave of increased racial discrimination toward Asian Americans. More studies are needed.

For young boys who are newly arrived from Asia, language barriers are great. They often are frustrated by their inability to show their competencies, and they are very careful not to make mistakes. But those gifted Asian American boys who rely upon their family strengths and their rich cultural heritage often become extraordinary achievers. If they are encouraged to assert their right to be considered fairly for gifted identification, for admission to

special programs, for admission to the best colleges, and for scholarships, they can get the high level of education and training that
they deserve.

Hispanic Gifted Boys

The Hispanic population, made up of people of Mexican,
Central American, Cuban, Puerto Rican, and South American descent,
is the fastest growing minority group in America and is soon to
become the largest (U.S. Census, 2001). Like most of the ethnic
groups described here, Hispanics are extraordinarily diverse when
considered collectively. However, despite the diversity of subcultures
making up this population, they also often have experienced shared
discrimination on the basis of skin color and, often, surname.

Hispanic gifted boys frequently come from strongly traditional, patriarchal families that encourage traditional gender roles. The
model of machismo insists that men be dominant, that they compete with other men, and that they prove their manhood through
feats of strength and courage. The machismo ethic is nearly impossible for the gifted boy to live up to. Since manhood cannot be
demonstrated to his peers through feats of intellect, the Hispanic
gifted boy risks "not being a man" unless he also demonstrates his
machismo in other ways as well.

Hispanic gifted boys may also be reluctant to take on the role
of being dominant over girls and women. In their home, their mother may have been the powerful one, even though the father was
allowed and even encouraged to *appear* as the dominant one in the
family. These boys also are well aware of mainstream society and
the changes there in women's roles, and they may feel uncomfort-
ably torn between the new and the old traditions. Most of the
Hispanic gifted boys we have counseled in our laboratory have
been gentle and loving toward their mothers, sisters, and girlfriends, and they believe that their behavior is what is true to their
tradition—despite the fact that they may be discouraged by their
peers from showing their gentle side.

One 14-year-old boy told us that his family had lived in Arizona for seven generations and had owned vineyards and ranches. His grandmother was his most admired person, because she had run the family business for many years after being widowed and was prominent in her community as a leader. He respected women's leadership potential and resented the disrespectful behavior of some of his friends toward girls.

Finally, Hispanic children are expected to value family above all else, and indeed, our studies (Kerr & Kurpius, 1998) of gifted young men in our Arizona laboratory bear this out: family security is named as their highest ranked value. While this means that some gifted young men have the support of a loving family, it can also mean that their leaving to go away to college might be interpreted as betraying their relatives or families. Hispanic gifted men will sometimes give up scholarships rather than move far away from home.

In addition, we have found that many of these young men feel a strong duty to support their families financially, particularly their younger brothers and sisters. They see the pursuit of their own individual goals as selfish. We suggest that gifted young Hispanic men may need help balancing their love for their families with their desires to achieve and to fulfill their intellectual potential.

One of the greatest difficulties faced by Hispanic gifted boys has to do with language. In many Western states, there is great prejudice against people who speak only Spanish, and support for laws against bilingual education and bilingualism in the public arena is prevalent. Like other non-English speakers, Hispanic boys who do not speak English must suffer through two or three years of school in which their gifts are masked while they learn English. We have also heard too many stories of boys with Spanish accents being discouraged from college preparatory programs in high school because it is simply expected that they will attend vocational school.

Fortunately, in areas where there are many Spanish-speaking children, gifted identification procedures are being developed that do not rely entirely upon language. Barkan and Bernal (1991) have shown how gifted Hispanic American children can be identified and guided into academic programs that emphasize their strengths rather than their weaknesses.

Many of the Hispanic boys with whom we have worked come from families that have braved much to provide for a life in this country. Their fathers and mothers often gave up homes and extended families, paid enormous sums to be able to move, and in some cases walked across miles of desert to find the life and education they wanted for their children. Their traditions of courage and sacrifice are alive in the minds of many Hispanic gifted boys.

For example, this Hispanic professor tells his story of success based on education:

> *Both my parents were from Mexico and they both came to the conclusion that education was "the way." That education would provide us with the wherewithal to succeed. My father would have been happy with whatever profession we got into—it didn't matter. Mother is unusual in that she came here and even she went back to school here.*
>
> *We were from the south side of El Paso, and lots of people have asked us—and I have wondered myself—what it was about our family that produced all of us with advanced degrees and all of us with jobs working with people. Well, the question in my family was not "Are you going to school?" but "What are you going to study?" My parents would do anything possible to ensure a good education for us. My mother enrolled us in summer reading programs; they took us to symphonies, and introduced us to many other kinds of art and music. I played sax, clarinet, and piano in band, and I played in the orchestra, as well.*
>
> *On my mother's side of the family, education had always been highly valued. The word "education" in Spanish doesn't have the same meaning as it does in English. "Educácion" is more broad based—not just school learning, but other things, too, such as appreciation of people, social conduct, etc.—a comprehensive concept. My brother was the*

first one who went to school, so he provided a lot of feedback and support to us. He also paved the way later for additional degrees. But my father would say to me, "When are you going to finish school? Mijo, when are you going to finish school?" He never understood what counseling psychology, my chosen career, was. But I knew that he and my mother were always proud of me.

My older brother was also involved in Latino causes and he got all of us involved. In the mainstream, the concept of responsibility means individual responsibility, but in my family and culture it means collective and social responsibility. That is what responsibility still means to me today—responsibility for all.

This quote illustrates well how Hispanic men view their giftedness. It is clear that giftedness, the capacity for "educácion," is the ability to learn not just facts, but ways of living well together. Giftedness is seen from the point of view of collective achievement. Also, an entire family is part of the giftedness of the child; it is expected that not just parents, but brothers and sisters and others mentor the growing talent in a child. Finally, there is a strong element of responsibility—being responsible for the development of one's gifts for the good of all.

American Indian Gifted Boys

Although African Americans and Hispanics receive short shrift from our society in schools and in the workplace, the most neglected minority in the United States is probably the American Indians. Many American Indians live in Third World conditions. One of the Navajo boys that we counseled in our program for gifted minority boys lived in a hogan without running water or electricity. The nearest hospital was over 100 miles away. To get to school, this Navajo boy walked several miles, stood waiting for a bus at 6 a.m., rode for two hours over bad roads, and did the same on the return, doing his homework on the bus and later at home by flashlight. He had been approached by gang members several times and had a brother whose gang had been caught burglarizing cars in a tourist parking lot. Nevertheless, his parents wanted him to go to college, and they borrowed a car to drive him nine hours to our campus for a special Saturday program, and then sat in the car all day waiting for him.

One of the reasons that it is so difficult to find information about gifted American Indian boys is that, as a minority, these First Nations peoples are an extremely diverse lot. American Indian groups span the length of the Americas and belong to hundreds of distinct cultural and language groupings. So even if one understands the traditions and concerns of one tribe, it does not follow that one understands American Indians in general. For instance, one tribe may have always owned its own land and be proudly independent today, another may have been forced to relocate far from its original home, and yet another may live in conditions of great poverty on the same land that once provided all its needs.

The cultures of the different groups vary greatly as well. One culture may honor women and girls and their contributions to society, while another may minimize their power, and still another may be in transition. Interestingly, even those cultures—such as the Navajo and the Apache—that have maintained their traditions for bringing girls into womanhood, have lost many of their traditions for bringing boys into manhood, largely because those rituals often involved raiding or hunting—activities that are now illegal or otherwise impossible.

Despite all these differences, there are some underlying themes and beliefs that connect all American Indian cultures (Herring, 1992). Most American Indians value and believe in a harmonious universe in which every object and being has a sacred life, that humans are simply one part of nature and not superior to it, that nature is sacred, that each individual has rights and dignity, and that leadership is based on earned respect. These beliefs affect bright American Indian boys in a number of ways.

First of all, these boys may be reluctant to show their intellectual abilities because of a strong wish not to stand out. This desire to not stand out is not just an individual preference, it is a cultural imperative. American Indian cultures are usually extremely communal, and special focus on any one individual is not just in bad taste, it is considered wrong.

Furthermore, gifted American Indian boys often feel so intensely rooted in their respective communities that any educational program that threatens to break their ties to home may be rejected. For many of these boys, their religion and traditions revolve around specific places. Often, even the name of their tribe refers to a sacred place—"the people of the river," for example, or "the people of the mountain." Leaving the community would mean leaving behind not only one's religion and sense of belonging, but also one's sacred place, because one cannot bring one's beloved and sacred natural places along.

We found that some of the American Indian boys who had opportunities for scholarships to prestigious schools did not wish to take advantage of them (Kerr & Colangelo, 1994). It may be important to help gifted young American Indian men find ways of keeping their ties to their homes without forgoing valuable educational opportunities elsewhere. Such ways could include honors programs at nearby universities or college programs that understand and support the wishes of gifted American Indian men to spend more time at their homes.

In addition, gifted American Indian boys usually do not wish to be as competitive or aggressive as their non-Indian counterparts, either inside or outside of class. Their cultures usually stress cooperation and harmony, and gifted American Indian boys will therefore usually respond better to techniques and classroom strategies that emphasize those same qualities.

The attainment of "balance" is also an important goal to many American Indian boys—balance between self and nature, body and spirit, masculine and feminine, and inward and outward. To the degree that programs for the development of these bright boys' talents allow for a search for balance, they will be successful.

We have also learned that the reservation is a very different world from that of mainstream America, and that our usual occupational stereotypes do not hold up there (Kerr & Kurpius, 1998). On the reservation, a social worker might be seen as a "non-helper," because so often, social workers have taken Indian children away from their families. (During the boarding school era, social workers persuaded or coerced families to send their children away to schools where they could be "assimilated.") On the other hand, an accountant might be seen as a "helper," because he might be able to help everyone figure out their tax forms so that they don't get in trouble with the government. And the role of the physician or mortician might be viewed with horror by certain groups such as the Navajo, who do not like contact with dead bodies. Therefore, it is necessary when counseling or teaching gifted American Indian boys to find out the unique meaning and reasons behind each educational and career goal that they may have.

Finally, most American Indian traditions have, or once had, special rites of passage into manhood for young men. The vision quest ceremony and the sweat lodge ceremony were central to young men's development. In many cases, these ceremonies were outlawed by white missionaries or the U.S. government, or they were lost or forgotten, as tribal elders were lost to disease or despair. There is a strong movement among First Nations people today to strengthen or revive these important symbolic ceremonies for young men. These rituals help build identity and pride, as well as inform the world that the boy has now become a man and is to be treated as a man. A gifted young man may be intrigued both intellectually and spiritually by investigating the ceremonies of his own people and by participating in their revival.

Guiding Gifted Boys of Color

Thomas Hebert's study (2000) provides several implications for the guidance of gifted minority boys and men. First and most important, he says, gifted minority men need a strong sense of self. The first author and Nick Colangelo (1994) found, also, that the gifted minority men who were happiest in college were those who had the strongest ethnic identities, rather than those who were "raceless." This does not mean that gifted boys of color must interpret all of their experience in terms of race—certainly Hebert's successful boys did not—but that they do need to be comfortable with their race, as well as tolerant of other groups. One of Hebert's most significant findings was the importance of multicultural awareness to these boys' success—these were boys who appreciated differences among people.

Second, these young men need help building resilience through the use of support systems and through self-care. Teachers have helped gifted minority men by providing them with models of resilience in biographies and in their own stories that they share. Parents can help their boys by providing the support system of the extended family or by creating an extended family from friends and teachers. Self-care means helping gifted boys of color learn to defend themselves against the stressors of growing up in a racist society and, in many cases, against the stressors of poverty. A healthy lifestyle and the capacity to resist substance abuse and violence is necessary to the development of the gifts of boys of color who are growing up in poor neighborhoods.

Third, gifted minority boys need mentors who will help them find their way into their colleges, their majors, and their professions. Mentors may constitute the crucial difference between success and failure in the young man's chosen career. Because men and women of color in the professions are sometimes hard to find (and are often overwhelmed by responsibilities), gifted minority boys may need the assistance of a teacher or other adult to help find and encourage the mentoring relationship. The Internet is a wonderful source of mentors for minority boys, and local college and university faculty may include people who would be happy to mentor a bright boy of great promise.

Conclusion

Even though minority groups are very diverse in their composition and in their life situations, some generalizations can be made. Minority gifted males are often under-identified and under-served. Each group of boys—African American, Asian American,

Hispanic, and American Indian—has unique issues and concerns. In addition, each group has its own conceptions of giftedness and of the meaning and purposes of education. Those gifted minority boys who are resilient, who have support systems, who have mentors, and who have a firm identity and belief in self are those most likely not only to survive a difficult youth, but to attain positions of leadership and high achievement.

Key Points:

1. Gifted minority boys may live in urban areas where they face issues of poverty, violence, and poor schools.

2. African American boys in urban settings often claim that their greatest accomplishment is their survival. Their African American families, communities, and churches can help provide the support that these boys need to achieve their goals.

3. Asian American gifted boys are often discriminated against in education because of stereotypes that they are overachieving, math/science-oriented, and not creative. In actuality, they are as interested in arts and humanities as they are in math and science, and are as creative as any other gifted boys. Their achievement motivation is often rooted in their concern for family and honor.

4. Hispanic gifted boys may suffer the masking of their talents by language barriers. They may struggle with traditional male roles that often conflict with their own intellectual and personal values. There is a stronger prejudice against Spanish speech and accents than most other languages—to the extent that in some Southwestern states bilingual education is under attack, and English-only laws have occasionally won support.

5. American Indian gifted boys' lives and identities are strongly rooted in their communities and traditions. Educational options that threaten their connection to the land and to the people they love, or that threaten their sense of harmony and balance, may be rejected.

References

Barkan, J. H. & Bernal, E. M. (1991). Gifted education for bilingual and limited English proficient students. *Gifted Child Quarterly*, 35, 144 -147.

Cleary, T. A., Humphreys, L. G., Kendrick, S. A., & Wesman, A. (1975). Educational uses of tests with disadvantaged students. *American Psychologist*, 30 (1), 15-41.

Ford, D. Y. (1993). Black students' achievement orientation as a function of perceived family achievement orientation and demographic variables. *Journal of Negro Education*, 62 (1), 47-66.

Ford, D. Y. & Harris, J. J. (1992). The American achievement ideology and achievement differentials among preadolescent gifted and nongifted African American males and females. *Journal of Negro Education*, 61 (1), 45-64.

Franklin, B., Franklin, N., & Toussaint, P. (2000). *Boys into men: Raising our African American teenage sons.* New York: Dutton/Penguin Books.

Heath, S. B. & McLaughlin, M. W. (1993). *Identity and inner-city youth: Beyond ethnicity and gender.* New York: Teachers College Press.

Hebert, T. (2000). Defining belief in self: Intelligent young men in an urban high school. *Gifted Child Quarterly*, 44 (2), 91-114.

Helms, J. E. (Ed.). (1994). *Black and white racial identity: Theory, research, and practice.* Westport, CT: Greenwood Press.

Herring, R. D. (1990). Understanding Native American values: Process and content concerns for counselors. *Counseling and Values*, 34, 134-137.

Kerr, B. A. & Colangelo, N. (1994). Something to prove: Academically talented minority students. In N. Colangelo & S. Assouline (Eds.), *Talent development* (pp. 361-374). Scottsdale, AZ: Gifted Psychology Press.

Kerr, B. A., Colangelo, N., Maxey, J., & Christensen, P. (1992). Characteristics of academically talented minority students. *Journal of Counseling and Development*, 70 (5), 606-670.

Kerr, B. A. & Kurpius, S. R. (1998). Talent, risk, and betrayal in the lives of gifted girls. In J. Leroux (Ed.), *Proceedings of the World Council on Gifted and Talented*. Montreal: WCGT.

Nobles, W. W. (1997). African American family life: An instrument of culture. In H. P. McAdoo (Ed.), *Black families* (pp. 83-93). Thousand Oaks, CA: Sage.

Staples, M. (1988). An overview of race and marital status. In H.P. McAdoo (Ed.), *Black Families* (pp. 187-189). Newberry Park, NY: Sage.

Stevens, E. (1973). Machismo and marianismo. *Transaction-Society*, 10, 57-63.

Sudarkarsa, S. I. (1997). African American families and family values. In H. P. McAdoo (Ed.), *Black families* (pp. 9-40). Thousand Oaks, CA: Sage.

United States Census Bureau (2001). *United States Census Report*. Washington, DC: U.S. Government Printing Office.

Valencia, A. A. (1985). Curriculum perspectives for gifted limited-English-proficient students. *The Journal for the National Association for Bilingual Education*, 10 (1), 65-67.

Van Tassel-Baska, J. (1984). The talent search as an identification model. *Gifted Child Quarterly*, 28 (4), 172-176.

Wright, R. (1969). *Native sons*. New York: Harper & Row.

Section IV:
Guiding Smart Boys

11

The Gifted Male in the Family

So far, we have focused on the gifted male as an individual. But of course, gifted boys and men live their lives in contexts of families, friendships, and mentoring and teaching relationships. We have shown that in many cases, it is difficult to be a gifted male. However, it is also sometimes difficult to be the parent, sibling, spouse, or partner of a gifted male. In this chapter, we will focus on some of the problems in parenting gifted boys, as well as ways of parenting effectively. We will discuss how some of the dynamics of a gifted boyhood are manifested later in adult relationships with women and partners, and we will go on to suggest a new vision for gifted men in such relationships.

In any successful family, it is important to respect the self of the gifted boy—to respect the boy's own tastes, interests, needs, opinions, and values, even when they sometimes differ from those of other family members. Because there is extraordinary variability in personality characteristics within a family, it is often the case that gifted boys are mysteriously different from one or both parents. For example, both parents are hippies, but the child is a perfectionist and a stickler for the rules; or both parents are professors in the humanities, but their child wants to be a mechanical engineer; or the whole family is musical except one who can't carry a tune.

Respecting the self of the gifted boy means acknowledging that he is different from the parents and the siblings and celebrating that difference, rather than being annoyed or frightened by it. Respecting the self of the gifted boy also means allowing the gifted boy to have boundaries—that is, to have some private space in his life. As a little boy, that means a room or workspace of his own. As an adolescent, it means a private intimate life. Even though parents must provide their son with information about his sexuality and health, they must recognize that his body is his own. As he becomes a young man, it means respecting his choices of relationships, work, religion, and home.

When parents refuse to allow a gifted boy to develop his own identity, he is more likely to develop a hidden self and a mask. Although all people who are forced to live a life that is incongruent with their own inclinations may protect themselves behind masks, the formidable intelligence of the gifted boy means that he may be almost too effective at walling away his true self behind a cleverly constructed façade—so effective that he may forget who he really is, or he may disguise his feelings so cleverly that others do not know when to provide comfort or assistance. People who live a life in the service of other people's expectations not only never know the joy of self actualization, they also suffer from illnesses and depression and often subject others in their lives to the same oppression that they themselves have endured. In the following sections, we show some common family and relationship patterns that can harm the self of the gifted boy, as well as ways of coming to the rescue of that self.

Parents and Gifted Boys

Significant controversy continues about the role of nurturing in children's lives. Psychoanalysts have long asserted that childhood experiences shape the adult by forming the unconscious, but there is disagreement about how and when, exactly, this takes place. Developmentalists claim that the first few years of life are crucial to the development of a well-adjusted person. And attachment theorists would have us believe that we have about five minutes to establish the parental bond or else all is ruined! On the other side of the controversy are the biologically oriented psychologists who write convincingly that genetic endowments of ability, temperament, and emotional health have much more to do with the adult product than parenting does. And social psychologists insist that it is the peer group, and not the parents, that primarily shapes behavior.

The position we take in this controversy is, more or less, right in the middle. We believe that there are heavy influences of genetic endowments upon behavior. Parents often note that their children showed very different temperaments virtually from birth. So we resist the notion that parents are to blame for every wrong thing their child does as an adult. However, we also believe that each child presents more or less of a challenge to his or her parents' skills—and that parents vary in those skills. So boys naturally respond differently to their various parental influences. Gifted boys, as is true for all children, are most often hurt by parents who simply lack basic parenting skills and who cannot see their child for who he is.

Parenting any gifted child can be a challenge, and having a gifted child is often a mixed blessing (Silverman, 1997; Strip & Hirsch, 2000). Parents of gifted children, though, sometimes band together to advocate for their children and to seek support from one another. Almost every state and many cities in the U.S. have parent groups devoted to the education and support of parents of gifted children. Only a few of these groups provide extensive information and support, however. Webb and DeVries (1998) describe the SENG (Supporting Emotional Needs of the Gifted) model for organizing and facilitating such parent groups, and they highlight the issues that are most important to parents of gifted children. They recommend that parents try to avoid, or at least minimize, power struggles by learning to "flow with" rather than "fight against" their gifted children. They point out that most parents of gifted children are as intense and as verbal as their children are, that parents are eager for information and support, and that parents are often quite angry at the public schools for their failure to provide for the needs of their children.

Parents need to be aware that power struggles may be particularly intense with gifted children. A gifted child's energy level and intelligence permits him to devise many strategies for gaining the upper hand with his parents. And in situations in which parents have many other tasks and responsibilities in their lives, the gifted child may have all the time and energy he needs to relentlessly pursue what he wants from his parents. Parents may be at a loss for how to discipline a gifted child who anticipates their every move, and they may be frustrated not only by their child's emotions, but also by their own feelings of anger, fear, and sadness over the realization that such a gift as a brilliant child can also turn out to be such a burden.

Parents of gifted boys experience all of these problems and concerns, and they often find that boys' activity levels and socialization for dominance may even exacerbate the power struggles and amplify the need for careful discipline and guidance. The SENG model of parenting, and advice from resource books such as *Guiding the Gifted Child* (Webb, et al., 1982), *Helping Gifted Children Soar* (Strip & Hirsch, 2000), and *The Survival Guide for Parents of Gifted Kids* (Walker, 1991), can help mothers and fathers create and maintain a healthy and loving relationship with their son(s).

Parenting Patterns that Inhibit the Growth of the Self of the Gifted Boy

Some parent-child patterns that we have observed in our clinical practice seem to be unique to the relationship between parents and gifted boys, and sometimes the boy's giftedness interacts with parents' needs in such a way as to create dysfunctional patterns of family life. These unproductive patterns can prevent a gifted boy from discovering his own unique identity and from fully maturing into a healthy adult. In *The Drama of the Gifted Child,* Alice Miller (1996) has written movingly about the plight of the gifted child with parents who seek to meet their own needs through their relationship with their child. As a psychoanalyst, she uses the term "narcissism" for the parents' failure to recognize the true self of the child and for their inclination to see in him only their own image or the projection of their own needs. (We should note that this is not how the word "narcissism" is used in common conversation, in which it means a vain and selfish person. Nor is it the same as the psychiatric definition, which is a very specific type of personality disorder.) In this section, we bring attention to the several special patterns that we have observed of parents' failure to recognize a gifted son's true self—the case of the Mother's Companion, the Father's Hero, and Nobody's Boy. We want to suggest that these are patterns that parents of gifted boys should be very careful to avoid, and for situations in which they are already in place, we describe ways of changing the dynamics of the family in order to create healthier ways of relating to one another.

The Mother's Companion

The Mother's Companion is the gifted boy who has been singled out as the child in the family who is responsible for accompanying, nursing, comforting, or speaking for the mother. Usually in these cases, the father is absent or uninvolved with his son's life. It may be that the father's attention is distracted by a talented older son who has absorbed all of his father's ambitions or that the father's emotions and attention are focused outside the family—in over-involvement in work or perhaps in an addiction of some kind. Or it may be that the gifted boy is being raised by a single mom.

Frequently, the mother is disabled physically or psychologically or is suffering through a crisis, and the mother involves the gifted boy in major family—and sometimes personal—decisions. In these cases, the boy can be said to be her "designated helper." She may create this role for her son because she is lonely and isolated and can find no adults to assist her. Since her son seems so intellectually mature, his mother may forget that he is not sufficiently emotionally mature, nor has he had sufficient life experience to have an appropriate sense of perspective about many life situations.

Why is it so frequently the gifted boy who is chosen for this role? Often, the son who has precocious verbal abilities is his mother's special conversational partner from the beginning. If his father is cold, forbidding, or angry, then his mother may provide the refuge he needs. Long past the time when most boys have been forced to separate from their mother psychologically, he remains her loyal ally. This attachment often even draws approval from society—for instance, the boy is commended for being so helpful to his mother. And if the boy is suffering bullying at school or feels isolated himself because of his special abilities, then being chosen for the special task of assisting his mother may come as a relief. Fulfilling this role of Mother's Companion, then, can diminish in him the sense of urgency that he might otherwise feel for the need to play with other boys. And it also mitigates, somewhat, his desire to spend time with his father.

Therefore, the role of Mother's Companion may be comfortable for both the mother and the son, and such a relationship pattern may be freely chosen by both. The mother gains a clever and endlessly resourceful young friend; the son gains sanctuary from the cruelties of other boys and men. When the father is virtually or completely absent, the boy may even become something like a surrogate spouse—the one person with whom the mother shares her problems, secrets, and hopes.

Problems only begin to arise when the gifted boy starts to wish for his independence. He might suddenly discover an activity he likes, or he might find the company of a new friend more enjoyable than he finds that of his mother. It may even be that he has found another adult who can offer mentoring and learning opportunities. Then, he begins to look for ways to strike out on his own.

For most boys, the process of gaining independence is a natural one. They begin to spend more time away from their mothers as they get older, they seek the company of other boys, and they spend a lot of time making fun of their moms and other females.

For the gifted boy who is his Mother's Companion, though, the problem of separating from her both physically and psychologically is more difficult. The easygoing way in which other boys sneer at their mother's wishes is impossible for the Mother's

Companion. If the mother is disabled but valiant, then showing even the mildest contempt for her is unthinkable. The Mother's Companion must maintain his stance of respect, admiration, and absolute love for his mother, while somehow finding a way to break free and create his own selfhood and masculine identity.

Mother's Companions sometimes cope with this dilemma by engaging in covert resistance to their mothers. They keep their independence hidden from her. They become congenial under-achievers, achieving just enough to stay out of trouble, but not so much as to require spending more time or energy away from their mother. Secretly, they yearn to be doing much more. But by "rebel-liously" underachieving in this way, they can appear to their friends to be separating from their mothers while appearing to their moth-ers to still be their closest ally. They may develop a secret and intense fantasy life. They may also be the sort of "runaway" who comes home before his absence is noticed. In the best cases, they find an outlet for their urge for autonomy in some creative pursuit. The gifted boy can separate from his mother while sitting right at her side—through writing, art, design, and music. He can draw dis-tant mountains, write epic poems, or design great battleships—right from the kitchen table.

If there is a father who is only occasionally available—who usually appears on the scene merely to "straighten the boy out"— then the stage is set for further division of the boy's personality. The father may be very threatened by the feminine qualities of intuition, verbal giftedness, and creativity that emerge in the intense contact of mother and son, and he may try to reverse the growth of these qualities. He may condemn the boy's activities in these areas and press him to develop more masculine pursuits in sports, science, and mechanical activities. As a result, the boy may develop these skills merely as a means of placating his father and without ever connecting them with his other identity as a creatively gifted per-son. But if this proves impossible, the boy may simply flee his father, avoiding contact with him as much as possible in order to maintain his integration.

Later, too, in their professions, Mother's Companions may vacillate between overt intense loyalty and covert escapism. Their working lives may be a tension between "man's work," on the one hand, and on the other, some creative outlet that is attractive to them but that is relegated to the past or to a hidden self. Additionally, they may resent women in the workplace who like to be with men doing masculine activities; nevertheless, they generally need women to stimulate their creative and emotional lives.

At their best, men who have been their Mother's Companions have the potential to be balanced men with strong feminine as well as masculine qualities. At their worst, Mother's Companions are fragmented men, maintaining a superficial appearance of obedience to authority and conventional relationships with women while engaging in hidden activities such as secret sexual liaisons, substance abuse, or subversion of authority figures.

What can be done for boys and men who have suffered this denial of selfhood? First of all, it is up to mothers who are ill, disabled, depressed, or lonely to refuse to put their sons in these roles. Mothers need friends their own age and caretakers who are adults, not children. They should not share the full force of their adult concerns with their boys or expect their sons to listen and to provide advice and support. Even very ill and disabled mothers can and should encourage their sons to develop their own interests and friends.

A father who recognizes that his son has bonded strongly with the mother needs to honor that bond while gently supporting the boy's attempts to establish his independence. This means helping the boy with the projects and activities that are selected by the boy and becoming involved with him. Gifted boys' most common plea of their fathers is to spend more time with them, but boys who hate sports or camping do not regard obligatory athletics and camping trips as quality time with Dad.

Recognizing the true self of the child means acknowledging the ways in which he is different from his parents and celebrating this uniqueness instead of feeling threatened by it. Often, a gifted boy will have extraordinary creative, intuitive, and spiritual gifts. If his preferred ways of expressing these go unrecognized, while only those activities that are approved by the mother and father are supported, then the boy may develop two or more separate lives—one that is public and socially acceptable, and one that is hidden and considered by the boy to be less than acceptable.

Boys need to be supported when they strike out on their own; they need to feel assured that their homes have open boundaries. This means that it is, at an appropriate age, okay for them to leave the house, to leave the family, and to embark on adventures of their own—but it should also be okay for them to come back home.

Furthermore, teachers who notice boys who are clearly their Mother's Companions may be able to help them develop their own interests and groups of friends. And although it may be difficult, a teacher can also help the mother recognize her son's true self by giving her an accurate understanding of the boy's interests and skills and by enlisting her in strategies for helping him develop them.

For the adult male who discovers that he is leading the life of a grown-up Mother's Companion, there are a few paths that can return him to his true self. One is psychotherapy. (Again, it must be remembered that the psychotherapist should be a capable one who is trained to deal with the special needs of gifted people.) In psychotherapy, the gifted man can begin the careful reintegration of the disparate parts of his self through honesty, reflection, and self-analysis. Honesty opens the windows of all of the closed compartments of the Mother's Companion's personality. When he begins to genuinely acknowledge each of his roles to all of the people in his life, he makes it possible for others to help him integrate his parts.

The process of opening up the secrets is often a painful one, because the Mother's Companion has convinced himself that he must protect others from the truth about himself. If he has partners or family members that he has "protected" from knowing about his secret life of substance abuse, infidelity, or adventurism, they may react with fury upon being presented with the real, integrated man. It is very difficult for relationships based on the false self he has presented to survive, partly because his partner may have grown too accustomed to his protection and good-son supportiveness—facets of the role he is no longer willing to play—and partly because of the difficulty that these partners have in supporting his new attempts at being integrated.

A rich spiritual life can provide a source of peace during this painful time and can open up the gifted adult male to the possibilities of wholeness. If his spirituality is integrated into his work, home, and daily life, it can become the cement that brings him back together. Spiritual exploration, like psychotherapy, can provide an opportunity for the gifted man to examine his images of the masculine and the feminine in his religious life and within his psyche. By claiming his own image of masculine and feminine and integrating these, the gifted adult male can reduce the conflicted feelings that have arisen from being a Mother's Companion.

Whether through psychotherapy, spiritual practice, or both, when the disparate parts of the self have been integrated, the gifted adult male will be less anxious, less depressed, and will feel more content. He will no longer feel the need to hide parts of himself, and he can focus his energies on discovering and developing his abilities and interests in a self-actualizing fashion.

The Father's Hero

Another parental pattern that inhibits the growth of the self in gifted boys is the creation of the Father's Hero. Unlike the Mother's Companion, the Father's Hero is often the firstborn son. He is the repository of all of his father's dreams and hopes and unrealized ambitions. The firstborn son, as R. S. Albert points out, is at a particularly high risk for becoming a Father's Hero in families in which the father is also a firstborn and in which the father's talents are similar to those of the son. When a boy is gifted, he often becomes the classic scholar-athlete. For as soon as the father recognizes that his son is intellectually gifted, he may become anxious about that child's masculine identity and fearful of what being a "brain" will mean for his boy's chances of survival in the face of bullying at school. He may begin to search for a sport that the boy can excel in at an early age so that he can have the protection of an athletic reputation. The father of the young gifted hero is likely to be found on Saturday mornings cheering tensely on the sidelines of a soccer, Tee-ball, or midget football game. No matter how hard the father tries to contain his emotions, he suffers with every foul incurred by his son and exults in every point scored. The Father's Hero may also have a "soccer mom," who helps plan and manage the team's affairs.

In academics, both the father and the mother of the Father's Hero are likely to encourage the boy to be competitive and highly achieving in school. More specifically, they may put a special emphasis on math and science, knowing that these skills are the keys to the most lucrative and high-status careers. Consequently, the son usually has the best education his parents can offer, although he may also be a victim of kindergarten redshirting (see Chapter 4), in an effort to place him at the top of his class both athletically and academically. He may be sent to selective summer camps and to talent search programs, and he may be signed up for a plethora of after-school activities to enrich his education. He is expected to get A's across the board, and he is often encouraged to be "well-rounded"—code for "good at everything."

Ironically, the tragedy of the gifted Father's Hero is often that he usually *is* good at everything he tries. He has excellent grades in all of his courses and scores above the 95th percentile on achievement tests. And it is unlikely that he will go through a period of underachievement, because he is monitored too closely to get away with it. He excels at several sports and by junior high is also a leader in social activities. He is a "golden boy"—admired by the other boys and pursued by the girls. He exhibits multipotentiality, and his guidance counselors and teachers smile at him and say that he can be anything he wants to be because he is capable of everything. And therein lies the tragedy: he is *able* to do everything, but he is unlikely to really *care* deeply about any one thing. He may be so uncertain about what to do with his future that he winds up attending his father's college, joining his father's fraternity, and following his father's path in business, medicine, law, or engineering.

At his best, the Father's Hero usually becomes a well-rounded, successful, nice guy. He is a pillar of the community and a paragon of masculine excellence. At his worst, though, the Father's Hero becomes an achiever without a center, a champion without a self. Because he has never been encouraged to fall in love with an idea, he is capable of seeking only extrinsic rewards. A high salary and a high-status occupation are important to him, no matter what that occupation might entail.

What can be done for the Father's Hero while he is still a boy? Somewhere along the line, someone has to subvert the plot line of the script that is his life. Often, fate takes a hand through the loss of a family member, a severe injury or illness, or a loss of home and friends in a wrenching move that may actually work to free the boy from the expectations that have controlled his life. With the family distracted by hardship or grief, it may then become possible for the gifted boy to begin to have an internal life of his own, without the constant scheduling that has stilled his own voice.

Sometimes a great failure can be a blessing in disguise. The young man who unaccountably is not accepted to the college he was prepared for; or the one who, because of some vagary of the process, is not accepted to medical school; or the one who loses his first big break because he didn't know the right people—each of these men now has an opportunity to learn how to face failure, to chart a new, original path, and to grow. A great failure teaches the gifted boy the hard lesson that life is not fair. This lesson is a late one for most of these boys, because throughout school, if they worked hard, they got the A. In life beyond school, it is not always the brilliant or the hardest working who get the rewards. Once this lesson is learned, the way is laid for learning to seek intrinsic rather than extrinsic rewards, and the growth of the self becomes possible.

What can be said to fathers and mothers who are creating Father's Heroes? I like what a 5th grade teacher said to two parents in an affluent suburban school: "Back off. Get a life." The father needs to give his son some alone time, and he also needs to be less involved in *coaching* his son and more involved in *listening to* and *being with* him in quiet ways. Parents need to encourage their boy to try activities that he is not the best at and to seek challenges that are unrelated to recognition and public reward.

Teachers can help the Father's Hero by becoming an ally in the boy's attempts to find a center inside himself. This means helping the boy discover a passion and allowing him to fall in love with an idea. Teachers who focus on the development of purpose and meaning and who care more about the actualization of their students' values than about raw achievement can be of great support to this kind of gifted boy. Sometimes this means discouraging the boy's attempts to do everything and be everything to everybody. Helping the boy prioritize his interests and activities and encouraging him to focus on just a few areas can go a long way toward protecting him from becoming an achiever without a center.

What about the adult Father's Hero? The gifted man who discovers, sometimes as late as midlife, that he has been living his father's life rather than his own is often an angry and embittered man. To recognize halfway through one's life that one's work is a bore and that one's partner is an empty, fading beauty is a misery that has informed much of modern literature. The suburban successes found in John Cheever's and John Updike's novels are often extraordinary portraits of gifted men who are Father's Heroes—intelligent men with a longing for meaning who have sold out their creative selves for external rewards.

The adult Father's Hero can seek, through men's groups or through therapy, to break the enslavement to the goals his father set for him. Other men who have suffered the same fate can often provide validation of his experience and support for developing his own true self. Becoming one's own self may mean a career change or a relationship change or both, and these experiences can be cataclysmic. Nevertheless, finding one's own true vocation as well as a respected partner can be worth the upheaval; it should never be too late to seek meaning in work and in love.

Nobody's Boy

There is yet another style of development that may be related to ineffective parenting of gifted boys—a pattern that results in what we call Nobody's Boy. Nobody's Boy is the gifted son who is often the third, fourth, or even later child. He is the child that the older parents are simply too tired to parent or who has little parental guidance for other reasons such as parents' substance abuse or neglect. Nobody's Boy spends a lot of time alone and has little guidance for how to spend that time. For one thing, he is not old enough to join his siblings on many of their "older kid" outings—dates, parties, movies unfit for younger children, etc. In the best of situations, he reads and plays games that enliven his imagination. In the worst of situations, he is bored at school and is neglected at home. Because his parents are tired or distracted, they do not seek appropriate educational opportunities for him. He languishes in a regular classroom in an inferior school. He seeks the easiest possible path, as children often will, and nobody stops him. He never learns any healthy work habits, and he gets by for a long time just with his extraordinary memory or his creativity. When it is clear that he has great gaps or unevenness in his achievement, he may be labeled as "gifted learning disabled" or some other psychiatric designation. Nevertheless, he is unlikely to be learning disabled and is more likely to simply be undereducated, poorly organized, or lacking clear goals. Because of his underachievement and lack of direction, he is unlikely to be admired or sought after by his intellectual equals. So he develops friendships with low achievers, finding that at least among these boys, he is accepted and even admired for his wit or sarcasm. Nobody's Boy is likely to be a substance abuser and sexually active at an early age because, again, there is no one to set limits on him and to guide him.

In a wealthy family, an adult Nobody's Boy is often the hanger-on who is given a lot of breaks and opportunities in the family businesses, but who doesn't make a good worker. If he tries to strike out on his own, he has to keep returning home because his jobs end or he gets fired. In a less affluent family, this gifted boy drops out of high school or college and goes to work with other lost boys; he may join the military or do wildcat work in construction, transportation, ranching, or service industries. He may continue to be a closet reader, writer, or musician, occasionally shocking his friends at the bar with his flights of extraordinarily imaginative storytelling or with a beautifully sung melody, but without intervention, his gifted potential will go largely unrealized.

What kind of intervention works? There are both unique problems and unique solutions to dealing with Nobody's Boys. One problem is that, unsurprisingly, many parents of these boys are unaware of their part in their boys' problems. Either because they have successfully parented other children or because they have had such easy children up to then that they haven't had to learn parenting, they may see themselves as more competent and involved with the boy than they actually are. Some parents of Nobody's Boys see themselves as liberal, permissive, enlightened parents who trust their children to know what is best for them. They are usually baffled by the boy's behavior and often don't know how to help. What these boys need is active parenting.

Sometimes teachers and counselors can help parents learn how best to intervene. For example, parents may need a system by which the teacher sends home a detailed list of assignments that the parents sign off on when it is completed. Many parents who grew up in other eras are shocked at how much homework is required in schools now, and they may need to learn time management skills themselves in order to be able to spend a few hours each evening assisting their child. Nobody's Boys who are already strongly influenced by negative peer groups may need a change of class or school. In addition, they will require careful monitoring of after-school time and evenings, curfews, and requirements for tasks around the house.

In addition to structure, parents need to provide active support and clear demonstrations of love. Plenty of affection, frequent praise for accomplishments, and a few rewards for positive behavior changes can be powerful reinforcers. Parents who themselves would balk at this kind of structuring are often surprised to find that their child enjoys it and responds to it.

At school, these boys can be helped by the same interventions recommended earlier in this book for underachievers and for oppositional defiant gifted boys—establishing a relationship within which to provide both challenge and meaning. However, for these boys, the challenge must be provided carefully so that the relationship is not negatively affected. Often, standard gifted programs do not provide either the time to cultivate the very important relationship, nor the study skills and time management skills needed by Nobody's Boys. Even more important, if the teacher is not a strong parental figure, the boy may successfully ignore his or her attempts to encourage him. But even in situations in which the parents refuse to change or intervene, a significant teacher or mentor can turn the life of a Nobody's Boy around. Many creatively gifted men who were underachievers or had behavior problems early in life tell stories of having had their lives changed forever by a strong and caring teacher who engaged their imaginations. Most Nobody's Boys are so hungry for affection, structure, and intellectual stimulation that they will attach themselves ferociously to a mentor, providing the same loyalty and hard work they would have liked to have shown their parents.

As adults, Nobody's Boys are likely to be as gifted in self-destructing as their luckier brothers are in constructing lives of meaning. They still need parenting if they didn't get it when they were younger. In addition, they need a community that is well structured if they hope to find a way to live. Alcoholics Anonymous and other recovery communities have often provided just that sort of environment for Nobody's Boys. Therapists with clear authority and the capacity to connect with the gifted male's longing for a parent may be able to successfully re-parent the gifted adult. These men need spouses, too, who are both strong enough to decline to be rescuers and sure enough of their own paths not to get caught up in the gifted male's self-destructiveness. Eventually, these men need to learn to become their own mothers and fathers. That is, they need to internalize unconditional love as well as the capacity for firm self-guidance. An exercise that we have used in therapy is to ask gifted men to imagine the Good Mother and the Good Father—and then to begin to shape those behaviors in themselves.

The Gifted Boy with Siblings

The gifted boy often grows up with brothers and sisters. Some of them may have been labeled gifted as well, and some may not have been. What happens to sibling relationships in each of these cases? According to Cornell (1984), the first-born child is the child most likely to be labeled gifted. If the younger children are also labeled gifted, as is often the case since intelligence scores of siblings are highly correlated (Silverman, 1993), then sibling rivalry issues are generally minimized. In fact, several experts advocate that the siblings of gifted children routinely be tested, because they are often gifted but overlooked (they may have been in a different school or may have moved after school testing took place, for example). In cases in which the first-born child is not labeled gifted but the second child is, then there appears to be more sibling tension (Tuttle, 1990). In addition, there is always the danger that the child who is not labeled gifted will underachieve, as a result of being self-labeled "the nongifted one."

Often, the gifted children receive more family attention and resources than do the other children in the family (Webb, 1993). Although it is, of course, an ideal of every family to generally treat every child alike and to divide resources as equally as seems reasonable, sometimes a child's giftedness demands more resources, in the same way that a child's disability might make greater claims on the family's time, energy, and money. This is particularly true when the child is highly gifted or extraordinarily talented in some domain.

Sometimes, treating every child equally is not the ideal, and it is more sensible to respond to a child's specific needs. The sister of a famous cellist once told me, "We knew from the time he was a little boy that he was special. As soon as it became apparent that he was a musical genius, our family knew that everything had changed forever. We would all need to commit ourselves to his development. I never resented it; it was just the way it was." There is evidence, as in this example, that the more extreme the giftedness (or the more obvious the giftedness), the less resentment arises.

Nicholas Colangelo and Penny Brower (1987) studied families of gifted children over five years to assess the long-term effects on a family of one child's being labeled gifted. They found that, as suggested above, the child not labeled gifted did have a lower academic self-concept than the gifted child did after five years. However, on all other measures of self-esteem, the non-labeled child fared very well—even scoring higher than gifted siblings did on some measures of psychological health.

What this means is that the matter of sibling relationships for gifted boys is a complex one, with the effects of his being labeled gifted dependent upon his birth order and upon the labeling of other children. A few cautions are also in order. In our practice with gifted men, we have often heard retrospective stories of second-born men identified as gifted who were bullied by resentful first-born, non-identified brothers—usually in secret, and usually over a long period of time. Even as adults, these men feared their brothers. If a gifted boy is in this particular situation, some caution is in order; sibling relationships need to be monitored closely to be sure that the older non-labeled boy does not underachieve and suffer loss of self-esteem, and that the younger, labeled boy is not secretly victimized.

Wives and Partners

Because many relationship and marital problems are related to behavior patterns learned in childhood, it might be helpful to show how the patterns described above manifest themselves in adult relationships.

Mother's Companions often grow up to be gifted men with several problems. First of all, they may tend to over-idealize women, particularly older women. They may fall in love with women who need caretaking, because that is how they learned to relate to women. However, they often have difficulties with fidelity and consistency, because they continue the covert resistance that first helped them establish their masculinity. On the positive side, their special understanding of women can help them achieve true intimacy with a woman.

Father's Heroes, as we have seen, are always looking for ways to gain approval and recognition. This being the case, boys like this often grow up to be men who seek women as achievements. Even if they don't pursue a "trophy wife," they may have difficulty looking beyond a partner's looks and sexual appeal to connect with the woman within. Because the gifted Father's Hero has no center of his own, he has a hard time recognizing the self of his spouse. He may expect her to act in ways that support his career, his hobbies, and his image of a successful life. Marriage and child rearing also become important achievements, and the gifted man seeks all of the external signs of success in these areas that he can. His wife has the biggest diamond and the best clothes, and his children are enrolled in the best schools before they are born.

It was interesting to us (Kerr & Anderson, 2001) that more gifted men seemed to have wives at home than men of average abilities in the same social class did. This may reflect their desire to appear affluent, or it may be because they marry women with lower achievement orientation. On the other hand, it may simply reflect a woman's conscious choice to be the primary caregiver of her own children-and of her husband's support for that choice.

Finally, a Nobody's Boy attracts rescuers, particularly women who fall in love with idle brilliance. There are gifted women who see the potential in these men and work tirelessly to get them to give up booze, drugs, or laziness and to get them going along a creative path. However, most of these men cannot hang onto a relationship—unless, of course, they find an extremely codependent partner.

In addition to these marital issues related to early family dynamics, there are other issues that arise from interaction with a gifted spouse. For instance, because gifted men usually exhibit high energy and high intensity, they may be exhausting for their partners. If they do not marry high-energy women, they may find themselves continually frustrated by these women's reluctance to travel, to have adventures, to explore new endeavors, and to stay up late. Similarly, because of the emotional and time demands of the Nobody's Boy, it can be quite difficult for his spouse to have her own career.

A problem that many of the men in our study mentioned was their difficulty with emotional expression. This difficulty, combined with an exquisite sensitivity, can be a fatal combination for a relationship. A man who shuts down when criticized or who deeply feels every little hurt but does not express it is likely to never get his needs met and even risks losing the relationship because of the fact that issues will linger unresolved. Another problem mentioned by the men in our study was their tendency to use sarcasm, irony, and contemptuous expressions when angry. Too often, they found themselves using their intellectual skills to hurt the one they loved most, simply because they were armed with words and were too angry not to use them. Still other gifted men who have trouble verbally expressing emotions lash out physically when angry or upset, when their pressure cooker of long suppressed emotions finally explodes.

In addition to these emotional issues, there are issues related to the work habits of gifted men that bear upon their relationships.

In interviews with male inventors (1991), for example, the first author and Nicholas Colangelo found that most of the inventors had spouses who functioned not only as wives, but also as lab assistants, secretaries, or business managers. Needless to say, it was nearly impossible for spouses of major inventors to have careers or lives of their own. Gifted men may make unreasonable demands upon their spouses to tolerate their lengthy and sometimes erratic work hours, their intense concentration, and their unconventional working environments. They may take over the house with their stacks of books and with the other materials of their work.

If the gifted man is in one of the common occupations of business, law, or medicine, the spouse may be expected to play the role of hostess, entertaining work associates and their wives, and the gifted man may simply think of this as the whole of their only social life. In short, the partners of gifted men may find themselves with much more work than they ever expected, and they may find their own goals for partnership or intimacy subtly compromised. In *Smart Girls* (Kerr, 1997), the first author shows how a generation of gifted women had given up their own dreams to support those of their husbands. It wasn't healthy for them, and it wasn't healthy for their marriages.

Gifted young men need help understanding the importance of sharing the responsibilities of a marriage. In "When Dreams Differ" (Kerr, 1998), the first author describes the difficulties that gifted young men have in contemplating their future marital roles. When we asked gifted college men and gifted college women to fantasize their "Perfect Future Day" from beginning to end, we found that both men and women imagined themselves in high-status occupations. However, whereas men fantasized about having a wife waiting for them at home, women fantasized years of dual career bliss! If women marry these bright men, they will have to confront conflicting expectations. While the majority of bright women expect to work all of their lives with one or more short maternity breaks, about a third of bright men don't want their wives to work at all. This means that, unless gifted men marry women with much less ambition (and possibly less intelligence) than they have themselves, they will have a rude awakening when they discover that their spouses have no intention of staying home to cook for them and raise their children single-handedly.

While many schools now offer instruction in sex education, we want to suggest that relationship education is perhaps more important. For gifted boys, relationship education, whether provided by schools, parents, or both, needs to include information on the impact of giftedness on relationships, on the realities of dual career families, on peer marriage or marriage between equals, and on the future of the family. While there are few books written to offer guidance to bright people in their search for loving and fulfilling relationships, we suggest Pepper Schwartz' book, *Love Between Equals* (1998) as a place to start, and the biographies of loving gifted couples such as philosophers Will and Ariel Durant, artist Georgia O'Keefe and photographer Alfred Steiglitz, and Marie and Pierre Curie (Kerr, 1997).

Key Points:

1. Parents of gifted boys can benefit from banding together in support and advocacy groups such as the SENG model.
2. Parenting the gifted child can be a challenge because of power struggles with the child, difficulties with schools, and problems of managing emotions and stress.
3. Certain unhealthy patterns of parenting gifted boys, in which parents' own needs dominate the relationship, may impede the growth of the gifted young man's identity.
4. Sibling relationships may involve rivalry, particularly when the first-born is non-identified and the second-born is labeled gifted, and when the level of giftedness is not extreme.

5. Research shows that while the academic self-concept of the "non-gifted" child in the family may decline, self-esteem and other measures of psychological health are unaffected in the long term by having a gifted sibling.

6. Marriage or commitment to a gifted man may make heavy demands upon the spouse or partner. Early relationship education can help gifted boys be more realistic about future relationships.

References

Colangelo, C. & Brower, P. (1987). Labeling gifted children: Long term impact on families. *Gifted Child Quarterly*, 31, 75-78.

Cornell, D. (1984). *Families of gifted children*. Ann Arbor, MI: UMI Research Press.

Kerr, B. A. (1998, March). When dreams differ: Gender relations on the college campus. *Chronicle of Higher Education*, Washington, DC.

Kerr, B. A. (1997). *Smart girls: A new psychology of girls, women and giftedness*. Scottsdale, AZ: Gifted Psychology Press.

Miller, A. (1996). *The drama of the gifted child: The search for the true self*. Translated from German by Ruth Ward. New York: Basic Books.

Schwartz, P. (1998). *Love between equals*. New York: Free Press.

Silverman, L. K. (1997). Family counseling with the gifted. In N. Colangelo & G. Davis (Eds.), *Handbook of gifted education*. Needham Heights, MA: Allyn & Bacon.

Silverman, L. K. (Ed.) (1993). *Counseling the gifted and talented*. Denver: Love Publishing.

Strip, C. A. & Hirsch, G. (2000). *Helping gifted children soar: A practical guide for parents and teachers.* Scottsdale, AZ: Gifted Psychology Press.

Tuttle, D. H. (1990). Positive labeling and the sibling relationship in families with gifted children. Unpublished doctoral dissertation, University of Virginia: Charlottesville, VA.

Walker, S. Y. & Perry, S. K. (1991). *The survival guide for parents of gifted kids: How to understand, live with, and stick up for your gifted child.* Minneapolis: Free Spirit Publishing.

Webb, J. T. (1993). Nurturing social-emotional development of gifted children. In K. A. Heller, F. J. Monks, & A. H. Passow (Eds.), *International handbook of research and development of giftedness and talent.* Oxford: Pergamon Press.

Webb, J. T. & Devries, A. R. (1998). *Gifted parent groups: The SENG model.* Scottsdale, AZ: Gifted Psychology Press.

Webb, J. T., Meckstroth, E. A., & Tolan, S. S. (1982). *Guiding the gifted child: A practical source for parents and teachers.* Scottsdale, AZ: Gifted Psychology Press (formerly Ohio Psychology Press).

12

Guiding the Intellectual, Emotional, and Spiritual Development of Gifted Males

Parents and teachers often ask us for practical suggestions for raising and guiding gifted boys. Many of the suggestions in such resources as *Guiding the Gifted Child* (Webb, et al., 1982), *The Survival Guide for Parents of Gifted Kids* (Walker & Perry, 1991), *Parenting Successful Children* (Webb, 1999), and *Keys to Parenting the Gifted Child* (Rimm, 1994) are applicable to nurturing gifted boys, and we recommend these resources as general guides.

However, throughout this book, we have reviewed research and theory that give us some additional specific ideas about the ways in which we can raise gifted boys to be more comfortable, both with their masculine identity and with their gifted identity. Gifted boys need intellectual, emotional, and spiritual guidance if they are to achieve their full potentials as gifted men. For each general stage of development, then, we will provide ideas for intellectual challenge, emotional support, and spiritual guidance. In addition, we hope to help with some of the more "everyday" dilemmas.

Preschool

Although some parents say they knew that their boy was gifted from the moment he was born, most parents of gifted boys first become aware of that fact in the first two or three years of his life when he begins to exhibit precocious behaviors that are different from his agemates. For example, he may begin talking in sentences at age one, or he may spontaneously put together a Lego® car at age two. And it is often sudden. The little boy who one day seemed content to read *The Adventures of Spot* on the next day picks up *Newsweek* and begins to read the first article aloud! Although there is little in the way of public education or enrichment for gifted preschoolers, parents can begin nurturing their boy's giftedness— and his attitudes about his giftedness—from that first moment on. Here are some suggestions for the preschool years.

Read to him every night, and watch for his own interest in reading. Let him look at picture books while you do your reading. Associate reading with cuddling and company. When he wants to try to sound out words, help him and praise him. Remember that much of his reading will be done electronically, so prepare him for this world. Have him sit on your lap and read to him from the screen of the computer, and show him fun Web sites for preschoolers. Or take a notebook computer to his bed at night and let him punch the key to bring up his favorite bookmarked Web site.

Dress your boy for preschool in the current fashions for little boys, but allow him to be creative and expressive in his attire. Allow him to choose the icons that he wants, even if they seem a little obnoxious to you. Gifted boys tend to get very involved with their favorite characters and may like to wear their images every day to preschool. One little boy insisted on wearing his Mickey Mouse shirt every single day. This was his way of saying, "This is me!" —a way of demonstrating his uniqueness. "Flow with it," and if you have to, try to get his clothes away from him while he's in the tub so you can wash them!

Boys of one and two are not yet infected with our society's homophobia. They may make a cape of Mom's lace slip or become fascinated by the stilt effect of her high heels. Don't overreact by shaming your little boy and drawing him into the fears of things feminine. Let him play, and he will learn soon enough what boys wear and what girls wear.

Be benignly indifferent to the more revolting characters in the media and toy stores—over-muscled he-men, gnashing killer monsters, and vicious robots—and offer a fascinating alternative. Say in a bored voice, "Oh yeah, Master Blasters, I'm not too interested in those guys. Hey, look at this! It's a magnifying glass that makes him look bigger! Let's see what else we can use it for." Find positive images of strong and caring males that he likes and buy him those toys and videos. The men on Sesame Street are wonderful models of kind, protective, active men. Talk about how much you like them, and ask him to imagine being on the show with them.

What about toy guns? We get tired of hearing, "If you take away guns, then he will just pick up a carrot and use it as a gun." Well, then, let him use a carrot; there is no need to give in if you don't want guns in the family. If you are gun owners, remember that gifted boys' curiosity and skills for getting what they want are much greater than other children's—and therefore, they may be even more at risk for a gun-related tragedy in the house.

Gifted boys may be ready for friendships based on shared interests long before average children are, and they may gravitate toward older playmates or adults. They may be very confused by the behaviors of average children. If there are no other bright children for your gifted boy to play with, then an older child may be suitable if you supervise them closely.

Young gifted boys often have one or more imaginary playmates, especially in circumstances where there are few other bright children around with whom they can interact. Gifted boys as preschoolers also often like to organize people or things—usually in complex games that they create. Both of these characteristics are often criticized by well-meaning but uninformed adults. Instead, permit these youngsters to explore these creative outlets.

Allow the gifted boy to have his intense feelings and sensitivities. He may have an aversion to rough clothes, you may have to cut the tags out of his shirts, he may complain about hearing fluorescent lights, or he may have intense likes or dislikes of certain foods. Avoid giving him the impression that sensitivity and strong feelings are wrong for boys.

The intensity usually also carries over into sleep and may cause the boy to receive needless criticism. Gifted boys often have vivid dreams—sometimes even night terrors—or may sleep so soundly that they continue to wet the bed long after other boys their age have stopped. Instead of criticism, ridicule, or punishment, a gentle comforting and understanding will allow the boy to learn how to accomplish this important self-management task.

Spiritual guidance for young gifted boys means sharing your own faith or philosophy of life in the simplest, most concrete terms. It is a time for him to become familiar with the symbols of your deepest values, whether those symbols are a medicine wheel, a cross, a flag, a revered place in nature, or an open book.

If he is tested with intelligence tests, remember these cautions. First of all, many gifted boys' abilities are obscured by their activity levels—that is, individual test administrators may not be able to get your little boy to sit still long enough for adequate testing. Second, many intelligence tests are not valid for predicting school ability until ages nine or ten. Third, many of the newer tests are not as good at identifying boys with precocious intellectual development as older versions of the tests. The newer tests, such as the *Stanford-Binet IV*, have lower ceilings. This means that they have been revised to be more inclusive of non-verbal skills, but are no longer as challenging to highly gifted students. Fourth, remember that it is difficult to get an accurate score for gifted minority children. Be sure that the psychologist administering the tests understands these cautions for gifted boys.

It is always a good idea to seek an assessment when a boy's precocious behavior seems to be indicating giftedness. At the very least, parents will need evidence to present to a school if they wish to request early admission or other special provisions.

Kindergarten and Primary

It is in these early school years that gifted boys display their giftedness the most—i.e., when their intensity, creativity, and activity levels are at their heights. However, underachievement also often begins around 3rd or 4th grade, when pressure to be "one of the guys" becomes intense. Boredom is another common culprit at this age, robbing boys of their love of learning. Parents are often puzzled by this change and don't know how to help. Here are some ways to ensure that the gifted boy at this stage both stays challenged and feels secure about his giftedness.

Kindergarten redshirting is one of the most destructive practices in our society for gifted boys (see Chapter 4). Do not hold your son back from entry into kindergarten so that he "has more time to grow" or so that he "will fit in socially" or "will be good at sports." It is a recipe for creating a big, bored kindergartener—one who may next become an unhappy bully. The only justification for giving him an extra year is if he is physically ill or if he has emotional or learning disabilities. Or if there has been a recent trauma in his life that may have temporarily impeded his development, then he might be able to use the extra time. Otherwise, send him to school or home-school him.

This is the time for parents to get really interested in children's television, in video games, and in Web sites. Watch and play alongside your son occasionally, searching for those images and stories that will help him grow and learn. Watch the children's television channels, and pick out the shows that will be intriguing and entertaining. Play the video games. One of the most common requests gifted boys have is, "I want my parents to play along with me." Remember that TV watching, video game playing, and computer use are all combining to decrease the amount of physical exercise children are getting, and the child's daily routine should also include some physical activity.

Make sure that he is allowed to learn to read and do math at his own pace. Remember that math skills, if not nurtured early, can fade, and that interest in reading, too, can diminish if a child is not allowed to read at his own pace. Parents should ask their son's teachers or school officials about the curriculum and about provisions for bright children.

Most public schools have very little funding for gifted children, and they may not be able to provide for your child's special needs. Most parents of gifted children become very angry at the lack of gifted education opportunities at their local school, particularly when provisions are less than what they experienced as children. If you are such a parent, try to be pro-active and positive. Join the association for parents of gifted children in your city or state to learn about resources and opportunities, and be an advocate who works alongside educators rather than against them.

Parents need to be aware that schools are usually not funded and teachers are generally not trained to nurture precocity; therefore, it is often up to the parents to educate the teachers about special ways of providing challenge. It is a delicate matter. Schools sometimes resent parents of gifted children because of their belief that these parents will approach them with an air of entitlement and resentment. Our own studies show that this is a false stereotype; nonetheless, parents should be aware of it. So approach the school as an informed, friendly partner, identify the resources available to your child, and suggest those resources, such as gifted parent-teacher associations, that might be helpful to the teacher. Give the teacher a few books that might help as well. Among the books with suggestions for how parents can work with schools are *Helping Gifted Children Soar* (Strip & Hirsch, 2000) and *Re-forming Gifted Education* (Rogers, 2001). Consider a conference with the school psychologist or counselor, and bring any privately attained assessments and observations that you might have.

If you have tried to work with the schools but without success, then perhaps you may need to consider other educational options for your gifted boy. Especially if your child is highly gifted, you will need to provide additional enrichment and accelerated education at home, or you may need to seek other educational alternatives such as private education, home-schooling, or moving to a different school district where resources are available.

Spatially-visually gifted boys are often labeled as underachievers because the curriculum does not tap spatial-visual intelligence. Be sure to check with the school psychologist to see if your son has highly discrepant scale scores—i.e., superior performance on nonverbal scales and average performance on verbal or math tests. If this is the case, he is not a true underachiever. If he has never been tested, you might ask for testing, giving evidence such as precocious abilities with art, chess, computer design, puzzles, mechanical toys, Lego® toys, etc.

If your boy is spatially-visually gifted, he may need and enjoy special opportunities to develop these talents. Plenty of art supplies, Lego® and construction toys, puzzles, chess and checkers, and some video games may feed this talent. Courses in photography, cartooning and animation, video production, painting, sculpture, and architecture that are developed for children may also be good bets. These boys also benefit from more hands-on learning in school, and they appreciate being able to put together slideshows, storyboards, and dioramas in the place of written reports.

Watch for Bartleby Syndrome (see Chapter 4), in which some gifted boys simply stop doing their homework because they "prefer not to"! This needs to be caught early, because the bad work habits and negative attitudes learned in the early grades can easily continue throughout a gifted boy's education. Teach him that choices about homework are family choices, not his personal choice, and that he should consult with you when his homework seems unfair. Help him to have good relationships with his teachers, teaching him to respect the men and women who are giving so much of their lives to him, but also help him understand that they may not have the resources to make all of his work at school seem interesting and fun.

If he loves sports, then support him in one or two physical activities—perhaps one team sport and one individual sport. Athletic teams can take up an enormous amount of time, so be careful not to overschedule him. If he dislikes athletics, support him in choosing other means of maintaining his physical fitness and in choosing other interests. Make physical fitness a family activity, and show him that healthy lifestyles help him learn more effectively.

Encourage his love of music and his participation in band or other music activities at school. There, he is likely to make friends who share interests in aesthetic and cultural areas. Some studies have noted that children who participate in band tend to get better grades, perhaps because of a feeling of acceptance by peers.

As the gifted boy grows older, he may become interested in role-playing games. An old myth is that *Dungeons and Dragons* and other such fantasy games are somehow dangerous to gifted kids' mental health—but there is no evidence to support this. Don't become alarmist over his fascination with games of the imagination; they have gotten a bad rap, but are generally good social activities for bright kids.

Similarly, don't become alarmed over the hours he spends at the computer surfing the Internet, as long as you provide supervision when he is still very young, and as long as his daily routine also includes some physical activity and family time. The Internet is where he can sometimes find kids like himself in the kids' chat rooms. Chat rooms run by Disney and other kids networks, by well-known toy companies, and by well-known film studios are usually well monitored. Networks of highly gifted kids provide an electronic community that will be a great support to him as he grows older. Many gifted children are finding new friends and using the Internet independently by the time they are seven years old. There are new programs that help children and parents filter and block inappropriate material; ask for suggestions at the children's section of your public library.

Arm him against bullies with humor, cleverness, and protective strategies. Take him seriously when he says that other kids are mean or that they are picking on him. If his giftedness causes him to be rejected by other kids, role-play with him ways of entering groups and playing with other children. Gifted kids often directly ask other kids, "Can I play with you?" which is often a bad strategy (the answer, even to a charming kid, is "no"). Instead, bright kids should enter a group by quietly joining in the play and by making their inclusion no big deal. Because young average children define friendships as "sharing toys," a gifted boy may need something to offer to share with other kids in the way of cool things in his pocket (a compass, a magnifying bug catcher, a flashlight with different colors).

Finally, teach him not to lecture other kids or constantly draw them into being educated by him; help him see that he can learn from others. If he chooses to be alone with his books or his computer, don't force him into social activities. It is very likely that when he needs social skills, he will use them. Parents should generally seek professional help for a loner boy only when the boy truly lacks social skills, rather than simply chooses not to use them, or when the boy himself is unhappy with his aloneness. If this is the case, social skills training programs recommended in Chapters 8 and 9 can be useful.

Give him a role in your family's spiritual or philosophical life, and share your beliefs with him. Teach him about the beliefs of other people, too, and help him find a balance between truth and tolerance. Rather than bludgeoning others with his faith or lack of faith, help him find comfort practicing his own values while also respecting those of others. Tell him, "This is our family's truth, here is what others believe, and here is how we can live with those who are different from us."

Try to find one or more male role model; if you are a single mom, find him a bright Big Brother or a mentor in a profession that he admires. Choose a godfather, even if you don't practice a religion that includes these, from among men who share your values.

Begin his career education by sharing your work life, taking him to work, and exposing him to many other careers as well. Give him a chance to focus on a few careers that might interest him, and help him learn about all of them.

Take him with you on travels. Go to museums and to special events related to his interests. Take a weekend day occasionally and have an adventure, letting him pick out a destination and a plan.

Adolescence

This time of turmoil for all teenagers can be particularly hard for the gifted boy as he struggles with choosing an educational and career direction, tries out relationships, and tries to understand his place in the world. A generation gap need not occur; parents can remain the trusted allies of their gifted boy if they respect the growth of his inner self and listen closely to the man that he is becoming, and allow him his independence while remaining supportive and available. Here are some suggested guidelines.

Create a unique and meaningful coming-of-age ceremony for him if your religion or community does not provide a Bar Mitzvah, communion, or similar ceremony. The Bar Mitzvah in the Jewish community shows that the young man has attained manhood through his mastering of the reading of the sacred texts before the community. Some American Indians send their boys on vision quests, in which over the course of a period alone in the wilderness, they seek the vision of their life path. The Eagle Scout ceremony is another symbolic induction into manhood. Find some way of showing the gifted boy that you honor his entry into manhood. Remember that this can be very embarrassing if other kids aren't doing it, so tailor the ceremony to the boy and attach it to some other event such as graduation from middle school, getting his driver's license (a "car mitzvah"), or some other achievement. The ceremony or ritual, no matter how informal, should include his most significant family members and friends, should recognize his accomplishments, and should suggest new responsibilities and give new privileges.

If he is not interested in the activities of the other adolescents—going to the mall, hanging out in friends' rooms, skateboarding, etc.—fine. Let him find his own way to be an adolescent, even if he chooses to spend substantial amounts of time by himself. It is good for him to have at least one best friend, so encourage his best friendship by making your home a welcome place for his friend. A welcoming home is one in which there is plenty of food that they like, a television and computer space that is private, and parents who are warmly welcoming but not constantly in their faces.

Sometimes gifted boys like to construct and invent together, so provide materials and a place to work. Gifted boys enjoy exploring together, too, so taking your son and a friend on hikes and turning them loose (with appropriate cautions) to explore on their own can be fun for them. Also, talk with your son about what it means to be a best friend and about what he is looking for in his friendships.

Many middle schools are wastelands for bright children because gifted programming is less common at this level. The middle school movement was anti-intellectual from its inception—the emphasis was and still is on social development—so there is still lingering hostility in some districts toward gifted education or anything involving rigorous curriculum and acceleration. This is a good time to get your boy involved in after-school, Saturday, or summer activities for gifted students. The Scouts and 4-H have excellent leadership programs that can challenge a gifted boy to achieve specific projects at his own rapid pace.

Some families have found foreign travel to be an antidote to anti-intellectualism (Westphal, 2001). Other countries often have far more appreciation for intellectual abilities, and the experience of traveling—or better yet, of living—in a foreign country can open up new ways of seeing the world, including recognizing the hollowness of the passing peer fads that so consume other teenagers.

If your son is interested in summer opportunities, be sure he signs up for the Talent Search in your state and takes the SAT. The Talent Searches are particularly appropriate for mathematically and verbally gifted middle school students. The Talent Identification Program at Duke University publishes a book of summer opportunities and camps that specialize in meeting the needs of bright children. It is at summer camps and institutes that many gifted adolescents create friendships that last all year long, and sometimes all life long. Remember not to push these activities, but to provide the opportunity and to ask that the adolescent gifted boy do *something* over the long summer.

When he is ready for relationships with girls, provide opportunities for him to be with bright girls—including at the same programs mentioned above. Talk with him seriously about gender issues. Describe the changing roles of men and women, and ask him how he sees himself fitting into this new world. Teach him to respect the young women with whom he associates, and help him learn the behaviors of equality—sharing work responsibilities, sharing relationship responsibilities, negotiating, and compromising.

Some gifted boys will not participate in student activities that they perceive to be run by or made up of lots of girls. Tell him that he is cheating himself out of valuable experiences by turning down extracurricular and leadership activities just because there are not a lot of guys involved. Talk with him about how sexism causes men to flee occupations and activities that are female dominated and how everyone loses when that happens.

If, despite your best efforts, he loses interest in school out of boredom during the middle school years, then look for a challenging high school in which he could enroll concurrently, or if that is not available, insist that he take more rigorous courses. Remember that it is better in the long run for bright boys to have B's in difficult courses than A's in easy ones. Despite the fact that some guidance counselors may try to pressure him to "keep up his grade point average," you should try to be more relaxed about grades while being serious about learning and challenge. Paradoxically, underachieving adolescent boys often require more challenge and more academic rigor rather than less, but high school advisors tend to drop them from Advanced Placement (AP) or honors courses if they enter with a mediocre middle school record. Help him challenge his way into at least one AP course in high school. Alternatively, gifted boys may enjoy on-line classes or classes at a local community college as a way of getting a taste of college learning.

Unfortunately, gifted boys are not immune to the lure of drugs, violence, and inappropriate sexual activity. Most of this takes place after school rather than at night, so be sure that he does not have long unsupervised hours after school, and talk frankly with him about activities that put him at risk. Start this communication when he is young, and he'll be more likely to confide later. Ask hypothetical questions: "What do you think you would do if…."

Many gifted boys like to associate with kids who live on the edge; they appeal to the gifted boy's sense of drama and love of intensity. Usually, gifted boys know how to enjoy the company of rebels without getting caught up in illegal activity, so don't automatically discourage him from befriending the angry poet or the lonely punk rocker. Provide a safe place for him and all of his friends to hang out.

If he is highly specialized in his interests, discourage school personnel and other people from forcing him to be "well-rounded."

Encourage him instead to discover and focus on his interests—in school, after school, or in his part-time work. Part-time work should be related to his career interests, whenever possible, and should not be just a fast food job. See if he can work a few hours with a friend who is a professional in the field in which he has interest.

A bright, multipotential boy who tries to be everything to everybody often has great difficulty later in prioritizing his interests. Help him limit his interests and focus on just those activities that are in accordance with his most deeply held values.

Increasingly include him in your adult social activities so that he is not just "listening at the stairwell." Bring the world home with you, exposing him to your colleagues and friends who are socially committed and courageous and who are accomplishing important work.

Give him the opportunity to go on a quest, to take on an important task, or to make a pilgrimage. A year abroad or a summer abroad can widen his horizons and help him define his identity. Or encourage him to be involved in a challenging service project that will provoke his sense of justice and give birth to commitment. Too many internships involve trivial work; help him find an organization in which he can be a leader in a meaningful project of his own and in which he will come into helpful contact with mentors.

Help him choose a college on some basis other than prestige alone. Harvard and Stanford are not the only places for gifted men. Make sure he takes into consideration what he wants to study, availability of mentors in his chosen field, and the quality of campus life. Visit the campuses with him if you can, and help him find a community of bright students with his values. Honors residence halls and residence halls specializing in particular themes—diversity, ecology, or technology, for example—can be havens for bright students.

College

It would seem that the parent's and teacher's job is done at this point, but it isn't. Gifted young men continue to need support, guidance, and counsel from caring adults throughout the college years. In fact, the decisions that they make in college may determine the course of much of their adult lives, for better or worse. It is important that they not make these decisions alone.

Help the gifted young man make imaginative decisions about a college major and about a career. Don't pressure him into choosing some field just because men in your family have always chosen it, and don't insist that he major in something just because it "pays well" or just because it will help him "get a good job." Career development for the gifted young man should be the search for meaning, not the search for a job. If he's talented and he loves his work, he'll get a job. So encourage him to follow his intellectual passion, which may mean creating his own major or combining majors in new ways if doing so better suits his interests.

Help him find honors housing and special communities while in college, and encourage him to get involved in research with a favorite professor. Have him offer to help a professor with his or her work; he is unlikely to be refused. Encourage him to do a senior thesis, if that option is available.

Talk with him seriously about the dangers of binge drinking, drugs, and unprotected sex, but assume that he will experiment. Talk with him about your own experiences, good and bad, and ask his opinions. Hazing is still an unfortunate reality in most fraternities, and bright men are often the targets of extraordinary bullying. Investigate any fraternity carefully, and check its rules about alcohol, substance abuse, hazing, and sexual harassment. Fraternities and residence halls can be miserable experiences for gifted men, and many older men have told us horror stories about roommates. Support him in finding the living arrangement that he needs.

Support him also in his attempts to find love; remember that too many parents provide much more career guidance than relationship guidance, and he needs both. Dating is an outmoded game that does not prepare young people for the changed relationship roles of the future, so encourage him to engage in more equitable structures for relationships. Remind him that love based on shared work, mutual interests, and compatible values is the strongest kind.

Keep alive his sense of social responsibility by continuing to encourage his participation in internships, travel, and special projects that take him out of his culture and instill in him an appreciation for diversity. Also, continue to encourage him to challenge himself intellectually and to use his creativity in choosing an identity and lifestyle all his own. Try to inspire in him the commitment to share his gifts with others, as well.

Encourage him to explore his own spirituality as well as the religions of others, visiting churches and temples and participating in the practices of Eastern religions, African-centered religions, and American Indian ceremony. Discuss with him his growing sense of his own philosophical and spiritual identity, allowing him to grow into his own faith (or absence of faith). Show him how to have his own truth and yet to tolerate the truths of others.

Be there for him. Keep his room the way he left it so that he has a place to return to when he needs a safe haven. Be there for long conversations and shared enthusiasms, and celebrate his adulthood by treating him as your equal, a trusted and beloved friend as well as a son.

It is our hope that all of these suggestions are helpful to parents of gifted boys and young men. However, just following suggested guidelines cannot alone provide the basis for a healthy, productive, and loving adulthood. It is necessary for all of us who parent, guide, and teach the gifted to share a proper vision of what a gifted man can be. With that in mind, we offer the following suggestions for school administrators, teachers, and guidance counselors:

1. Institute early identification programs for preschoolers and kindergarteners.

2. Discourage kindergarten redshirting, explaining to parents the hazards of delayed schooling.

3. Create gifted education programs that will challenge gifted boys before Bartleby Syndrome sets in. Early elementary programs need to include some special grouping of gifted that allows for advanced reading and problem-solving activities.

4. When underachievement occurs, teachers need not take it personally. It is important to explain to parents the ways of preventing and overcoming underachievement.

5. Later elementary programs should be based on acceleration and challenge within specific domains. Gifted boys need to have their specific talents diagnosed and programming provided that teaches to their talents.

6. Middle school gifted programming should focus on academic rigor as well as social and emotional development.

7. High schools need gifted programs that encourage critical thinking in advanced classes (including college level language, mathematics, and science classes).

8. Career education and guidance for gifted boys should focus on resolving multipotentiality. Gifted boys need help finding those career paths that are most in keeping with their deepest values.

9. Gifted programming in high school should include relationship education or special discussions of gender relations.

10. High schools might consider providing after-school activities that lead toward a rite of passage experience for bright boys, such as Outward Bound experiences.

11. Gifted boys need encouragement to engage in service learning, internships, and volunteer work to strengthen their social commitment and enhance their moral and spiritual development.

In the next chapter, we take on the task of developing our vision of the ideal gifted man. We present this not to provide a rigid blueprint for the optimum gifted male, but instead to provide our own conclusions about the best we can hope for—a man of intellectual and emotional courage, a man who is creative in his lifestyle and in the fruits of his work, and a man who is committed to the common good.

References

Rimm, S. B. (1994). *Keys to parenting the gifted child.* New York: Baron's Educational Series.

Walker, S. Y. & Perry, S. K. (1991). *The survival guide for parents of gifted kids: How to understand, live with, and stick up for your gifted child.* Minneapolis: Free Spirit Publishing.

Webb, J. T. (1999). *Parenting successful children* (video). Scottsdale, AZ: Gifted Psychology Press.

Webb, J. T., Meckstroth, E. A., & Tolan, S. S. (1982). *Guiding the gifted child: A practical source for parents and teachers.* Scottsdale, AZ: Gifted Psychology Press (formerly Ohio Psychology Press).

Westphal, C. (2001). *A family year abroad: How to live outside the borders.* Scottsdale, AZ: Gifted Psychology Press.

13

Realization of Potential for Gifted Males: Courage, Creativity, and Commitment

Here at the end of our book, we find ourselves reflecting on all that we have learned about gifted boys and men since we began the research and writing of *Smart Boys*. Our initial motivation for writing this book was our observation that many of the gifted boys whom we have counseled and taught over the years are disengaging from achievement and leadership. It seems to us that while gifted girls and young women are rapidly transforming themselves and their society, gifted boys and young men are hanging back, in part because they do not know how to respond to society's changing gender roles. Instead of taking their places at the sides of young women who are now behaving as their equals, we see young men increasingly isolating themselves or taking shelter in the remaining very narrowly defined masculine roles. What is stopping gifted boys from achieving and leading? We found that there are several likely contributing factors, which we will now discuss in some detail.

A Rigid Masculine Role

We have learned that, despite major changes in gender roles, the culture of boys continues to discourage them from association with the feminine. Unfortunately, emotional sensitivity, creativity, spirituality, and even intellectuality are associated in our culture with femininity—or at least, with a questionable kind of masculinity. And as more and more females pour into once-masculine realms, these areas become suspect, too, and therefore seemingly off-limits. Many of the authors of books on boys show movingly how the myths of boyhood and the emotional mis-education of boys has led them to deny their own creativity and sensitivity. We have seen how this kind of socialization might be especially agonizing for the gifted boy, whose special sensitivities and talents are often hidden or suppressed in order to maintain a masculine facade. Furthermore, we saw that a gifted boy might sometimes avoid activities, organizations, or even classroom discussions in which girls play major roles in order to protect his precarious male image. Therefore, socialization for a rigid male role that does not fit the experience or inclinations of gifted boys is one of the primary barriers to their successful development.

Boredom

A second barrier is boredom. Kindergarten redshirting, delays in identification, and lack of appropriate gifted education all conspire to create a mismatch between the gifted boy's abilities and the challenges offered him. In the absence of intellectual challenge, by third grade, the gifted boy may be so bored that he acts out his frustrations and is then labeled with Attention Deficit Disorder or Oppositional Defiant Disorder. Or he may go underground as a bored and congenial Bartleby, preferring to do the least possible amount of work to get by—which is sometimes none at all. Or sadly, he may simply adjust to boredom as a way of life, choosing a dull career because he has come to expect so little from his world.

Deviance Fatigue

In many parts of this book, we have bemoaned the tendency of gifted boys to conform to societal expectations of them in their academic choices, in their career choices, and even in their relationship choices. Longitudinal studies of gifted men, for example, have shown a clear tendency for many gifted young men to choose from a rather narrow sampling of college majors and to follow a fairly linear, almost pre-ordained, career path. One need only examine the strange trajectory of most gifted men's careers, from initial promise to fast track academic training to lucrative career to a sort of career plateau marked by good citizenship and mild regret—to see that potentials are often not being met. Among the men in our own study, for example, there appeared to be many caring, good gifted men who might have been compassionate, creative leaders in their talent domains had they not been doomed to obscurity by their perceived need to conform to standards of mediocre masculinity.

Certainly, there are gifted boys at the other end—the drifters—who do not go in a straight path. They stay in college seemingly forever trying various college majors, or they meander from one career to another. But these young men feel the pressures to "settle down" and to develop a career path that is thoughtfully planned and more traditional.

In addition, we saw that there is some evidence that gifted men's choices of partners may also be influenced by their need to conform to societal expectations. This may at least partly explain why so many of the gifted men in our study who exhibited such good spirits and kind demeanors had such troubled relationships.

And our explorations of the lives of overweight, overly intellectual, and feminine gifted boys showed the high price that gifted boys often pay for nonconformity in any realm—physical, mental, or emotional. It should not be surprising that many gifted boys choose not to pay this price, opting instead to conform—at least outwardly.

However, it is not useful to gifted boys to belabor the fact of their conformity. After all of our interactions with gifted boys and men, we are convinced that it is not that they wish to take the easy way out and conform, but rather that they simply get tired of being different—in other words, they have deviance fatigue. If boys are labeled gifted but are given no understanding of what that means for them, they may reject the label. If they are bullied or belittled by their peers for being gifted, it only makes sense that they would seek cover in conformist behavior. If they feel that they have been separated from their friends by their intellectual status, they may spend their whole lives trying to prove that they are really just "one of the boys."

Lack of Guidance and Mentoring

The painful lack of guidance in the lives of gifted boys often begins with their hunger for their fathers' attention. Our review of the Alvino study showed that, for gifted boys, the father is often "everywhere and nowhere"—that is, boys have a pervasive sense of their fathers' expectations of them and therefore carry their fathers with them everywhere. Nevertheless, they miss their fathers and wish that they would spend more time with them doing ordinary things.

The lack of appropriate guidance in high school contributes to gifted young men making stereotypical college and career decisions, or to their just floating along with a pre-packaged plan that is not truly their own. And in preparing for college, many gifted young men are steered toward large, prestigious schools where they will find few mentors. Unfortunately, those gifted men who do not have mentors are less likely to achieve their full potential in their careers, partly because they often do not know the career ladders and do not have access to the proper networks.

Finally, many of the theorists on the psychology of men have been alarmed by the absence of "rites of passage" for boys as they grow into men. One of the most important roles in the rites of passage in traditional cultures is the male mentor or sponsor—the one who teaches or supplements the parents' teaching of what it means to be a man. Without this male ally, the gifted man may flounder spiritually, may fail to develop his own unique masculine identity, and may never be sure of who he is.

A Vision and a Quest

Related to the importance of a rite of passage is the importance of both a vision and a quest. Both are important because those gifted boys who do not have a vision of their vocation, but who do receive the gift of a quest—a task to do—may never find their way toward self-actualization. According to Robert Johnson (1989), the author of *He*, all young men have a glimpse, like the young Parsifal, of the Grail—and then somehow, through foolishness or through the drudgery of daily routine, they lose that beautiful vision. If and when young gifted men have a glimpse of their life's vision, too often it is discounted ("Why look for life on Mars? It's pretty clear it's a dead planet." Or "Nobody ever makes any money in creative writing!"). Even if they enter adulthood with their vision intact, somehow it gets lost later along the way as they struggle to meet others' expectations and as they encounter the inevitable dragons on the path to the Grail. Seldom do we give young gifted men the opportunity and encouragement to pursue a vision; instead, we try to create their visions for them by plying them with job market statistics and giving them well meaning but dismal advice.

Gifted boys need permission to seek a vision, and they need support for their dreams. In American Indian cultures, a young man's dreams are attended to with great care by the family, because those dreams may carry within them the secrets of his future. The "Perfect Future Day" Exercise, used in our programs for talented at-risk young men at Arizona State University, is a guided visualization exercise that takes the students on a trip 10 years into their own future, allowing them to imagine an ideal day from morning till night. Just as exercises such as these are important, so are the caring, serious conversations that one can have with adolescent boys, in which they are shown that their dreams are respected and that they will be held accountable for their visions. That is, we expect them to endeavor as hard as they can to fulfill their visions, and we offer our loving support to them in that process.

Similarly, our society rarely sends our young gifted men on a legitimate quest—they are seldom encouraged to take on a task and engage in a struggle for a cause larger than themselves. Yet gifted boys long for a task to do and for work that has meaning and dignity. In a touching scene in *Mansfield Park*, Jane Austen depicts a father ruefully remembering his erring adult son as a child demanding, "Father, give me a Quest!" We must have the will to send our young gifted men out into the world to seek their visions through quests. Such quests can be as simple as a year abroad for the young man who hungers to know another culture, a year of missionary work for the religious young man who wishes to put his faith into action, or an actual guided vision quest through a program such as Outward Bound.

Resilience and Resolution of Crises

One of the most disturbing observations we made in our work concerned gifted boys from privileged backgrounds who not only turned their backs on achievement, but also even used their intelligence for antisocial or violent action. We learned that intelligence alone guarantees neither adult achievement nor social commitment. We learned that, sadly, gifted boys who are bored, alienated, and bullied may themselves become people who hurt others.

However, as we began to examine the research on those men on the margins—including poor boys, sissies, fat boys, and nerds—we saw that there were many gifted men who had used their giftedness to overcome rejection in positive ways. And men of color often felt that they had "something to prove," and they took advantage of mentors and special educational programs to achieve high academic and career goals. In all of these cases, being an outsider seemed to help gifted boys become men of accomplishment. A special resilience that was learned through struggle and the support of at least one significant teacher, mentor, or family member marked the lives of these successful men.

We also learned that even those gifted men who were exempt from proving their masculinity—either because of superb athletic achievement or because of an upbringing in which nonconformity was valued—were often able to fully manifest their intellect and creativity, though this sometimes came about only after they had faced a challenge that led to "positive disintegration." That is, their lives disintegrated and seemingly fell apart for a period of time, and only after experiencing that failure or crisis in their lives did they come to reexamine their values and priorities, and were then able to re-integrate themselves in a positive way that allowed them to more fully develop their inner lives.

From the beginning, as psychologists who work with gifted boys and men, we have believed that gifted men are happiest and at their best when they are able to use their talents to the fullest in the service of deeply held values and when they are able to create meaningful friendships and true intimacy with a partner. Like Sigmund Freud, the first psychotherapist, we too believe that healthy men are capable of being successful in both their relationships and in their work lives.

But where are the models for gifted men who are able to both love fully and work effectively toward their goals? Too often, as we read the biographies of eminent men, we have been struck by the fact that so many of those men who are held up as paragons by society have often failed miserably in their relationships. Throughout the annals of history, we see holy men neglecting their families, powerful men using women, and creative men leading irresponsible lives. Gandhi seemed to ignore his wife, Franklin D. Roosevelt and Bill Clinton betrayed their wives, and Frank Lloyd Wright and Dylan Thomas left behind unpaid bills and broken promises.

Even many eminent men who had responsible and loving relationships often had trouble leading balanced lives. Too often, they were all intellect—men who paid little attention to their own bodies, to their emotional lives, or to the possibilities of a spiritual life.

In *Smart Girls*, Kerr (1997) said that the world should expect more of gifted women than cheerful compliance and good children. Perhaps we can say now that the world should expect more of gifted men than conformity and good salaries. At some point, the gift must be shared and finally passed on to others. And the gift should not be fulfilled at the expense of body, heart, and soul.

In an article entitled "Cultivating Courage, Creativity, and Caring," James Webb (in press) suggests that we add to the commonly used model of giftedness—which encompasses intelligence, creativity, and task commitment (Renzulli, 1981)—two other traits: courage and caring. Intelligence and task commitment seem to create the kind of hardworking and dutiful gifted men that showed up in so many of the studies, including our own, of the lives of bright men. In this article, Webb proposes that the true realization of giftedness is only possible by adding the triad of courage, creativity, and caring. The lives of gifted individuals are incomplete without these, for courage without creativity and caring leads to heartless bravado, creativity without caring and courage leads to trivial imaginative pursuits, and caring without creativity and courage leads to much kindness but little activism in the service of others.

We now look to three researchers to help us understand what a courageously self-actualizing, creative, and caringly committed gifted man might look like—the research of Abraham Maslow on self-actualizing individuals; the research of Mihaly Csikszentmihalyi on creative people; and the work of Daloz, Keen, Keen, and Daloz on socially committed people. Their work gives us intriguing lists of characteristics that might be shaped in gifted boys. Here, then, are some models of self-actualization and our attempt to draw from them some ideas for guiding gifted boys and men.

The Courage to Realize Potential: Maslow's Self-Actualized People

In this first attempt by a psychologist to explore the optimum state of being, a group of historical and contemporary people, each of whom seemed to have realized their full potential as a human being, was selected by Maslow's research team. These were people who had fulfilled the promise of their gifts, who led satisfying and rich lives, and who left behind them a world that was more beautiful, more orderly, more just, or more comprehensible than the one they had been born into. These people included such historical figures as Abraham Lincoln, Thomas Jefferson, Eleanor Roosevelt,

Albert Einstein, Jane Addams, William James, Albert Schweitzer, Aldous Huxley, and Baruch Spinoza. There were also a number of unnamed contemporaries—people who had not achieved fame but who seemed to be living full, actualized lives.

Reading Maslow today from the new perspectives of multiculturalism and feminism, it is striking how much his perception of the self-actualized person was based on individualism. The very term "self-actualization" calls to mind a lone person pursuing his own development. However, no matter where his team of researchers began, and no matter what their original assumptions were about individual achievement, exposure to these people inevitably led to a very different viewpoint: each of these individuals, while having attained personal satisfaction and happiness, was someone more interested in the greater community of humanity and the great mysteries of the universe than in his or her own enlightenment or achievements.

It is also striking when reading this study how static Maslow's original notion of self-actualization was. It was as if this state of being was a product rather than a process. There is little retrospection in the study; instead, it is a snapshot of how these people were—either at the end of their lives or as they were when interviewed. However, the subjects themselves were anything but static; they referred to their lives as a process, as an ongoing quest, rather than as a tale of a completed quest.

Through biographical study, interviews, and reports of peers, data was gathered about the characteristics that these people had in common. Maslow searched for those personality traits and those behaviors that seemed to be most clearly related to their capacity to express their deepest self and to fulfill the potential of their character and gifts.

One of his first findings was that these people had a more efficient perception of reality than most people did. Maslow said, "They seemed as a group to be able to see concealed or confused realities more swiftly and correctly than others.... They distinguished the fresh, concrete, and idiographic from the generic, abstract, and rubricized" (153-154). There was also in these people a lack of guilt, shame, and anxiety, as well as a comfortable acceptance of their own shortcomings—not in a self-satisfied way, but as one accepts the things of nature. They extended this acceptance to others and bowed serenely to those forces of the universe around them. They were, Maslow said, "good animals, hearty in their appetites." Maslow stressed that the spontaneity of these people was much more internal than external. They usually behaved according to their society's conventions, but in the workings of their inner selves, they were extraordinarily unconventional. There was no artifice in their behavior, and they never strained for an effect on others.

Another finding was that the self-actualized people were strongly focused on problems outside of themselves. They had a mission or a calling to fulfill, and that is how they tended to expend their energy, rather than in introspection upon their own needs. These people tended to stay with their own assessments of situations rather than being swept up in other people's opinions and emotions. As a result, they could occasionally seem aloof and serene at the same time. They liked solitude and sought privacy. Although they loved their friends and enjoyed people, they did not need other people in the ordinary sense. Self-actualized people, Maslow found, were dependent for their own growth on their own potentialities; they did not need others to meet their needs. Rewards, prestige, and status were much less important to them than was their own inner development.

Self-actualized people seem to love the basic things in life and to see the beauty in common things. They derive inspiration from nature or children or art and do not require exquisite stimulation. Nevertheless, self-actualizing people do have the capacity for mystical experiences—experiences of limitless horizons opening up, of ecstasy, wonder, and awe. Such peak experiences involve a loss of self and transcendence.

Self-actualizing people, Maslow said, have a deep sympathy and identification with humanity despite an understanding of the foolishness and weakness that limits us. This brotherly attitude prevents the self-actualized man from becoming bitter when he is rejected because of his differences from others.

These people have deeper and more profound relationships— closer friends and greater love. They can transcend ego boundaries to truly connect with those they love. They are friendly with any-one, regardless of color, creed, or educational level. Maslow said, "They seem not to even be aware of these differences" (167). Self-actualized people appear to be citizens of the world and resist becoming embedded in one culture.

Self-actualizing people also have strong feelings about right and wrong. Their standards may be different from the community's, but they are strongly ethical and uncompromising in their under-standing of good and evil. However, though they are staunch in their ethics, they are not short on humor. And their humor is based not on hurting or laughing at someone, but on poking fun at humans in general—it is a kindly humor.

There was one characteristic identified by Maslow as being universal in this group, and that was creativity. They each had a gift for creative living. Perhaps one of the sources of their creativity lay in their ability to resolve the polarities of selfish-unselfish, mascu-line-feminine, introverted-extroverted, mystic-realistic, and so on. They were both and neither, and saw no dichotomy. They seemed to live instead in the tension between opposites—happily balanced there between extremes that they did not even recognize.

Creativity: Csikszentmihalyi's Study

It was Mihaly Csikszentmihalyi (1996) who took the next step in studying people who shared that one common trait—creativity. These people were not those who lived particularly creative lives or behaved in original and interesting ways, but instead were women and men who had produced publicly acknowledged creative works. Csikszentmihalyi referred to them as people who had changed—or were changing—the culture in some important way. These people were all creative in some respect, but they were not all self-actualized.

The participants in the study included such men as musician Ravi Shankar; physicist Manfred Eigen; novelist Robertson Davies; John Reed, CEO of Citicorp; John Gardner, public policy expert; Benjamin Spock, pediatrician and social activist; and Barry

Commoner, environmentalist. Each was interviewed about his childhood, adolescence, and adulthood, about his creative process, and about his personal life, his career development, and his philosophy of life.

The creative people in Csikszentmihalyi's study had, for the most part, normal childhoods, as opposed to the desperately unhappy childhoods assumed by previous scholars of eminence to be the origin of creative lives. In fact, most of the people in this study praised their parents for giving them a solid set of values, the freedom to explore their interests, and the support they needed to receive the training necessary for their careers. Of all the values instilled by their parents, the one named most often by these creative people was honesty. In all of the domains—science, the arts, and leadership—truthfulness was seen by these people as absolutely necessary for success. They were grateful to their parents for giving them this gift.

The family lives of these creative people were dissimilar to ordinary families in one important way: a high proportion of the creative people, particularly the men, were fatherless. Many scholars have speculated about the meaning of this commonly observed fact. Jean Paul Sartre, the existentialist philosopher, quipped that the greatest favor a father could do for his son would be to die young. However, Csikszentmihalyi resisted the notion that losing a father somehow enhanced creativity. Instead, he said, it was the set of conditions surrounding that loss that affected creativity. If the boy had the support of significant adult others, if he used his loss as an opportunity to define his own identity, and if he transformed his loss into a precocious empathy and sensitivity, then creativity might be enhanced.

Another trait that characterized the creative people as children was a prodigious curiosity. Most of them fell in love with their fields of interest when they were still quite young. Although most were very bright, not all would be considered highly gifted. What distinguished them instead was a sustained interest in learning everything they could about their chosen passion. And their curiosity was supported by adults who gave them the knowledge or skills they needed to pursue their interests. As their knowledge increased, their curiosity drove them on to mastery of the techniques of their domain. This gave them a competitive edge over others.

School seemed to have had little effect on these creative people; in fact, few had much to say about the benefits of their education. Like most gifted children, they seemed to have spent a good deal of time in school being bored. In addition, there is little evidence that they received unusual recognition from others for their abilities. On the other hand, these creative people had much to say about particular teachers. There were teachers who inspired, teachers who supported, and teachers who challenged. Nearly all of these people could name at least one teacher who had given them extra attention and who had recognized, challenged, and affirmed their talents.

Adolescence was a difficult time for most of these creative people. One interesting observation made by Csikszentmihalyi was that these people were less sexually active and more attached to their families than average adolescents were. He speculated that this made possible a longer period of playful exploration and provided a safe distance from the programming of their genes. By avoiding early marriage, these young people had the time and the resources to continue their educations and to enter into their careers.

Nevertheless, adolescence was often a time of loneliness and marginality. Even these conditions, though, might have served the creative process by teaching the young people how to work alone and how to be an outsider—both prerequisites for making changes in a profession or a culture.

College and graduate school were often remembered by creative people as the finest times of their lives. It was during this period that their thirst for learning and mentoring was at last slaked. Here, they often discovered their true direction. Most of them had great luck in that they were at the right place at the right time—the resources and people were there when they needed them to fulfill their interests.

Most of these creative people met their life's partners when they were quite young, although they delayed marriage until other goals were achieved. They usually were blessed with supportive partners, and in most cases, the two stayed together for life. Although there were a few unhappy marriages, most of the participants in the study named their marriages as great sources of stability and strength.

After observing the career paths of these creative individuals, Csikszentmihalyi found that there was no such thing as a straight path to career success. In fact, for most of the people, the path had been a circuitous one. Indeed, many of them found it necessary to invent their own careers. Unlike most people who begin at the entry level of an established field, work up the ladder, and then settle in at some level of competence, these people often had to search out a place where they could create their own environment for working. They had to begin their own laboratories, set up their own studios, or start their own companies. As the author says, one could not be an aeronautical engineer before the Wright brothers.

There were so many exceptions to even the broadest generalities that could be made about these people that Csikszentmihalyi concluded that there was no one path to creative eminence. Instead of being shaped by their genes or by external events, these people had, he said, seized upon whatever opportunities they had been given and then shaped events to meet their own ends. They had, in many cases, transformed loss, loneliness, and deprivation into creation and action. He says, "According to this view, a creative life is still determined, but what determines it is a will moving across time—the fierce determination to succeed, to make sense of the world, to use whatever means to unravel some of the mysteries of the universe" (p. 182).

Commitment: Daloz, Keen, Keen, and Park's Caring People

Lawrent Daloz, Cheryl Keen, James Keen, and Sharon Daloz Parks are four scholars who share a strong belief in the importance of social commitment to the fulfillment of the self. In *Common Fire: Lives of Commitment in a Complex World* (1996), these authors tell of the lives of people who have committed themselves to a common good. These are people who have recognized their connectedness to the environment, to the creatures with whom we share the earth, and to the rest of the human race. They range from famous politicians to little known but extraordinary community activists.

The criteria for selection for the 100 people who were interviewed were the following: a demonstrated commitment to the common good, perseverance and resilience, ethical congruence between life and work, and engagement with diversity and complexity. The method used to find the interviewees was the "snowball" method—that is, one interview led to another, as people who met the criteria were asked to identify others like themselves. Half of the participants were male, and half of them were female. They were representative of diverse cultures: one-third of the participants were either Black, Hispanic, Asian, or American Indian. Gender, ethnicity, and even sexual orientation matched typical U.S. patterns. Each participant, though, according to the authors, was a person capable of sustaining commitment to the common good in the face of global complexity.

What else did the authors find out about these people? First of all, they investigated the childhoods of these people. They found "at the heart's core" that these people had all been loved as children. They had all grown up in loving homes that had provided shelter, safety, nourishment, and a chance to learn that they could count on the world being a good place most of the time.

There was more, however. They had, for the most part, come from homes with open doors—homes that other children loved to visit and that were often full of neighbors, friends, and people who came from the outside world to tell stories and share experiences. Often, there was at least one public parent—that is, a parent deeply engaged in caring activities on behalf of other people. And because the home was a busy place, the children who were to become committed people frequently "listened from the stairway"—that is, they were drawn to the adult conversations in the living room below. And as they grew, these children became part of their parents' hospitality, learning to host foreign exchange students, their parents' colleagues, and visiting speakers. They lived in neighborhoods in which they were known and recognized, and they became comfortable with this community.

As adolescents, they did not so much leave home as transform the meaning of home. They moved about quite a bit, but they felt safely anchored to their homes. They seemed to be able to carry the security of their homes with them. For with the teen years came adventure—these people traveled, participated in foreign exchanges and youth leadership programs, and did volunteer work in other communities. They made pilgrimages that held great importance for them.

Interestingly, school was not mentioned as very important to these people, although they did well—it was more of a "background hum" for them. They did acquire important knowledge and skills, though, and some were also fortunate enough to have schools that were caring and productive places. All of the interviewees, however, could tell of coaches or teachers who had made a vast difference in their lives. Most could recall many teachers by name who had given them a sense of being special and who had taught them something that they were hungry to know. They had met people who had given them a sense of "can do"—a belief in their own efficacy.

They also learned the difference between justice and injustice. Their elders taught them from an early age the nature of injustice—how it begins in intolerance and ends in dehumanization and destruction. They learned to recognize injustice in human relationships, in communities, and in governments. Finally, their elders taught them how to fight injustice and how to work for fairness for all, and they did this by modeling a way of life that was committed to overcoming inequities.

One striking difference between these young people's adolescence and that of so many American teenagers' experience is that they were given a task to do. They had work that was meaningful at an early age—work in which they strove with others, for others. They learned leadership skills, they acquired the capacity to mobilize others in positive ways, and they learned the art of serious and productive conversation. These young people had a community that acknowledged their passage into adulthood primarily by trusting

them with the responsibility of caring for others. And unlike
"Mother's Companions," they were given responsibilities that were
appropriate to their age and abilities and were not left caring for
people who should have been caring for them. Nevertheless, the
tasks that they were given were challenging and represented work
of real importance. They had mentors who saw them through this
passage—and these were often people who shared their parents'
values but who represented the new lives that the young people
were about to enter, separate from their parents.

It was in college that many of these young people met the
mentors who helped them find their work in the world. They found
their vocations, and as they moved from college into the world of
work, their commitment to these callings deepened. Few of these
young people entered adulthood floundering about, not knowing
what they wanted to do. They had a clear set of values, they had
mentors to show them the way, and they took to their paths with
enthusiasm. Young adulthood, therefore, was not a protracted period of exploration, but a time of intensification of their already-
formed sense of mission and purpose.

As for their relationships, they married at a rate lower than the
nation's average. Twenty-four of them had never married or were
divorced, 67 were married, five lived in other partnerships, and four
had taken religious vows of celibacy. Those who were single felt
that it had been the right choice, giving them more time for their
work—although sometimes it led to their feeling "different" in a
world of couples. The most salient aspects of the partnerships of
these people were sustaining conversations, emotional support, and
a richness of shared experience.

What about the characteristics that distinguished these people
from others? First of all, the authors said, these people had gone
"beyond the tribe." Going beyond the tribe means that they had
become interested and concerned with people who were outside of
their family, neighborhood, community, socioeconomic group, ethnic group, or religion. They had become engaged with otherness.
Such a perspective is a challenge in today's world, as tribalism—
the narrow concern for one's own people—seems to dominate the
public mind. However, these people were supported from an early

age in their interests in people who were different from themselves.

There was something else that helped them go beyond the tribe, and that was a lingering feeling of marginality. Although most of these people had loving families and fairly happy childhoods, they all felt different in important ways. Some were disabled; some were "too small" or "too fat" or "too smart;" some came from families that were outsiders by virtue of religion, race, or class. In the end, though, marginality for these people was a gift, because they learned empathy with outsiders and learned independence of mind. This allowed for a strong connection to the people they served and for a sense of compassion that seemed to well up from the depths of their souls. Each one along the path of his life came to the conviction that everyone counts—even those who oppose one's own point of view.

Indeed, another aspect of these committed lives was conviction. The authors say that their interviewees saw their convictions as arising out of critical habits of mind. They had cultivated intellectual habits that allowed them to deal with complex issues and with diverse people. These habits of mind included that of dialogue, the idea that meaning is constructed through ongoing interaction between oneself and others; interpersonal perspective taking, or the ability to see through the eyes of others; critical, systemic thought that looks for patterns and reflects upon them; dialectical thought, the ability to recognize and deal with contradictions by resisting easy answers and premature closure; and holistic thought, the ability to intuit life as an interconnected whole.

Imagination was another critical element in their committed lives. The authors talk about "responsible imagination"—that is, an imagination that responds. These people used their imaginations to create new services and programs, to devise responses to injustice, and to create an image of a better world. This kind of imagination has several components. First, there is conscious conflict, a period in which the individual becomes curious or troubled about some conflict he or she sees between the way things are and the way things ought to be. Often, an observed injustice, which they experience either directly or indirectly, leads to this feeling of conflict. Then comes a pause, in which the person steps back to consider the meaning of this experience. During that fertile rest, an "aha!" experience is born, in which the person has a new insight about the situation. Then, the whole pattern is reframed, and the insight is integrated into the reality of the situation. Finally, the insight is articulated in dialogue with others. Often, the insight is a powerful image or vision that becomes a guide for the person's own behavior.

For many of these people, religion was never far away, and it often provided the source of these insights, images, and visions. However, the authors pointed out that often it was not religion in the traditional sense, but a faith in the interconnectedness of being—a belief in oneness. Often a particular image—the Crucifixion, the medicine wheel, or the seated Buddha—became the source of imaginative power, the metaphor that guided the individual's service. In other cases, it was a saying, such as "Do justice, love tenderly, and walk humbly with your God." Sometimes it was a more idiosyncratic vision. Nevertheless, all of these people had used their imaginations to create new ways of seeing the world, relying upon rich imagery and verbal wisdom to guide them to insights concerning ways of acting for the common good.

Another characteristic common to these people was recognition of their own fallibility. Often, these people believed that they fell short of their own ideals. They worried about "taboo motivations" for helping, such as anger, pride, the need to please, ambition, fear, perfectionism, and the need for control. What made these powerful, intelligent, socially adept people different from manipulators and tyrants, though, was their sense of fallibility and their inner urge to constantly examine their own motivations. They acknowledged inner wounds and tried to heal those wounds through introspection and service and by seeking the guidance of others.

Conclusion

These sweeping and inspirational studies of what is best in human beings provide us with many ideas for overcoming the barriers we presented at the beginning of this chapter. The people in these studies leapt over the rigid barrier of masculine roles by cultivating in themselves a true androgyny. Self-actualized subjects reconciled the polarities of masculine and feminine, creative subjects ignored the fear of the feminine aspects of creativity, and committed subjects combined feminine nurturing qualities with masculine instrumentality and drive.

Boredom could not conquer these people, because all of them were involved with an idea and a vocation that kept them vividly occupied. And most were fortunate enough to have had at least one great teacher who had kept their intellect alive in school, and many had more than one. Both the creative subjects and the committed subjects had benefited from rigorous training in their talent domains; some trained formally in excellent schools, and others were apprenticed to master teachers who helped them hone their skills. Although ordinary education very seldom provided what these young people needed, they and their families sought alternatives to a mediocre education or found ways to supplement schooling with tutoring and out-of-school activities. The combination of a powerful idea to hold the young people's interest and access to special educational opportunities to nurture their gifts was an effective antidote to the monotony of the average school.

"Deviance fatigue" may have hit these people occasionally, but they were inoculated against the fear of being different by parents who were themselves different or who simply encouraged their children to be different. They had teachers who valued their gifts and who respected and were not fazed by the fact that gifts often come with sharp edges. By the time these subjects were adults, their excitement about their work and their dedication to their goals eclipsed the fear of being different and replaced the contentment of conformity with the joy of action.

These people had mentors and guides who helped them seek their visions. They made pilgrimages—quests for their particular visions. Especially creative people usually had a master who took them on as an apprentice, if only informally. Committed people had someone in their lives who ignited their fire for social activism and who served as a model. Many of them even "listened at the stairwell" to the conversations of admired adults, engaging in a kind of vicarious mentoring process.

The beautiful words of Daloz, Keen, Keen, and Daloz (1996, p. 211) summarize well the way in which these courageous, creative, and caring gifted people achieved their visions:

> Over the years, their hearts' deep gladness became so integrated with the world's deep hunger that they found a home...where everything connects and were finally unable to turn away from its claim on them.... Almost without their noticing, their roots had taken a fierce and luxuriant hold in the soil of the world, and they had become dedicated spirits, the people we need.

We believe that we have presented a very different vision of what a gifted boy can be by emphasizing three essential traits: the courage to actualize talent and free the inner self; the creativity to live spontaneous and innovative lives, as well as to produce works of lasting significance; and the commitment to nurture the lives of others, share their gifts, and work for the common good.

Some writers in the field of gifted education seem to be content with speeding a gifted boy through his education just as quickly as possible, with the implicit goal being that of creating a 20-year-old Ph.D. And then what? While we favor acceleration—whether single-subject or whole-grade acceleration—as the best educational strategy for gifted children, we disagree with the emphasis on precocity for the sake of precocity. Why boost a rocket out of the atmosphere at warp speed if there is no destination in mind? Therefore, we suggest that all accelerated programs for gifted children have strong guidance components, as well as moral education that instills a respect for the gifts that have been given as well as a desire to give back to society.

Other writers in gifted education do indeed have a destination in mind, and that is eminence, or becoming the "king of the hill" in a particular talent domain. It is interesting that they consider this the ultimate end toward which gifted men should strive, while politely excusing women from this goal, given the latter's waning tendency to compromise their talents in order to support their gifted husbands' and sons' quests for eminence! And therein lies one problem with an eminence-based model of talent development—it does not take into account the fact that eminence is often achieved with the support of others, and sometimes at the expense of others.

Self-fulfillment, the actualization of one's deepest values and interests, is certainly a more humanistic goal and, we assume, one that leads to greater life satisfaction. But it, too, has its shortcomings as a model of talent development. The exclusive focus upon one's own self-realization can lead to the worst kind of New Age narcissism and to the kind of men who neglect their families while mistakenly seeking their true selves in some distant land. Therefore, we reject speedy achievement, eminence, and self-fulfillment as optimum models of gifted men's talent development. Instead, we suggest the possibility of gifted boys' growth toward courageous self-challenge, creative lifestyle, and commitment to the common good. We want to help boys acquire the courage to challenge themselves—through rigorous education, apprenticeship with a mentor, and a meaningful quest. We want to urge them to be creative in planning their lives and in forging new products of the intellect, forgoing the roads most often taken. They can invent their own educations with after-school activities, travel, camps, and the Internet. They can create new kinds of friendships and intimate partnerships, becoming the vanguard of young people living in truly egalitarian relationships. They can imagine careers that do not yet exist. They can be courageous enough to choose the most rigorous courses of study and specific, intensive training in their talent domains, so that their creative products are truly disciplined works of art, science, or service.

Finally, we want to guide gifted boys toward commitment— toward work for the common good. For the gift to be actualized, the gift must be shared. This means that the ultimate goal of talent development is a person's development of the talents of others— through teaching, loving relations, and service. Rather than individual eminence and actualization, we encourage gifted boys to strive for a kind of collective actualization, to engage in work that liberates not only their *own* hearts, minds, and spirits, but also those of others. Become all that you are, we tell gifted boys, so that others can become all that they can be.

Many times during the writing of this book, people have asked us to name men whom we believe fit this model of courage, creativity, and commitment to the common good. Any time one attempts to list those people who seemed to live lives of gentleness and strength, vigor and reflection, brilliance and kindness, someone will mention a flaw here and there—an unhappy marriage or an unfinished task. But given what little we know of the mystery of gifted lives, there are indeed some men who come to mind. So we offer up, here at the end, an idiosyncratic, purely personal list of slightly flawed, truly great men: Antonio Vivaldi, Abraham Lincoln, Geronimo, Jimmy Carter, Muhammed Ali, Steven Spielberg, Carl Rogers, Crazy Horse, Auguste Renoir, Oskar Schindler, Nelson Mandela, Albert Einstein, Cesar Chavez, Stephen Hawking, Jackie Robinson, Walter Cronkite, Akira Kurosawa, e e cummings, Victor Frankl, Antoine St. Exupery, Carl Jung, Lech Walesa, Martin Buber, W. E. B. DuBois, Vaclav Havel. These are the names of but a few gifted boys who became gifted, courageous, creative, committed, caring men.

Stephen Spender, in his poem "I Think Continually of Those Who Were Truly Great," wrote of men such as these, saying that they were:

> *"...those who in their lives fought for life,*
> *Who wore in their hearts the fire's centre*
> *Born of the sun, they traveled a short while*
> *toward the sun*
> *And left the vivid air signed with their honor."*

We believe that all gifted boys have the potential to become men of courage, creativity, and commitment like these men did. As parents and teachers, we have our gifted boys only for a short while. If we help them fight for the life of their mind and help them find their heart's fire, we honor them and the gifts they give us.

References

Austen, J. (1996). *Mansfield park*. New York: Modern Library.

Csikszentmihalyi, M. (1996). *Creativity: Flow and the psychology of discovery and invention*. New York: Harper-Collins.

Daloz, L., Keen, C., Keen, J., & Parks, S. D. (1996). *Common fire: Lives of commitment in a complex world*. Boston: Beacon Press.

Johnson, R. (1989). *He: Understanding masculine psychology*. New York: Harper-Collins.

Kerr, B. A. (1997). *Smart girls: A new psychology of girls, women and giftedness*. Scottsdale, AZ: Gifted Psychology Press (formerly Ohio Psychology Press).

Maslow, A. H. (1968). *Toward a psychology of being*. New York: Van Nostrand Reinhold.

Renzulli, J. S. (1981). What makes giftedness? Reexamining a definition. In W. B. Barbe & J. S. Renzulli (Eds.), *Psychology and education of the gifted*. New York: Irvington.

Spender, Stephen (reprinted 2001). "I Think Continually," *Poetry Parlor*, .

Webb, J. T. (in press). Cultivating courage, creativity, and caring. *Gifted Education Press Quarterly*.

INDEX

A

able learner   39

academic
  achievement   70, 72, 107,
    258-259, 263
  performance   63, 177,
    182-183, 190, 195, 258
  placement   194-195, 198

Accelerated Learners Program
  159

achievement/IQ
  discrepancies   181-182
  tests   177-178, 181, 186,
    188, 191-193, 259, 287

ACT studies   263

adolescence   4, 18, 70, 114,
  122, 126-128, 131-132,
  135, 147, 150-152, 184,
  246, 251-252, 309-313,
  330-331, 334

adversity   67, 158, 171-172

African American culture   41,
  65, 185, 255-262, 267,
  271-272

Albert, R. S.   68, 77, 152,
  172, 286

alienation   128, 147, 196, 208,
  211, 234, 248, 252

Alvino, J.   57, 77, 152, 172

American
  Indian   41, 127, 166, 185,
    255, 267-273, 315, 323,
    333
  Psychological Association
    45, 78

androgynous   96, 102, 232-
  233

anti-intellectualism   45, 221,
  311

V

W

About the Authors

Dr. Barbara A. Kerr was born in St. Louis, MO, and received her M.A. from Ohio State University and her Ph.D. from the University of Missouri, both in counseling psychology. She has taught at the University of Nebraska, where she established the Guidance Laboratory for Gifted and Talented, and at the University of Iowa, where she was Associate Director of the Connie Belin National Center for Gifted Education. She is now Professor of Psychology in Education at Arizona State University. She is the author of four books: *A Handbook for Counseling Gifted and Talented*; *Smart Girls*; *Smart Boys*; and *Letters to the Medicine Man: The Shaping of Spiritual Intelligence*. She also has written over a hundred articles and papers on the topics of guiding and nurturing talent. Her research ranges from case studies of inventors, artists, writers, and architects to large-scale studies of students who attained the highest scores on the ACT college admissions tests. She is a Project Director for the National Science Foundation gender equity program, and director of a nonprofit retreat and professional development center called Cascabel.

Dr. Sanford J. Cohn completed his Ph.D. in the psychology of mathematically precocious youth at The Johns Hopkins University and subsequently joined the faculty of the College of Education at Arizona State University (ASU). His focus there has been on the education and development of academically talented young people, and in 1979, he started the Center for Academic Precocity (CAP). Dr. Cohn co-edited with William C. George and Julian C. Stanley *Educating the Gifted: Acceleration and*

Enrichment and is the author of numerous articles on assessment and identification of academically talented youth, program evaluation, and intellectual talent. In 1990, he began to explore alternative behavior sampling techniques to identify talented migrant education students. The resultant program, called *Conexiones*, brings secondary school-aged migrant students to ASU for a two-week workshop and introduces them to state-of-the-art technology, which they use to build and program a robot using the *Lego Dacta®* materials, learn techniques of video-ethnography, or write articles for the *Conexiones* Web site.

Dr. Cohn currently is a professor in the Division of Curriculum and Instruction and the Division of Psychology in Education at ASU. His research interests remain focused on issues related to growing up gifted, but have also evolved to consider all aspects of the development of talent and the creation of optimal learning environments. Of special interest to him is the important role technology can play in this process.

Dr. Cohn is also a licensed psychologist in the state of Arizona, where he has a small clinical practice devoted to highly able youths and their families.

Other Great Books from Great Potential Press

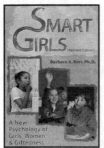

Smart Girls: A New Psychology of Girls, Women, and Giftedness
by Barbara A. Kerr, Ph.D.
Over 70,000 copies sold!
Why do so many talented girls often fail to realize their potential as adults? Dr. Kerr investigates this question and also offers practical advice to parents, teachers, and smart women about ways to help gifted girls continue to grow and succeed.
ISBN 0-910707-26-X / 270 pp. / paperback / $24.00

Helping Gifted Children Soar: A Practical Guide for Parents and Teachers
by Carol A. Strip, Ph.D. with Gretchen Hirsch (winner, 2001 Glyph Award)
This user-friendly guidebook educates parents and teachers about gifted issues such as working together, choosing curriculum, meeting emotional needs, and finding support. A must-read to establish a solid foundation for gifted education.
ISBN 0-910707-41-3 / 288 pp. / paperback / $18.00
Also available in Spanish!

Guiding the Gifted Child: A Practical Source for Parents and Teachers
by James T. Webb, Ph.D., Elizabeth A. Meckstroth, M.S.W., and Stephanie S. Tolan, M.A.
Over 100,000 copies sold!
Called the Dr. Spock book for parents of gifted children, this award-winning book covers important information on the unique social and emotional concerns regarding gifted children. Chapters focus on motivation, discipline, relationships, peers, stress, and depression.
ISBN 0-910707-00-6 / 266 pp. / paperback / $18.00

To order materials or to request a free catalog,
please write, call, email, or visit our Web site:
Great Potential Press
P.O. Box 5057 Scottsdale, AZ 85261
Toll-free 1.877.954.4200 fax 602.954.0185
giftedbook@earthlink.net
www.giftedbooks.com

Other Great Videos from Great Potential Press